THE ORAGEAN VERSION

THE ORAGEAN VERSION

As
presented
by

C. Daly King

REGISTER

PREMISES

This treatise is not written for publication, which I forbid. The reasons upon which I base my decision in this respect will appear in fuller detail later.

My reasons for writing down what follows, however, are clear and simple. It constitutes one version of the approach to the Hidden Learning, an approach which I now know full well will surely be lost unless it is carefully set down at the present time.

And indeed the season is late for this task already; many of those who were once acquainted unambiguously with its principles, and even with its details, have wandered during the past fifteen years into other paths, perhaps as legitimate but assuredly very different. For them this version has become subtly distorted, overlaid with other attitudes as the colors of an original painting alter not only with the passage of fading time but, as it may be, are also changed by well-intentioned efforts to improve upon the original through the further application of a supposedly better technique. It is not my purpose here to render any judgment regarding the wisdom of such efforts; what remains is simply that they inevitably obscure and eventually destroy the integrity of the version thus affected, and with its integrity its validity also. To me it appears of importance that the version be preserved.

The Hidden Learning has existed (as it exists today) at all times of which we know, although only seldom appearing upon the surface of what the late M. Ouspensky called Public History or the History of Crime, viz., the history of the school books, which deals with wars, conspiracies, violence and tyrannies. As now and then we catch vague glimpses of the Hidden Learning, it appears in many different guises or versions—the East Indian version of the Bhagavad Gita, the medieval rendition of the Orders of Chivalry and of the original Rosy Cross, perhaps in the very earliest of the Christian and Mohammedan accounts, perhaps also in the initial interpretation of the Lamaists whose descendants still inhabit Thibet, and so on. And once it even appeared with accustomed clarity in Public History itself, in the official religion of Ancient Egypt whose complexities are rendered only the more dubious by the anthropological naïveté of professional Egyptology but which shine with an almost unbelievable illumination when a few key principles of the Hidden Learning have been achieved.

The exegeses dealt with in this treatise may be called a "straight" version, formulated rigorously but without the slightest double entendre; no artificial impediments are involved and a clear understanding of the formulations is limited solely by the degree of individual development already gained by the inquirer. In other expositions (in fact in all of them with which I have any acquaintance) many safeguards of an artificial and deliberate kind are thrown about the student or postulant; in this there are none. Thus the reason for non-publication is not merely of a pearls-before-swine character. For perhaps this is the most dangerous version whose formulations are in any way available.

The field of these formulations is that of objective truth, both personal and non-personal. And in such a field common sense will warn us that we must take into account not only what is written, in a treatise like the present one, but likewise who it is that writes. And although, generally, the authority for any serious statement lies in its truth and not in its enunciator—when the case is that of a factual report of what precisely a given series of formulations has been, it is advisable to have some assurance that the reporter himself really knows what these formulations were. For that reason I conceive it necessary to declare merely the relevant details of my own relation to the version which I have undertaken to set down.

In the year 1924, M. Georges Gurdjieff came to New York City. He was then the founder and head of The Institute for the Harmonious Development of Man, at Fontainebleau, France; and he brought with him a considerable number of his instructors and pupils, with whose assistance he produced a succession of exhibitions, first at the Neighborhood Playhouse in downtown New York, later at Carnegie hall, and still later in Chicago. The performances consisted of "tricks, half-tricks, and real phenomena," and included a number of dance-ceremonies, some original and some replications of ancient dervish and sacred dances. These exhibitions were totally unusual and impressive to a degree. My wife and I (I had then been married somewhat more than a year) attended one at The Neighborhood Playhouse and another at Carnegie Hall. I have forgotten who informed me of them; it may have been Miss Jessie Dwight, then a mere acquaintance of mine, who was part-owner and operator of the Sunwise Turn Bookshop on 44th Street. M. Gurdjieff returned to France and for a time I heard no more of him.

It was the following autumn, of 1924, when Miss Dwight (at whose shop I purchased all my books) informed me that a Mr. A. R. Orage had remained in New York City as the representative of M. Gurdjieff and that he was proposing to hold a series of informal groups for those interested, in order to explain the nature of the Institute and its work. She urged me to attend.

I was then twenty-nine years of age. Eight years earlier, in 1916, I had graduated from Yale College with the degree of BA, where my courses had been generally in what are called the liberal arts. My major subject had been Latin; I had also studied Greek, French, German, a good deal of professional philosophy, constitutional law, American and ancient history, some mathematics and a bit of physics. That was my educational background then. Immediately following graduation I had served with the American field artillery in World War I, a year of it in France; shortly after my return my father had died and I had found myself the junior general partner in the factoring business which he had founded and built up in New York City. It was an honorable, successful and lucrative enterprise but, strive as I would, I could not succeed in becoming seriously interested in carrying it on as my father had hoped that I would. My widowed mother had been left very comfortably off and I myself had a small but adequate income even after I presently married, so that necessity did not come to my aid. I had, however, become interested in a new technique called psychoanalysis and at this period I had undergone an analysis of such a kind under Dr. Edward J. Kempf, who was somewhat of an eclectic in the field and based his theories more upon the functions of the autonomic nervous system than upon the entirely subjective foundations of analogical speculations. My chief, and perhaps unusual, motive had been to discover what it was all about through personal experience but I had been fairly thoroughly taken apart in the fashion of this technique and it had effected two results in my case, although I believed then—and it is still my conviction—that the disadvantages of the psychoanalytic technique far outweigh its scientific advantages. The first of these results was the initiation of my interest in psychology proper; the second was my first realization that it was possible for me to view the man, C. Daly King, from the outside as well as from the inside, i.e. as some purely external observer might view him and especially without the necessity of being identified with his wishes, his hopes or his fears.

This, then, was my situation when Miss Jessie Dwight urged me to attend one of the groups conducted by Alfred Richard Orage. Certainly I was far from unhappy but I was definitely dissatisfied with my business life and I was seriously seeking another activity which would occupy me more seriously and to which my growing interest in the so-called science of psychology would possibly furnish the answer. The fundamental questions of philosophy aroused my curiosity, but not the philosophical verbalisms by means of which they were dealt with by philosophers. And there was more than this, too. I had by now encountered the Gnostic literature, the Hermes Trismegistos of G. R. S. Mead, and other fragments. Also, I was interested in Egyptology and, as I considered that long parade of strange gods and goddesses, I could not believe that anyone of a lively or inquiring intellect could possibly view them seriously for more than a few moments without receiving the conviction that there was some real significance there, something quite other than the childish totemism attributed to them by those who fairly obviously were totemists themselves. These were riddles I could not read; and yet I became more and more convinced that they were readable if one could only discover the key. I was looking for that key, and not by any means consciously, either.

The previous exhibitions by M. Gurdjieff had certainly stimulated some kind of response in me; but my own picture of informal groups of fanatics meeting privately to discuss strange notions, did not attract me. I had already superficially investigated fortune tellers, numerologists and astrologers, and my conclusion was that all of them were either quacks-on-the-make or else were their own sincere dupes. Very nearly I did not attend any of Mr. Orage's groups.

I think it fully just to say that Miss Dwight's accounts and repeated invitations were solely responsible for my initial attendance. She did not seem to me to be a fanatic. In any case, eventually, I selected an afternoon and presented myself among strangers. I went alone.

The afternoon was dark; I have forgotten the address but I suppose the meeting place must have been some sort of private school, for the room was equipped with rows of small desks, as if for young pupils. I had arrived reasonably early and had some time to wait while others gradually congregated. I knew none of them and presently wandered out into a small, dim, adjoining hallway. There I encountered an entering gentleman of whom I made out only that he was tall and slender, and dressed inconspicuously in a dark business suit; actually I could see only his eyes with any distinctness, no doubt because of some shaft of light from the illuminated room within. In the gloom he extended his hand, shook mine and said that he was very happy to see me again. Peering more closely, for the first time I saw Alfred Richard Orage and felt well assured that I had never seen him before. Possibly he mistook me for someone else in the darkness or perhaps he had actually seen me at one of the exhibitions, without my having seen him in turn. We entered the room together and he at once proceeded to conduct the groups by a modified Socratic method.

I think what impressed me most at this first meeting was the complete and utter rationality of what I heard. Perhaps I had gone in the expectation of a proselytizing harangue; and certainly I had taken with me an incredulous attitude, prone to raise objection to everything put forward. My incredulity was not admitted; instead, it was demanded that I adopt skepticism toward what I heard, i.e., that I should neither believe nor disbelieve, that for the moment I should not even judge, and certainly that I should be neither credulous nor incredulous.

This is not the place in which to reproduce the discussion that then occurred but I may say that my reaction was without delay, immediate and vivid. Even now, my recollection of this first meeting I attended is more clearly detailed than that of the many later ones in which I took part. The topics went to the real heart of what had always intrigued me, those questions which I had always hitherto found hedged about by qualifications, by half-statements, sometimes even a shame-faced avoidance, always a lack of specificity which had convinced me that the speaker didn't actually know the truth about such subjects. I was not merely fascinated; I received such an interior lift of pure exultation at the discovery that these questions could be considered seriously, fully and without equivocation, as had never occurred to me before and has never been as fully repeated since. To cap it all was the assurance of skepticism, the rational demand that I must not believe until I myself had obtained the proof. That reassurance was very necessary to me and it set the seal upon my determination to investigate this extraordinary doctrine, or whatever it was, further. I went home exuberantly and made a most unusually excited report to my wife. Thereafter she accompanied me to all of these groups.

They continued through the winter and well into the next year, 1925. There had then taken place abroad the serious automobile accident suffered by M. Gurdjieff (late 1924), which closed the Institute, incapacitated the man himself for a long period, transformed his whole program out of recognition to me (as I now realize) and left Mr. Orage holding the bag, as it were, in New York. The next summer (1926) I was in Europe with my family and essayed a visit to Fontainebleau; however, I found nobody of much authority about when I sought entrance and, not insisting, was turned away.

The following fall, back in New York, Mr. Orage's groups were resumed and he also consented to come out to Orange, NJ, where I was then living, to conduct a weekly group there. At that time I was studying technical psychology at Columbia University where I was accorded the degree of MA the next year, having finally resigned from my father's firm and retired from the business. At this time, too, I had written out a careful formulation of so much of the Oragean system as I had yet been acquainted with, submitted it to Mr. Orage himself for correctness and had it acknowledged as accurate. I also wrote a small book, Beyond Behaviorism (1927), in which I sought to show the relation between scientific psychology and the ideas with which I was now becoming more familiar. This took me into the late spring of 1928.

That summer I went to California where I collaborated with Dr. William M. Marston upon Integrative Psychology; he had been the professor under whom I took my Columbia degree and I left there with him in order to help formulate his own approach to psychological problems, an approach which I continue to think of the highest importance for the science.

In the fall my wife and I were back in New Jersey and resumed our work with the Orage groups. I was now conducting two groups of my own, one in New York City and one in Orange, NJ. These I had undertaken with the encouragement of Mr. Orage but perhaps with a bit of apprehension upon his part, too; however, at first he supervised some of the meetings and later dropped in once in a while unexpectedly to look them over, at length professing his unqualified approval and withdrawing from any further supervision. But of course he was always in the background, he was always there, and indeed without the possibility of his aid in a perplexity or crisis I should not have consented to take these responsibilities upon myself.

They continued into the year, 1930, while we were also continuing to attend the groups conducted by Mr. Orage in New York City. It should be said here, also, that during the preceding years I had formed a close personal friendship with Mr. Orage; very frequently I lunched or dined with him, sometimes in the company of others and often alone. Thus I obtained an exceptional opportunity to discuss with him all sorts of details of the formulations he was presenting in the work of his groups, to consult with him concerning my own work with the groups which I was conducting, and to maintain with him the closest liaison in regard to the accurate and a rigorous statement of the propositions, doctrines and ideas that formed both the core and the superstructure of this version of the Hidden Learning. It had been in the summer of 1927, three years previously, that Miss Dwight, my wife and I, and Orage had taken a vacation trip together in Canada but even before that he had often been our house guest and our friendship was now of a number of years' standing.

This summer, 1930, Mr. Orage left for England with his wife (Miss Jessie Dwight and he had been married some two years before) and my own wife accompanied them for an extended visit. I remained behind and later made only a brief trip to rejoin my wife and accompany her upon the return journey, spending only one or two days with the Orages at their English home.

Before this vacation trip Mr. Orage had been applying the principles of his version of the Hidden Learning to the interpretation of the early copy of M. Gurdjieff's series of books, the first of which was not to be published until 1950 but which already existed in ms. form. When he left for England, it was decided to continue his groups straight though the year (it had been the custom to close them in late spring and to re-open them in the early fall) and it was in this year, I believe, that in Mr. Orage's absence I conducted his own groups for some two or three months, acting as his deputy.

The winter and spring of 1930–1931 brought the final crisis in all this activity. Mr. Orage, returning to New York, had resumed his groups for the reading of M. Gurdjieff's books and had also expanded the program to include separate groups working upon psychological exercises and upon the principles of literature as seen from this special perspective. All this presented me with a rather full calendar and, since the pupils from my own groups had gradually been fed into the Orage groups, I now discontinued my own.

It was at this point that M. Gurdjieff once more came to New York. During the preceding years he had visited America on a number of occasions, spending by far the greater part of his time in New York City. During such periods the other groups had been discontinued temporarily and their members had met with M. Gurdjieff on a similar schedule for private readings from his manuscripts; there had been also opportunities for personal consultations with M. Gurdjieff. Upon his departure the activities of the Orage groups had been resumed in the same manner as before their interruptions. Now, however, suddenly and without warning (at least this was true in my case), M. Gurdjieff repudiated Mr. Orage, the latter's previous activities, and in especial the Oragean version of the Hidden Learning; and demanded that the former pupils and associates of Mr. Orage should have nothing further to do with him, upon pain of exclusion from the meetings conducted by M. Gurdjieff. Many of the former members of the Orage groups actually signed pledges to such an effect; naturally I did not, and I remember that there were one or two others who, acting for themselves, joined me in this refusal. Apparently the whole thing was a bluff, for all of us continued to attend the meetings held by M. Gurdjieff, as did Mr. Orage himself, also. Such an outcome, after all the fuss that had been raised, went far to persuade me at that time that the repudiation of Mr. Orage's formulations was no more serious than that of himself personally. But I have come to the later conclusion that in this I was mistaken.

M. Gurdjieff now departed from his former custom and, in addition to occasional readings, constituted separate groups to which he gave the titles of "esoteric," "mesoteric," and "exoteric" but as between which I was never able to distinguish any difference at all. They were concerned with a series of peculiar, sometimes juvenile, exercises whose significance (if they had any) I was never able to grasp. At one point I conjectured that their real purpose was to re-establish a sort of faith or credulity, which all of Mr. Orage's work had done much to undermine, of course. But, if so, they produced no effect upon me, who am naturally not a very credulous person. And, after all, my notion about them was no more than a wild surmise. These episodes marked, however, the final break between M. Gurdjieff and Mr. Orage; in the summer of 1931 the latter left for England permanently with his family. He never returned to America, nor do I think that he ever again saw M. Gurdjieff. And of course his New York groups were abandoned.

In New York, with M. Gurdjieff's departure, matters naturally were left in some confusion. Certain of the former group members arranged to meet for further readings from the Gurdjieff manuscripts and I myself organized a small group, not conducted as previously, but concerned solely with a particular experimental work in connection with that Method which will be formulated in the body of this treatise. The next year, 1932, I published the Psychology of Consciousness, a much more detailed, technical and expanded version of the earlier Beyond Behaviorism.

In 1933 this experimental group of mine was continued, resulting in the accumulation of much data which even yet I have been unable adequately to analyze and publish. In October of that year I made a trip to England in connection with my writing but primarily to see the Orages and to renew my friendship with them. Mr. Orage was now the editor of the New English Weekly and had severed all connections with M. Gurdjieff. I shall always remember the pleasure I then had in his company and the profit from his advice; he appeared at the time to be in the best of health but almost exactly a year after my departure from England he died suddenly and unexpectedly, toward the end of 1934.

With his death and the absence of M. Gurdjieff from New York, activity of the kind relevant to the present treatise ceased for me. The five years, 1935–1940, I spent with my family in Bermuda, engaged upon the writing that had now become my profession. With World War II I returned to the United States and spent the next five years, 1940–1945, at Yale University in New haven, prosecuting research in physiological psychology and as a result being accorded the degrees of MA and PhD in Psychology from that university. During this time M. Ouspensky, a former colleague of M. Gurdjieff, came to New York and a number of the former Orage group members joined themselves with the groups he proceeded to conduct. I came down from New Haven to attend two such meetings and had one private interview with M. Ouspensky but I found nothing of serious interest to me in his formulations and had no further contact with these groups.

During the winter of 1948–1949 M. Gurdjieff paid a short visit to New York City for the first time in many years and, although I was now living far out in the country, I succeeded twice in attending his meetings. One was for a reading from the final version of the first of his series of books, soon to be published, the other was a class in the extraordinary and interesting type of dancing in which he still continued to instruct.

As a result of my experiences at these meetings and of conversations with former members of the Orage groups whom I had known well for many years, I came to the final conclusion that the Oragean version of the Hidden Learning no longer remained extant and that it was in fact upon the verge of being irrecoverably lost. For that reason I propose now to set it down in accurate detail. This is a difficult and exacting task, which I should be well content to avoid if I knew of anyone else competent and willing to undertake it. Since I cannot find any such person, I must do it myself.

*

These Premises would be far from complete, were I not to remark further upon the break which took place in 1931 between Mr. Orage and M. Gurdjieff. I shall deal with this matter with all the fairness of which I am capable and certainly without any misplacement of emphasis upon these details with which personally I was acquainted.

The charge against Mr. Orage's activities upon behalf of the Gurdjieff Institute and specifically against that version of the Hidden Learning which Mr. Orage had been expounding to his groups in New York City for some seven years, was that this version was intellectually lopsided, that it placed an undue stress upon mental activities at the expense of emotional and practical activities; and that thus, far from being of objective benefit to the pupils and students who sat under Mr. Orage, it could be guaranteed to render them even more abnormal, objectively, than they had been in the first instance. Frankly, I never heard M. Gurdjieff put the matter in terms so specific as these but, then, I have never heard him put any matter in clear and specific terms at any time; his position in this case seemed to me as I have formulated it above, and I find that other members have received the same impression. I have no hesitation in presenting the above charge as that which was in fact made.

It is difficult to speak of this charge in moderate and serious terms, for to me personally it appears to be brash and blatant nonsense, quite on a par with those "esoteric" exercises with which we were being entertained at the same time when this charge was being brought. Nevertheless, it is necessary to say that not a few former members of the Orage groups—including some whom I myself believe to be perfectly competent to hold a respectable judgment—still feel the charge to have been, and to be, a proper one. Upon such a point, therefore, I have no wish to be dogmatic and I prefer to leave the correct answer to this question to any reader who has seen, and even partially understood, the mentioned version, which it is the purpose of this treatise to formulate.

Perhaps a more important question is this: whose is the version here considered, Gurdjieff's or Orage's? As to this, I can only state the personal opinion which I have had some unusual advantages to form, which I have pondered long and seriously; and after, of course, mentioning certain facts which are incontestable.

The first fact is that Alfred Richard Orage always stated without equivocation or qualification that what he was formulating, derived directly from the teachings and ideas of M. Gurdjieff. To me personally he made those statements many times over and for a long period I had no reason whatsoever to doubt them. Nonetheless, I do now seriously doubt them. Yet the question is one which is insusceptible of a positive yes-or-no answer.

I recall that I myself once composed several short, poetic "translations" from the ancient Egyptian hieroglyphic and, when asked whether or not they were mine, I replied: indeed no, that they were properly to be attributed to certain unknown Egyptians who had lived thousands of years ago. Now this in a sense was true, and in another sense it was not true at all. It was true that the sentiments expressed and a number of the terms used in translation, were genuinely those of a certain period of ancient Egyptian history. But it was not true that the poems themselves had ever been written in ancient Egypt or, for that matter, by any Egyptian at any time—at least, I should be more surprised than anyone else to hear of it if they had. Now, although this instance is so minor and trivial, I personally suspect that the case of Orage and Gurdjieff is very similar upon another level.

I entertain no doubt at all that Mr. Orage became acquainted with the general, and even with some of the specific, ideas and principles which he later formulated in his New York groups, during the time of his acquaintance at the Institute for the Harmonious Development of Man, in the years before the occurrence of M. Gurdjieff's automobile accident. And undoubtedly it was to this origin of his formulations that he referred when stating that they derived directly from M. Gurdjieff. But the formulations were those of Mr. Orage; as formulations, they derived directly from the latter's individual understanding and realizations concerning those principles with which he had become acquainted through his connection with M. Gurdjieff. And what they expressed was certainly as nearly and probably more directly, related to the individual realizations of Orage as to the original hints or statements which he had received from Gurdjieff.

In this connection two further facts must be taken into consideration: during the years when he was inaugurating and conducting his groups in New York City Mr. Orage had little or no direct contact with M. Gurdjieff, who sustained his injuries shortly after the group work in New York began; and although I myself never met or spoke with M. Gurdjieff before his accident and to the best of my knowledge only saw him once in the distance in those times, I cannot fail to suppose that the serious head injuries the latter then sustained, very greatly altered his later activities and his whole approach to the task to which he devotes his energies. Indeed, M. Gurdjieff himself has stated this to be the case and has gone so far as to speak of the period following his recovery as constituting "another life," in which he has first liquidated all the undertakings of his former existence and then adopted another and new occupation. One difference too obvious for anyone to miss is that previously he conducted an institute and that later he has altered his chief occupation to one of writing books.

This circumstance makes it impossible to say just how close the connection may be between the version taught by Orage and the actual pronouncements of the earlier Gurdjieff Institute. It may even be that the whole system expounded by Mr. Orage, including the details themselves, is a mere replication of what was taught at the Institute in earlier days and that M. Gurdjieff's later repudiation of it is of a piece with his "total liquidation" of all his previous undertakings. Since I myself never attended the Institute, I cannot answer this question of my own personal knowledge; and having become only too well aware of how unreliable are the memories of my former colleagues in the Orage group work, I fear that I would not place too much reliance upon the assertions even of those among them who in fact did attend the Institute in those times.

I can only say that personally I do not think that the Oragean version was ever a word-for-word repetition of the Institute lectures or of what was taught there. I feel certain that it was based upon what was taught there, for I do not think that Mr. Orage could have become acquainted with these particular ideas anywhere else where he had been; as to how closely his formulations and those of Gurdjieff resembled each other or as to how widely they diverged, of course I cannot say. But for one thing I do not suppose M. Gurdjieff to be capable of the type of formulation employed by Mr. Orage. M. Gurdjieff made statements very difficult to understand correctly, if indeed at all. Mr. Orage analyzed and fathomed such indications of M. Gurdjieff and then reformulated them with great care and skill; that is precisely what Mr. Orage did in the case of the famous Method later repudiated by M. Gurdjieff on the grounds that he, that is M. Gurdjieff had noticed during his visits to New York certain signs of aberration in the faces of Mr. Orage's pupils. What M. Gurdjieff claimed to have noticed, may perhaps have been the case but, if so, it resulted not from his pupils' having followed Mr. Orage's instructions but precisely from their not having followed them. In such an instance it would seem more reasonable to me for M. Gurdjieff to have placed the blame where it belonged and to have instituted more apposite remedies.

There is likewise the matter of the entirely different personalities of these two men to be taken into account, as concerns the question now before us. No doubt for many years to come there will be discussion regarding the character and personality of M. Gurdjieff. Unquestionably they are complex and devious but I can see no reason to make a mystery of them. As in other cases, different persons have received different impressions of M. Gurdjieff; as for my own, I do not hesitate to say that in my opinion he is not a teacher, and I have seen him both privately and at the meetings conducted by him many times. He is evasive, and I have never yet heard him give a direct answer to any inquiry, however sincere and straightforward the question may have been. When not evasive, he blusters; in these bullying moods there is more contempt for his followers than of animosity, but in any case it is scarcely an attitude conducive either to loyalty or to successful instruction. It may well be that he does not wish to instruct—others besides myself have received the idea that he knows much but isn't telling—and my own view is that, insofar as he desires to assist anyone, his principle is that this cannot be done through intellectual information.

Of a similar nature is M. Gurdjieff's demand that his followers become his "voluntary slaves." Now upon a very high level a very superior man may be able to adopt such an attitude successfully—in the earliest times the officiating priests in the Egyptian temples were called "the slaves of the deity"; but I do not have the impression that the persons who have surrounded M. Gurdjieff, or who surround him now, are of so superior a kind and for them, as for myself, I feel convinced that what M. Gurdjieff demands can result only in an attitude of faithful credulity toward everything he says and does, and the attribution to him of an often absurd degree of omniscience. It appears to me that such a result must be far worse for the pupil than any possible intellectual formulation, no matter how clear or rigorous the latter may be. It will be seen that I neither respect, not approve, nor intend to adopt any such attitude myself. It is not that I consider myself the equal of M. Gurdjieff, for there is no Equalitarian Lie involved here at all. It is not even that I would deny the legitimacy of my becoming his voluntary slave. I simply realize that as yet I am not even approximately so superior a man as to be able to become anyone's voluntary slave. And this is one of the reasons for which I have found that I have little to gain personally from association with M. Gurdjieff.

Since it appears that he does not consider an intellectual approach to serious problems suitable, it would seem that his approach must be either emotional or practical, because there are no other approaches feasible for human beings. But the people surrounding him are certainly not for the most part of the practical type and thus it remains that his approach must be emotional so far as they are concerned. Now the advantages of an emotional approach are these: that it may be sincere, that it may bring into play the great reservoir of energetic force which carries into effect the hopes and strivings of mankind and that it appeals directly to any person's immediate apperception of his own wishes. But it also contains disadvantages, and especially does it contain them for those who are not as yet fully human individuals: that is as likely to lead in an incorrect as in a correct direction; that it relies in the first instance not upon the realizations of the subject himself but rather upon the plausible suggestions of another person; that it may as easily be used to the appetitive benefit of the suggestor as to the objective benefit of the recipient and more often than not it is just so used; that it confirms in the subject that very disease of suggestibility which does so much to render the latter subhuman and is so typical a symptom of his subhumanity.

Against all of these inherent disadvantages the mental attributes of the subject (if they function at all as mental attributes) are specifically designed to guard and, at least to begin with, that is their prime function. The emotional approach is by definition lopsided in this especial fashion, in that it not only seeks to, but by its own nature must, delete the very safeguards included by nature against the hasty, credulous and fanatic acceptance of falsities or, at best, of partial truths. It has occurred to me that M. Gurdjieff's prime error and fault in his later activities is precisely the overestimation of his followers' abilities, an overestimation which seems quite clearly to achieve its compensation in his exaggerated contempt for them. Of course I may be wrong; the fact that such an interpretation is a rather too "clever" one, in no way guarantees its truth.

These are the sincere and honestly reported impressions which I personally have received from my association, such as it has been with M. Gurdjieff over a number of years. For me they are confirmed, although they have not been originated, by the very definite types of people who surround him. He presents to me the appearance of a dubious messiah, even if of an extremely sophisticated one; and he presents also to me the very picture of what I expected to encounter when I first attended that group meeting of Orage's to which I went with so much foreboding and incredulity. I honestly constate that Gurdjieff merits the incredulity. And if my judgment be incorrect, as much as my own bias it is *his* own behavior which has initiated and which justifies that judgment.

It would be disingenuous of me, however, having said so much, to deny or omit another aspect of M. Gurdjieff which has impressed me with assuredly as great an impact as any of the above. For while I have received no impression that M. Gurdjieff is by any means as outstanding intellectually, emotionally or practically as his faithful disciples suppose him to be, I am convinced by my personal experience of him that he possesses another quality that may be more important than any of the foregoing. This quality he possesses to a degree not merely superior to that of any other man whom I have ever encountered but to a degree greater than it would ever have occurred to me could exist, had I not met M. Gurdjieff. It is the quality, not of mind or of feeling; or of successful accomplishment, but simply of being. I have never failed to experience this in his presence; one (or I) cannot "put one's finger upon it" but it is most certainly there. It has always prevented the slightest show of impertinence toward him upon my part but, more than that, it has always prevented my (otherwise frequently demonstrated) ability to challenge him even upon those grounds to which he constantly lays himself open to the most obvious challenge. I cannot account to myself for this, in other ways, inexplicable respect in which I hold him that by my admission of the remarkable degree of being with which I am always impressed when in personal contact with him. . . . So much for M. Gurdjieff.

There could hardly be a greater contrast to the above type of personality than that of Mr. Orage. He was a brilliant intellectualist but, far more than that, he was also a very great teacher. It happens that I have spent most of my life among men of the intellectual type and some of them have been brilliant men; one or two of them have been great teachers. But I have never encountered any other mind of the shining clarity which Orage's achieved nor have I met any other teacher who so completely understood that no human being can ever be taught anything, that the true teacher's task is to assist another to learn. To assist hopefully, willingly and with every possible aid at the former's disposal, to dismiss no question as being too ignorant or too obvious to merit an answer provided the desire to learn be present, to encourage that desire in every possible way without ever consenting to pander to it; and never to permit the relationship of him-with-more-knowledge toward him-with-less either to deny itself or to imply any inherent superiority in the possessor. Never in my experience did Orage permit an ignorant man to assume an equality with him in respect of knowledge nor did he ever take the attitude that his own superiority was more than a temporary and unimportant one, if the other were impelled to learn.

Incidentally we touch here upon the reason for which I have called the subject of these ideas the Hidden Learning and not the Hidden Teaching. It is because, if such subjects are to be mastered and although the efforts of the teacher must be great; the most severe effort involved must proceed upon the part of the pupil. They cannot be taught. But they can be learned.

That I personally found Alfred Richard Orage to be a congenial friend is doubtless no more than a matter of type, chemical affinity and polarity. Upon my best self-searching I do not believe that this fact, which is indubitable, has escaped the allowances which I have made for it in the judgments upon him that I have stated above.

But there is more involved in this matter than the contrasting personalities of Orage and Gurdjieff; beneath it is the whole distinction between rational teaching and inspirational teaching. It may be that for a certain type of learner the inspirational approach is not only convenient but also possibly successful. I personally am not of that type. And even if I had access to such a form of communication with one greater than I (which I have no reason to suppose that I possess), nevertheless I should refuse to make use of it; for I fail to perceive that there is any measure or standard by which one inspiration may be distinguished from another in respect of its validity and I take it as self-evident that many inspirations are bogus. Thus, to repose one's confidence in an inspirational process of learning is to expose oneself to the blind chance that the inspiration selected is that exceptional one that may be correct, whereas the simple mathematical chances are very heavily against the probability of such an outcome. For within the inspirational technique itself there is offered no assurance, not any means, of distinguishing between the bogus and the objectively correct inspiration. Such a means can be founded only upon the learner's trained critical faculty and thus it can only be rational (or intellectual) in kind. Perhaps it would be unreflective to assert at this point that the path of rationality is necessary for everyone; I do assert, however, that it is necessary for me.

I take it that a learner is, by definition, one who desires to learn; I take it, further, if the learner proposes anything practical to himself, that he is already convinced, in whatever field he has selected, that there is something specific to learn; and finally I take it that the learner must be willing and must be able to expend the energy required for his proposed purpose. I am prepared to admit, as an assumption for which I have some evidence, that M. Gurdjieff possesses a fund of very serious and important knowledge. At the same time I know of my own experience that he either will not or cannot disclose it to me, that in contemporary fact he is not a teacher. But specific knowledge can be acquired by a learner only through the assistance of a teacher; and my experience has again informed me that the only real teacher I have ever known to be associated with the Gurdjieff knowledge was Mr. Orage. Vague and general inspirations are neither the hallmark nor the guarantee of a really serious quest concerned with the most important subject any human being can confront—namely, the meaning and aim of his existence.

Upon this matter Orage had something specific to teach and he was both willing and able to teach it. What he had to teach was nothing less than the specific key to that barred door which neither speculating nor wishing can open to those who seek entrance, which can be obtained only through its deliberate disclosure to the postulate by someone who antecedently knows what it is, because previously it has been disclosed to him. This, as it were, initiatory secret has nothing whatever to do with good intentions, a virtuous outlook, a benevolent interest in mankind or any sort of morality emotion or inspiration. It is as defined and specific as any actual key that has ever unlocked any actual door. It is that key which Orage had in his keeping to disclose. And it is that key which he did disclose.

Of course he did not invent it, or even discover it, by himself. Neither, of course, did M. Gurdjieff. It seems as certain as may be that Orage did obtain it from Gurdjieff and that that was the immediate sequence of its availability during the period of the Orage groups in and about New York City in the nineteen-twenties. How much of what followed from it, was due to Orage's individual realizations and how much attributable to Gurdjieff's specific instruction of Orage, is problematical and scarcely seems of very great importance. But the disclosure in New York was made by Orage and all the dependant and sequential formulations were made by him too. Moreover, it is precisely these which were later repudiated by Gurdjieff.

That is why I attach the title Oragean Version to the body of statements that I propose to delineate here.

*

It is entertaining, although not especially profitable, to speculate upon the possible explanations of the extraordinary recent history of these ideas concerning the Hidden Learning—their introduction and exposition in modern New York, their expansion and their carefully formulated consequences, their sudden repudiation and attempted destruction. Two theories have been advanced in this regard which bear at least some initial plausibility.

The first is that the information herein contained is really secret, really hidden and really forbidden. To make it public is prohibited and to reveal it even to a very highly selected number of candidates for initiation can be allowed only after the passage of severe tests and the inauguration of complex safeguards. Nevertheless, Gurdjieff did formulate this information at his Institute for the Harmonious Development of Man, it being unknown to me whether with or without the adequate safeguards. Orage formulated it later in New York without any especial safeguards but with an explanation of the necessity for doing so which will appear at the proper place. There was then the accident that so nearly cost M. Gurdjieff his life. At this point it is supposed that the latter repented of his program or came to an interior realization of warning against it, thereupon doing his best to destroy both the teaching itself and its further results so far as concerned those who had been taught by it. The history of this sort of activity is full of accidents on roads, of sudden illuminations and of subsequent reversals of behavior; and here we have an accident that really happened. That is one of the theories.

The other is that Gurdjieff has not really repudiated these ideas at all. He has merely suppressed them temporarily. As is known, he is engaged upon the writing of a series of three "books"; the first is undoubtedly destructive, to clear the ground of rubbish, as it were; the second is alleged to provide constructive data upon which new building may commence; and the third and last is said to disclose true and objective information of the most serious character. According to this second theory, then, the formulated ideas which I am here calling the Oragean Version will reappear as a part at least of Gurdjieff's third and final "book." At the moment, however, he prefers, that they be forgotten, that they remain for the present non-extant. In other words, he does not care to have the climax of his writings anticipated.

There is also a third notion, circulated in more or less shamefaced whispers since it supposed to reflect upon M. Gurdjieff personally, although (unless he is to be taken with some sort of superstitious dread) I do not myself see anything derogatory in it. There is no doubt that the man received very serious head injuries at the time of his accident nor that this time coincided with his change of program. It may be supposed that these injuries were sustained by the frontal lobes, either directly or contrecoup. But the general region of the frontal lobes of the human brain mediates both formulatory ability and recent memory; and its injury might well produce such effects as a) the retention of former realizations and understandings without the continuing ability of previous formulation, or b) the loss of both the clarity of realization and of the formulatory ability, or c) the loss of the former and the retention of the latter. In all of these cases the previous kind of work could be carried no farther and therefore M. Gurdjieff, without abandoning his general aim, after his accident adopted entirely different means and an entirely different method of teaching in carrying it out. Naturally this implies a certain kind of inability upon his part resulting from harm to his physical organism, just as it also implies a highly competent adaptation to altered circumstances.

Certainly the first of these theories is more in accord with the traditions of the Hidden Learning, although the proposed indiscriminate broadcasting of M. Gurdjieff's writings will scarcely fit that picture. And perhaps the third theory may contain more ordinary common sense. But I have no personal means of judging which of them may be the most plausible and indeed it may easily be that none of them is even applicable to the situation. Actually I should consider them all to be more or less empty and useless speculations.

What is neither empty nor useless, is the information itself. This I propose to preserve but the first of the above theories at least impresses me sufficiently so that I shall not permit its publication. I shall merely set it down, just now.

*

To sum it up, I possess the following qualifications to do so. For a number of years I personally stated these formulations to a series of the Orage groups in New York City and its neighborhood. My familiarity with these propositions was constantly checked with Mr. Orage himself at that time. Nor am I forced altogether to rely upon my recollections of what was then stated, for I retain in my possession the detailed notes upon which I conducted one full group course from its beginning to its conclusion. Likewise there lie in my files numerous notes which I took down when attending both groups and lectures conducted by Mr. Orage, as well as careful copies of the diagrams elucidating certain of the fundamental principles expounded. Finally, I have a whole series of rigorous technical definitions of the verbal terms employed by Mr. Orage in his formulations; and these were not written down later from memory but were taken at the time when they were first introduced, and often thereafter compared and confirmed with the man himself.

Such, then, are the sources, upon which I rely for the account to follow.

*

Since my writing of the above introductory Premises there has taken place a further happening which I think should be mentioned here. Having recently been invited to attend a series of private readings from the late M. Ouspensky's so-far unpublished book entitled In Search of the Miraculous or Fragments of an Unknown Teaching, I have thus become acquainted with the contents of most of that work.

The book purports to be a chronicle of the original meeting of M. Ouspensky and M. Gurdjieff and to render an account of the talks and lectures then given by M. Gurdjieff at Moscow, St. Petersburg and other places in Russia before the Bolshevik revolution. It is so accepted by the followers of the late M. Ouspensky, who are in the best position to know, and I am told that it is also so accepted by M. Gurdjieff himself. It is said that the latter was much angered when first told of M. Ouspensky's book but later, when he had heard it read, that he altered his attitude and endorsed it as a correct account.

The bearing of those events upon the matter of these Premises is obvious when I say that the subjects discussed in M. Ouspensky's book are identical with the formulations of Mr. Orage and that here, once again, they are attributed unequivocally to M. Gurdjieff. It is therefore impossible to doubt that at least the intermediate origin of these ideas is from M. Gurdjieff himself directly; as to whence he in turn had earlier received them, I am not in a position to know.

However, the same circumstance arises again in relation to the version of Ouspensky as with that of Orage, viz., that any version at all must vary at least slightly from the original. And of course it is this accumulation of variations which inevitably, and after the lapse of no long time, always destroys the integrity of the original and may even terminate by reversing the original meaning, as so obviously has been the case, for instance, with the early Christian teachings. As to the body of the Gurdjieffian ideas, however, I am convinced that as yet no serious distortion has occurred with them. After all, I myself have known Gurdjieff and listened to him many times.

The differences between the versions of Orage and Ouspensky are chiefly those of approach and treatment, the former being rational and what might be called scientific, the latter suffering from a hint of the hortatory and at least a tinge of mysticism. But differences do exist, consisting for the most part in a differing placement of emphasis upon various concepts connected with these ideas. Thus, that entire Method by which the first actual work is conducted, and especially the ground work and the first steps in it, has been very much more fully formulated by Mr. Orage than by M. Ouspensky, so far as I am acquainted with the latter's writing, and, by contrast, certain psychological aspects of mechanical personality and certain physical statements, as in the case of the concept of the Cosmic Ray, have received a much more detailed formulation by M. Ouspensky.

For reasons such as those just mentioned I remain of the opinion that the formulations made by Mr. Orage may properly be called the Oragean Version and likewise that the importance of preserving them before they are either lost or distorted, also remains.

*

I must make a final observation regarding what is to follow. The terminology, the concepts and the propositions of this version will be solely those expounded by Mr. Orage; I shall endeavor to exclude not only any later constatations of my own but also all information of a similar character which I may have acquired from the writings of M. Gurdjieff, from those of M. Ouspensky, or from any other source. Except, of course, when such later information may serve to clarify the original concepts proposed by Mr. Orage himself.

However, it should be understood that the form and structure of the representation are my own and not those of Mr. Orage. This must be so because the outline form in which a series of groups may be conducted by means of the Socratic method, simply does not correspond to the necessities of the structure of a treatise. The demands of holding the immediate attentions of many different hearers by the introduction of various quite different ideas in the same discourse, do not arise in the case of a treatise which will only be read by one reader at a time, and by the same token the requirements of a single reader will better be met by assembling all the congruous subjects together while nonetheless separating each subtopic from the others, and especially by including at one place all the statements relating to a single subtopic rather than returning again and again to succeedingly fuller expositions of such subtopic, as is more suitable in work with a consecutively meeting group of people.

There will be only one exception to the above procedure. Manifestly the simpler ideas must be presented before the more complex and difficult. And thus the section entitled The Local Map must precede that which is called The Greater Map, and indeed is separated from the latter by the portion entitled, The Boat. These titles, incidentally, were suggested by Mr. Orage and are not my own inventions. And it will be understood that, as between the two Map sections, there are necessarily similarities, consisting in the less or more expanded exposition of some of the same subjects.

The body of the treatise will be written in Roman typeface, and will relate directly to the Oragean Version. Whenever I may find it of advantage to add some further formulation of my own in order to provide added information upon a point under discussion, such contributions will be distinguished from the main body of the exposition by being indicated in italics.

––––

And so, I wish you good hunting.

C. Daly King

Per Ketet,
Long Valley, N.J.
26 May, 1949

Georges Ivanovitch Gurdjieff died at the American Hospital at Neuilly, outside Paris, in France, 28 October, 1949. These Premises, therefore, were written while he still lived.

I. THE SUBJECT AND THE ATTITUDE

The subject of which we shall treat is the Hidden Learning, not the history of its appearances but the actual content as expounded in the Oragean Version. Tales, legends, romances and traditions have grown up about the Hidden Learning over the course of many centuries, but with these we shall not deal. Our subject is the Learning itself and there shall be only incidental remarks as to what may have happened to it from time to time. This body of knowledge has existed longer than can adequately be traced and, as mentioned above, has existed in many different formulations which, however, have all, if genuine, had reference to the same truths.

With what are these truths concerned? Primarily with the destiny of Man and with that of individual men, with their genuine human functions and the obstacle that prevents the fulfillment of them, and with those procedures that may hold out promise of being used effectually to alter the situation. This was the sort of thing taught in the ancient Mysteries, now mostly lost and almost entirely unintelligible because the key of those teachings has vanished. Confronted with fragments of the merely verbal skeleton of such teachings and in absence of the key, all attempted contemporary interpretations of their real meaning are either fantastic or plainly speculative in a philosophic or romantic sense; and without exception they are ignorant interpretations. But that somehow those original teachings refer to serious and important truths is a widespread belief even today.

There will be no endeavor here to reconstitute the Mysteries nor will their terms be employed except possibly in occasional illustration. But the same verities, to which they pointed, shall be our subject too; for the truth, if genuine, is unique and single. But the terms presently to be defined, will be modern terms and thus more readily comprehensible to the contemporary reader.

It will be seen immediately that our subject is a very serious one indeed. But it does not on that account demand to be approached with a long face; a mournful sense of sin is no more to the point than would be an attitude of drunken levity. What is required of the investigator is that he should understand from the beginning that more is at stake here than the mere satisfaction of his possible curiosity. Curiosity alone may suffice to bring one into a first contact with the Hidden Learning at times like the present; after the preliminary contact has been established, however, this stimulus by itself will progressively wane and another must take its place. It is one of the functions of the Hidden Learning to make such further stimuli available to those who may be able to respond to them.

The scope of the present subject is as broad as that of Science and may be taken in a similar fashion. The term, Science, is given in our vocabulary to a certain, defined method employed in the investigation of reality and, since it is alleged that every sort of phenomenon and real relationship may be investigated by the scientific method, it follows that the subject-matter of Science embraces all reality. The scope of *this* subject-matter is equally inclusive and the procedure employed is likewise very similar to that of Science, which comprises four steps in the solution of any problem—viz., 1) the accumulation or observation of many items of the data relevant to a given question, 2) the formation of a theory or hypothesis subsuming large numbers of such data in a more or less broad generalization, 3) the setting-up of an experimental technique whereby the deductive consequences of the hypothesis may be tested in an unknown instance, 4) the resulting disproof or lack of disproof of the hypothesis.

It is not intended to be stated that we are here engaged upon a formulation of Science, for this treatise concerns solely the general body of Gurdjieffian ideas as they exist in the Oragean Version; but the identity of the subject (reality) and the similarity of the approach to it (the four consecutive steps of procedure) with the comparable aspects of Science, constitute an advantage of familiarity to the inquirer with which it would be foolish to dispense.

For just as scientific efforts may be, and are, subdivided among various fields of knowledge, here we encounter a similar case. The Gurdjieffian ideas and procedures are directed towards the same fields in which Science works, as for instance physics, chemistry, biology, psychology, sociology, astronomy, cosmogony, religion and philosophy (which later are also subject to scientific investigation), and many others. In addition they invade fields so far almost untouched by Science, such as telepathy, clairvoyance, ESP, astrology, and so on, but as to which scientists expect their own technique to be applicable eventually. In other words the entire realm of Science, both actual and potential, is covered.

At the outset by far the greatest attention will be given to the field of psychology—i.e. to a formulation of the objective behavior and of the subjective experience of the human being—but it must not be supposed on that account that the further aspects of reality are to be disregarded; and indeed it will be found necessary that the investigation of many of these should go hand in hand with the primary inquiry. But naturally, for a human being, any serious critique of reality must *commence* with himself, that is, with him who is making the critique in the first place.

There is also another aspect of Science which is identical with the present approach. Above all else scientific method is *impartial*. It does not seek to prove a foregone conclusion by the laborious accumulation of unnecessary supports nor does it expediently seek the disproof of some position whose validity is still a matter of conjecture. It constantly seeks to discover what is, but neither what might be or what ought to be. It has no axe to grind.

Now while it is a fact that many scientists personally fall far short of this scientific ideal—contemporarily they do so most blatantly in the fields of psychology and sociology, wherein all kinds of *ad hoc* projects are prosecuted—that circumstance does not impugn the nature of Science itself but only signifies that a considerable number of scientists are in fact unworthy of the name. In present scientific work such imposture is often quite feasible but with regard to the procedures to be detailed below it will be found that masquerading is entirely out of the question. For impartiality is their heart and core and very essence; and if this attitude be lost at any time, then for that time the procedures followed will not be those here formulated but instead they will be, by definition and in fact, some other sort of procedures altogether.

It may be said now, also, that in the predominant position accorded to psychology there are two aspects, the theoretical position treating of the nature of the human being as such and of the relevant psychological concepts, and the practical or "applied psychology" aspect wherein the individual begins and continues the application of such principles to his own case, i.e., he inaugurates work upon himself. It is the efforts involved in this last procedure which demand a continuing reinforcement from outside and among the reinforcements required are not only the theoretical concepts pertaining to psychology itself but also many further statements relating to what are usually called other branches of Science. These are needed both as aids to the efforts to which he is making personally and, in addition, in order to keep him as orientated as possible while he may himself gradually begin to change during his prosecution of his personal work.

For the questions to be answered here are the fundamental questions with which all human beings must be confronted eventually, simply by reason of the fact that they are human beings: What is a human being? Why is a human being? What is the meaning and aim of human existence? How may such aims be fulfilled personally and individually? As regards these questions it will be well to establish the same approach that will be used generally concerning every question dealt with in this Version.

2.

In the first place there is an arresting assumption presented to those unconversant with the Gurdjieff system of ideas. This assumption is that, for serious human beings knowledge exists upon three different stages or at three different levels. The first of these stages may be denoted as the general level of Science, the second as the level of Moonshine (including such knowledge as possessed by religions, cults, various ethical systems, etc.) and the third stage or level may be called that of genuine and correct knowledge. These various divisions in respect of knowledge may also be referred to as; A—Knowledge; B—Moonshine; C—Science. They are all included within the general field of knowledge, thus:

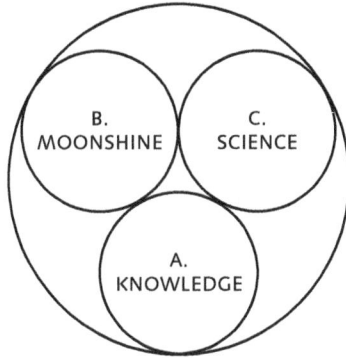

Figure 1. The General Field of Knowledge.

Within this general situation C knows only C and believes A to be inherent in C; B knows both B and C and mistakes B for A; A knows A, B and C. Within any general population only a few of its members are within the field of B; and of these only a few again ever meet within the field of A, by chance.... This formulation, of course, is not offered for the purpose of arousing credulous belief. It is a simple, graphic portrayal of the situation in respect of knowledge, as the Oragean Version states that that situation exists.

What comes as a surprise to many persons is the subordinate position accorded to Science in this order of the degrees of knowledge, for it is placed below the status of even credulous cults. A word of explanation is obviously required. From the viewpoint of this Version scientific work is a perfectly respectable activity and the general personality balance of most scientists is plainly at a higher order than that of religious fanatics. The question here, however, is not one of general respectability; it is the question of potential access to a full, genuine and correct knowledge of reality as the latter actually exists. In this matter the religionist, despite all his lopsidedness, possesses a distinct advantage over the scientist, for the former is not antagonistic to the unusual, the bizarre or the wonderful, while the cut-and-dried attitude of the latter is a continual hindrance to him just so soon as he makes contact with any phenomenon not readily to be assimilated into the current orthodox view. Although at first it may seem like a paradox, to be sincerely in search of wonders and receptive to their possible recognition is an approach to the profounder aspects of reality more likely to be successful than is the cautious timidity of the scientist, forever fearful of unorthodoxy. Few B-type persons will ever meet those of the A-type but, when they do, at least they have some chance of profiting by it. Very often the "academic integrity" of the scientist is little more than an unreasoning terror of the unfamiliar. And any genuine truth, at all approaching to completeness, must be very unfamiliar indeed.

One can scarcely expect the above remarks to hold an especial appeal to scientists but there is another unfortunate aspect of science upon which all the best scientists will agree. This is the circumstance that the scientific method can never offer a valid affirmative proof of any proposition or theory. That is because the method consists in the experimental verification of the logically deduced consequences of a hypothesis. Such verification can never establish the correctness of the original hypothesis in any final sense, the reason being that the particular consequence confirmed may be a logically correct deduction not only of the selected hypothesis but likewise it may be an equally correct deduction from an altogether different hypothesis. It may be both at the same time and in extreme cases it may be a common deduction derivable alike from two different hypotheses which may even state opposite views of the same phenomenon. Thus, the statement that the sun will rise at 7 a.m. on a given day is equally derivable from the hypothesis that the sun moves around the earth or from the opposite hypothesis that the earth revolves on its own axis. In such a case the verification of the given deduced consequence will as readily confirm hypothesis M as hypothesis P; in other words it is generally confirmative of neither of them. The fallacy here involved is termed by logicians the Fallacy of Affirming the Consequent; and although many poorly qualified scientists continue in bland ignorance of it and thus remain entirely at ease, every first-rate scientific worker on the planet is well aware of it and will often go to great lengths in his investigations to modify it so far as possible, without at some time ever fully being able to overcome it. Naturally this disability does not extend to the case of negative proof, or disproof; if any rigorously deduced consequence of an hypothesis is shown by experiment to be characterized by non-occurrence, then that hypothesis is shown, pari passu, to be an incorrect one.

For these reasons, also, the C-field of knowledge, which is called Science, is the more incapable of approaching actual reality directly since, even though it may light upon some perfectly genuine aspect of the truth, no means lie at its disposal whereby the proposition may be shown to be finally correct. That Science has very large practical effects is not relevant to the present question; so have the operations of the field artillery brigade but they do not on that account provide any access to genuine knowledge.

In the exposition of that knowledge of the A-type which this Version claims that it possesses, a few common sense rules of formulation must be kept in mind. One of them is well instanced by the numeral, 124. In verbalizing that number one must first say "one hundred" (but this is not only not the full statement, it is even an actual misstatement of the information intended to be conveyed); then one must next say "twenty" (and still the information is both incomplete and incorrect, though somewhat less so); and then finally one says "four," and the deed is done. This rather halting accomplishment of the task is due to the nature of speech itself, it being impossible to pronounce "one" and "four" simultaneously; and it is necessary therefore to make the full statement by successive degrees or steps. In just the same way it has not been possible since the days of ancient Egypt to condense a complex subject into a single symbol or hieroglyph. The nature itself of our form of writing renders impossible the complete and simultaneous statement of anything worth stating in the first place; and the reader must understand, with regard to any subject considered, that he is not acquainted with the intended exposition until the full formulation has been completed. Very often a preliminary misunderstanding may be due only to the circumstance that a partial formulation is first demanded as a requirement for the arrival later of a complete formulation. And, similarly, many of the questions which will automatically arise in the reader when some subject is first introduced will later be found to have obtained their answers when the subject has been dealt with fully. But plainly enough one must begin somewhere; the first step is not the whole journey, yet without it, there will never be any journey at all.

Moreover, in dealing with matters difficult to understand, it is important that one does not lose one's place in the argument. Side topics must often be considered and these involve digressions from the main line of the discussion. Indeed, it is well to think of the discussion of any large subject as compromising a straight line of exposition from which there will usually depend a number of circular lines representing formulations of subtopics interrupting the main course of the exposition and then returning to it at the point of the interruption. Within these circles of the first degree there may also be smaller circles of the second degree representing a consideration of a subtopic of a subtopic. A very simple diagram may be made of the situation:

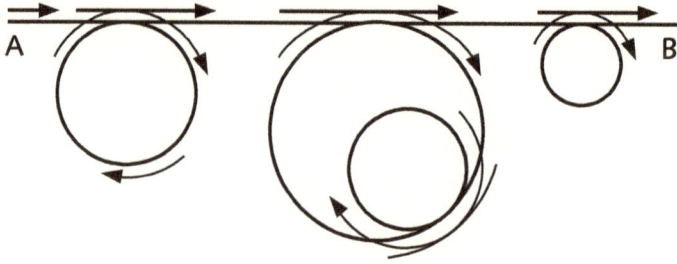

Figure 2. The Course of Exposition.
The circles represent digressions from the main (straight) line of discussion.
The inner circle represents a digression within a digression. A—beginning
of exposition; B—conclusion of exposition.

The point to be kept always in mind is one's current location during the
passage from A to B, whether it be at some position on the straight line or
upon the circumference of one of the circles. If confusion commences to
arise, that is the time to stop, to visualize the diagram and to discover the
position of the argument at that moment.

Another matter to be understood is the necessity for technical terms. All
careful scientists very soon adopt such terms and one of the first requirements which their students face, is the demand that they be familiar with the
exact meanings of the terms employed by the science. There is an excellent
reason for this; and it is neither pedantry nor a love of hocus-pocus. The
reason is that words in themselves have no meaning whatsoever but acquire
meaning only in connection with the association which they arouse in us.
But since our associations are formed haphazardly by our circumstances
and experiences and without reference to any form of logic or reason, it
results that none of us has the identical associations with a given word that
is possessed by someone else. Obviously, then, the significance received is often quite different from the significance intended. In ordinary conversation
this does not greatly matter, for most of it is either mere chattering or else
is concerned with practical matters of so plain a kind that mistakes are difficult to make. But with regard to matters that must be formulated carefully
and which are not easy of comprehension under the best of conditions, the
stumbling-block of verbal misunderstanding can become of serious import.

This misfortune, inherent in the nature of verbal communication, can no
more be fully overcome than can the scientific fallacy inherent in the scientific method. Its solution lies finally in the adoption of a more accurate sort of
communication than the verbal kind; but meantime something can be done.
By defining words in terms of other words at least some of the incongruous
associations may be deleted; and by inventing brand-new terms which lack
any great associational history we may in some degree start afresh upon a

common ground. That is why rigorous definition is not a mere academic luxury and why newly invented technical terms, often appearing artificial and pretentious, are in fact of much scientific value.

But if a technical language is valuable to Science, it is even more desirable here. Eventually we shall have to deal with concepts that make Einsteinian relativity appear relatively simple, and to attempt to do so in the *argot* of everyday life would probably render them entirely incomprehensible. Therefore our definitions will be at least as strict and rigorous as the most rigorous in Science, and whenever assistance can be obtained by the coining of a new and technically defined term, there will be no hesitancy in adopting such a means to a clearer understanding. This signifies that the reader must sincerely try to grasp the exactitude of the definitions, to learn the technical language employed by this Version and not to wander irresponsibly outside the limits carefully set in the definition used. When the term, normal, is employed, for example, it will have a careful technical significance quite other than that related to its ordinary use and abuse; if the reader fails to learn and to accept and to employ that special significance, he will simply fail to understand what is said. No one is going to levy a fine against the culprit. The fine is automatic; the loose and careless user of words shall surely lose his way. Very certainly there is a penalty; but the penalty is assessed against the man by the man himself. He has no more right to blame his instructor than has his chemistry student whose test tube explodes in his hand because he failed to learn the definitory properties of hydrogen. All versions of the Hidden Learning have always suffered from the self-justifying excuses of would-be converts who have failed in their very first duty of at least *knowing* what is said.

This is very important indeed in a practical sense. If the inquirer is told *not* to engage in a certain activity, if he then does so and receives harm as a result, the fault and the blame are his own alone.

Clear distinctions are also related to rigorous definitions; and the ability to make distinctions clearly and with a considerable degree of preciseness is essential to an understanding of many serious subjects. Let us make such a distinction now and let it be the distinction between Reality and Unreality.

Reality comprises both the Actual and the Potential. The Actual is what in fact exists or takes place; the Potential is what might or may exist or take place. Thus I am now sitting in a particular chair and this fact is a part of the Actual. But it is possible that a cat might be now sitting here and it is even likely that a cat may be later sitting here; and these circumstances, especially the future one, form a part of the Potential. It is also to be noted that these different matters are actual and potential regardless of the reader's knowledge of them; the nature of the Actual and of the Potential, and thus of the Real, is not dependent upon anyone's correct or incorrect knowledge of it. Nor is it related to a total absence of knowledge concerning it.

Now with the regard to the actuality of being in the chair a number of potentialities immediately exist. I may continue to sit in it; I may rise from it in the usual fashion; I may swing it backwards and thus leave it more unconventionally; its supporting structure may collapse and force an undignified exit upon me; and so on, in the case of numerous eventualities. All of these circumstances are real potentialities, which is to say that they are among the potentialities that constitute a part of Reality. There are, however, a number of impossibilities associated with my sitting in this chair. One is that I should suddenly take on the form and appearance of the cat; another is that I should reach under the chair and, extending my arm beneath, then up and over the back of the chair, should touch my fingers to the back of my neck; another is that within the next few moments I should find myself travelling in a New York subway fifty miles away; and so on. These constitute unreal potentialities and are a part of the realm of Unreality.

Thus we see that Reality is what exists or happens or may exist or may happen; and that it comprises the really Actual and the really Potential. Unreality is what cannot exist or happen or what it is impossible may exist or may happen, and is thus synonymous with the really Impossible; it comprises both the actually Impossible and the impossible Potential. These distinctions are more than mere verbalisms. They should be kept in mind, memorized if necessary, as the definitions and meanings, used here, of the terms, real, actual, potential, unreal, impossible. Those are the senses in which these words have been used in this treatise.

There is also an application of these distinctions to one of our first projects, the consideration of the subject of human psychology. The science of psychology, as known today, treats of only one section of Reality, that is, it treats of the Actual. It approaches Man as a datum given, as a creature to be investigated solely as he is now found to be, and it seeks to formulate adequately both a description of the human being as he is and the laws governing the activities which he is found in fact to manifest. There it stops; as to any further fundamental potentiality in the nature of human beings, apparently it holds no opinions whatever. It does not deny such potentialities, it does not affirm them, nor does it investigate them. It simply remains oblivious to them.

This Version takes a different point of view, since its own necessity is to deal with the full field of Reality including both the Actual and the Potential. Thus it raises no objection at all to the attitude of scientific psychology in treating of the Actual; it is very necessary that we should understand the nature of men as they are and that we should understand it as completely as possible. But when psychology investigates human beings solely as they are now found to be, it is to that word, solely, that this Version objects. For men, even as they are now found to be, do possess basic potentialities, which though in fact unactualized, remain real.

And by far the most interesting thing about Man is not what he is, but what he *may become*.

Here, too, it is necessary that our distinctions should hold. A man cannot become an angel, nor can he become a planet, nor can he become God. All propositions of such a character are really impossible and thus they are within the field of Unreality. The actuality about men is that they are humanly undeveloped; their potentiality lies exactly in the real possibility of their fuller and more harmonious development. The real Potential in relation to men is that they may become Men.

3.

Before we can take up the concrete details, however, our general orientation toward these subjects must be established. What is to be our attitude regarding the statements and propositions put forward in this exposition? What really is our personal relationship to what shall be said? Certainly it is not generally one of prior acquaintance with the assertions to be made.

The reader will here be invited to explore new continents of knowledge; and continents, moreover, of which he has now either a vague and incorrect opinion, or else none at all. In order to have any real value such new knowledge must be both precise and detailed to the one hand and accurate to the other. How is the precise knowledge of a new continent presented ordinarily? It is done by means of a detailed map. Accordingly we may consider that the specific propositions and assertions advanced here, comprise in their entirety the map of a new continent of knowledge of which, as in the case of a cartographer's work, the general outlines will appear first, then the broad features, and finally the local elements will be filled in increasing detail. Naturally in the beginning, as in the case of any explorer, we must be concerned primarily with that locality at which a landing is to be effected and at other times, too, it will be necessary for us to pay a greater attention to some localized area of the map than to the whole document, to study as it were some special feature of the map. But gradually more and more of it shall be completed. In the present Version all of the details will not be entirely filled in even at the end, for this Version does not take us so far; but a general working acquaintanceship shall have been achieved and in respect to some of its portions a very particularized local map shall be available.

How, then, shall we have a proper assurance concerning the accuracy of such a map? In the ordinary case we simply rely upon the *bona fides* and the assumed competence of those who furnish the map; but it is to be doubted, if we were actually setting out upon an exploration in which our own lives were at stake, that we should accept our master-map with the same ease of unverification that suffices for mere stay-at-home curiosity. In the present instance we are truly going to explore the new continent personally; it is truly unknown to us at the start; and it holds some truly dangerous localities. We need a truly first class map, not just for fun but for keeps. So what shall be our attitude towards the map which is offered? Credulity? Disbelief? Well, what?

In sanity our attitude can only be one of skepticism, i.e., of suspended judgment until such time as we are able to say for ourselves that we have been at such and such a described location and that our knowledge of it is our own, no longer relying on travellers' tales. Until we can say that, we simply do not know, so why not admit it? A credulous acceptance of everything we hear about this new continent would scarcely be a sound foundation for our proceeding; the exploration is too important for that and we do not wish to be led into even an innocently contrived ambush. But surely a blind disbelief will hardly advance us upon our way, for to reject the map in that fashion will only leave us exactly where we are now. The reverse of the coin is just as much the coin as the obverse; and obstinate incredulity is just as credulous, in a merely negative sense, as is credulity itself. The dupe can serve neither himself nor his quest nor anyone else by his dupiness; and the inverse, i.e., the disbelieving, dupe stands in the selfsame position.

Moreover, the two sides of the coin of credulity represent two aspects of a common human disease, the very literal disease of suggestibility. Vast numbers of persons in these times follow blindly after a Hitler, a Roosevelt, a Stalin; other hordes not only grasp for suggested economic gold bricks of a kind preposterous to any reflections at all, but even swallow them whole. Perhaps it would be as well if we did not too quickly convince each other that we ourselves are of course immune to the same disease of suggestibility. For we shall find a little later that we are not, that though our fallacies may take a different turn than those of certain other people, they are not the less fantastic on that account.

Agnosticism or skepticism is the antidote to the poison of suggestibility; and even though it may be uncongenial to some of us, we shall have to adopt it now. At the very start it is required to preserve one's rational self-respect by taking an attitude of sane and truthful skepticism, neither foolishly believing what one may later discover to be false nor stupidly disbelieving and even denying that of which one now can only be ignorant.

Such an attitude is *required*. The present Version welcomes skeptics, it rejects either positive or negative dupes.

4.

It will now quite properly be asked how one is ever to come to any reasonable conclusions concerning the alleged continent. A map is all very well but, upon the recommended ground of agnosticism, how shall one verify it or ever know for oneself whether it be accurate or not? That the mapmaker invites such personal verification by others, argues a high degree of confidence in his map upon his part; but this, of course, is no sufficient ground for accepting it as correct. It is necessary that we visit the localities described and see for ourselves how accurate the description has been. For this purpose we shall need some transportation and to meet the necessity our Version provides a boat.

The boat consists in a certain method of procedure, in something specific to do, in a meticulously described program of action which, if followed successfully, will bring the explorer into a close relationship with the localities represented on the map. Thus there is offered the possibility of eventual verification, in a personal sense, of the statements that comprise the map.

There are provided in this Version the Map (the body of statements and propositions contained in the system of Gurdjieff ideas) and the Boat (a specific Method of a practical kind, designed to bring the user into a personal relationship to the Map). For the moment we need say no more about the Boat and we may return to a first and general glance at the Map.

5.

One of our very first questions may well concern the position of mankind to the Universe in which it finds itself. Here is the answer, and a preliminary glimpse of the Map. Mankind constitutes a part of the organic kingdom, which itself is a part of this planet; this planet, in turn, is one of a system of planets and that system of planets, together with its central sun, comprises the solar system in which we live; our sun is one of the countless others in the particular galactic system which we call the Milky Way and which is itself only one among other galactic systems; together all of these latter very large systems make up the universe. We then have the following sequence of steps:

galactic systems (or Universe)
Milky Way (a single galactic system)
Sun (a single star in the above galactic system)
planetary system (attached to the Sun)
Earth (a single planet of the planetary system)
organic kingdom (a part of the Earth)
Mankind (a part of the organic kingdom)

It will be seen that in this sequence no fundamental element is omitted nor are any included which are not in themselves both natural and complete subdivisions. We have therefore oriented ourselves in relation to the Universe in the most general, but an accurate, way.

We have also come upon a form of sequence which is interesting in itself, apart from the elements that in this case compose it. It must be acknowledged that the structure of this sequence has not been invented artificially nor has it artificially been imposed upon the elements that make it up; it has in fact appeared of its own motion and nature in answer to the question which we first proposed. Because this particular kind of sequence is a general feature of the whole Map, we may well now make a preliminary survey of it.

The sequence comprises a series of seven degrees of magnitude or, in general, of seven distinct steps. It is a special instance of the universal Law of Seven, called in the Gurdjieff writings Heptaparabarshinokh, in the Oragean Version the Law of the Octave and scientifically the Law of Octaves as proposed by J. A. R. Newlands many years ago. Its traditional recognition is so ancient as to be lost in antique mists, it appears upon the keyboards of our familiar pianos in the musical octaves there represented,* its application is plainly to be seen in the periodic table of the chemical elements and in the deduced structures and electromagnetic fields of the atoms studied by physics.

The constitution of our own planetary system, taken by itself, shows the same relationships. In fact, the more fundamental the phenomena which we may investigate, the more plainly and openly does the octavic principle manifest itself.

The relationship is a simple sequence made up of three successive unitary steps, followed by a step half again as large, followed by two unitary steps and then once more by another step half again as large, whereupon the succession repeats itself. Proceeding from below upwards, thus:

new octave	do	1 unit (subsuming the octave below)
seventh step	si	1½ units
sixth step	la	1 unit
fifth step	sol	1 unit
fourth step	fa	1½ units
third step	mi	1 unit
second step	re	1 unit
first step	do	1 unit

This is the pure form of the octavic relationship; but because each step or note of the succession usually comprises another octave (and often subordinate octaves within itself in addition) it is seldom presented to us in nature in so obvious a fashion.

---

* Due to the incorporation of 'temperament,' for practical reasons, in the construction of the piano, the authentically pure relationships of the octavic principle do not exactly appear there in the vibration-rates of the notes.

The units will be relevant to whatever phenomenon may take the octavic relationship and may be, for instance, in terms of length, time, magnitude, and so on. The inequality of the fourth and seventh steps to the others, is what constitutes the definitory characteristic of the octavic principle. It is here that the step-like progression of the octave is interrupted by two, as it were, foreign intervals, the first intervening between the third and fourth steps, the second between the seventh step and the beginning of the next octave. These intervals also constitute barriers to the continuation of the natural sequence from one step to the next and at these special points in the progression, proceeding so far perhaps by its own momentum, will cease, unless reinforced by further energy of an external kind not characteristic of the particular octavic phenomenon in question. For example, in the propagation of musical sound the note, do, can be transformed into the note, re, without outside assistance; but the transformation from mi to fa can take place only when, in addition to the presence of the note (rhythmical vibration in air), noise (unrhythmical or chaotic vibration in air) is also available.

As another example we may take the case of atomic structure. In the modern scientific view the atomic series begins with hydrogen, having a central nucleus with a positive charge and a single external electron circling about it, whose negative charge neutralizes the atom electrically. Since these units are deductively reached concepts, it may be that future research will alter the picture now accepted; but the arrangement, even though possibly analogical, is sufficiently close an approximation to the actual phenomenon. From the hydrogen atom the series builds itself up until the uranium atom is reached, each successive atom being formed by the addition of one more external electron to the orbits surrounding the succeedingly denser and heavier nuclei. But these additional electrons are not added just uniformly; they take their places successively in a series of differently spaced rings or orbits and these successive rings fall into the octavic relationship. Each ring accommodates just enough added electrons to satisfy the case, whereupon the next electron to be added is found circling the nucleus at a distance corresponding to the position of the next octavic ring. There is thus produced the general series of atomic structure; and since the properties of the chemical elements depend upon the arrangements of the external electrons of the respective atoms, there is also produced the periodic table of the chemical elements which likewise manifests a similar octavic arrangement.

Energy can pass either up or down such octavic scales, undergoing the comparable transformations, but always in accordance with the octavic principle, i.e., whether the movement be up or down, there will always be encountered between the points, mi and fa, and between the points, si and do, those special intervals at which the reinforcement of outside energy is required in order that the movement may continue. (In the case of the atomic progression this outside energy is perhaps furnished through the electro-magnetic field of the atom itself.)

This same octavic principle holds in very many other cases, ranging from learning curves (where it applies to energy expenditure) to sociological phenomena and to the familiar spectrum of visible light. The last indeed is but a single octave from among the total vibration-rates known to science, which reach from the long waves of radio through the short and Hertzian waves, the heat radiations, the infra-red, the spectrum of visible light, the ultra-violet, Schumann and X waves to the gamma and so-called cosmic waves; a continuous series of more than forty octaves and possibly, when fully explored, of forty-nine. Throughout this whole range the laws of octavic relationship hold undisputed sway. We shall see later in what further applications to specifically human problems the Law of Octaves is manifested.

In this first view of the Map we may well now also make a preliminary observation of another of its large features, a second law which, with the Law of the Octave, constitutes one of the two primary laws of the Universe. In the Gurdjieff writings the name of this second law is Triamasikamno, in the Oragean Version it is called the Law of the Three.

The law states that in every total phenomenon there are always present three independent factors or forces. They are denominated the positive force, the negative force, and the neutralizing force. The first two of these can be observed with little difficulty but the third appears mysterious and difficult to apprehend because in the large part we are third-force-blind. Nevertheless, with effort the presence of the third force can be seen and its effect appreciated. For instance, in the atom the positive nucleus and the negative electrons are distinguishable at once; but where is the third factor entering into the constitution of the atom? An understanding of this kind of problem has led to the development of now recognized field theories in modern physics, for the third factor in the phenomenon of the atom is the electromagnetic field permeating its component parts. The effect of a magnetic field has long been demonstrated upon iron filings; in the same way the paths or orbits of the external electrons and the constitution of the inner nucleus are accounted for by the electromagnetic field, in the case of the atom. It will be seen that the third force in this case is a *force*, actively participating in the phenomenon, that is, it is just as much an active force in its own right as are either the positive or the negative forces. Everywhere else this is also the case.

We might take innumerable other examples, for all phenomena are the results of these three forces working together. In the settlement of a dispute the plaintiff and the defendant represent the positive and negative forces, the judge who brings to bear upon the matter his interpretation of the law, occupies the position of the neutralizing force; the result is the settlement, and in this example it is easy to see that the third force is an active one, for the judge ordinarily will have little difficulty in enforcing his decision.

Another example is a town or city, in which the positive force is the desires and plans of those who wish to occupy the place, the negative force is the actual work necessitated in building the constructions which make up the town, and the neutralizing force is the site itself, whose configuration has decisive effect upon the design that the town must have. Cities on islands or in lakes, at river junctions, on hilltops or in ravines very obviously show the effect of the third force, while in other cases it is equally present without being equally noticeable. New York City on Manhattan Island has had to grow upwards with skyscrapers, Newark could just spread. Still another instance is that of the human body, its positive factor being its energy intake, the negative factor being the chemical constituents of which its cells and organs are composed, and the neutralizing factor being the biological steady-state DC *electrical field of the whole organism, which determines that specific organic design that we call a human body. And in the case of the human being the same situation holds, for his subjective experience (positive factor) is based upon the objective neurological functioning of his body (negative factor) and it is his consciousness (neutralizing factor) which mediates the transformation of neuron activity into experiential content. We may condense these examples as follows:*

Physics

first force, positive	nucleus (positrons, neutrons, etc.)
second force, negative	outer elements (electrons)
third force, neutralizing	electromagnetic field (including "exclusion principle," etc.)
total phenomenon	atom

Engineering

first force, positive	architectural decision and planning
second force, negative	constructional work
third force, neutralizing	geographical site
total phenomenon	city

Law

first force, positive	plaintiff
second force, negative	defendant
third force, neutralizing	judge
total phenomenon	settlement of dispute

Biology

first force, positive	thermo-dynamic energies
second force, negative	chemical entities
third force, neutralizing	electro-dynamic organic field
total phenomenon	biological organism

Psychology

first force, positive	experiential content (e.g., blue, anger, introspection)
second force, negative	neurological functioning (sensory, basal ganglia and cerebro-integrative processes)
third force, neutralizing	conscious entity (whose transforming mediation is consciousness or pure awareness)
total phenomenon	human being

The more naïve error in regard to the Law of the Three is the view that the positive and negative forces account for the neutralizing force, i.e., that the interaction of positive and negative forces in itself produces that reconciliation between them which is both the design of the final product and also the product itself. This is merely a hasty failure to make the proper distinctions among the factors and product involved, for it can be seen at once neither that the plaintiff and defendant together constitute the judge, much less the settlement of the dispute, nor that engineering intentions plus constructional work ever create the actual geographical location of the town.

An only somewhat less naïve and apparently inevitable error concerning the relation of the third force or factor is the other elements should also be mentioned here. This error earlier took place in physics (where it has now been largely remedied); when the significance of the third force was first deduced, there immediately arose a tendency to over-exaggerate it and thus to attribute to the electromagnetic field the actual appearance of both nucleus and electrons, as if the latter were in fact the creation of the former. The same error has occurred in psychology, in the Gestalt contention either that the total phenomenon is solely due to the inherent patterning factor which is the third force involved or that this patterning factor is properly to be identified with the total phenomenon itself. In psychology this fallacy has not even been entirely repudiated. Likewise in biology, when field theories first appeared upon the scene and the steady-state DC field of the organism was established by definite potential-difference measurements, there at once followed the impulse to attribute a primary importance to the field force in the constitution of the organism.

There is, however, nothing primary about this third factor. The positive, the negative and the neutralizing forces are all equally required in order that there should take place any phenomenon whatsoever. This can be seen very clearly in the instance of the city: in the absence of the geographical site there can certainly be no city but in the same fashion the site itself neither does, nor can, create the city. The total phenomenon, or the city, demands for its actualization not only the site but also the work done upon that site and the planned intention to accomplish that work; and in the same way a biological organism, in the absence of thermo-dynamical energies and con-stituent chemical entities, remains only an unactualized potentiality in the design of the electro-dynamic steady-state organic field. The last statement is by no means simply a theoretical one; in the unfertilized frog's egg, for instance, the steady-state organic field which may contribute to the typi-cal formation of the adult frog, has often been measured with the relevant electrical recorders and always manifests the typical frog organic pattern; if the egg is fertilized, the frog subsequently appears but, if not, then the field forces remain so long as the egg lives but in the absence of the positive factor of fertilization the maturing frog of course does not result.

It will be noticed that, in whatever instance we take, the three forces, positive, negative and neutralizing, are incommensurable with each other; but this does not mean that any one of them is superior, or primary, to the others. The Law of Three states only that in the totality of all real phenom-ena all three forces are *equally* required and are *equally* contributive to the result.

For the moment this is all that need be said concerning the two funda-mental Laws of the Three and of the Seven. Already, however, we may make an important distinction between them. The Law of the Octave is an op-erational law, i.e., it applies to *what happens* and is determinative of the sequence and progression of such happening. The Law of the Three finds its application in what is. And since there can be no interaction or happening until there exists something between which interaction may take place or in regard to which something can happen, in this sense the Law of the Three is the more basic creational law.

6.

At the beginning of these expositions it is frequently asked what is the origin of this information and why it should be believed. The answer to the second of these questions can be given first: the information is not to be believed; it is offered simply and solely as a series of statements which in fact are correct but which cannot be properly accepted as correct by the inquirer until he himself has achieved a personal verification of them. This at once raises the question of the nature of genuine proof and it may be said here that there are three kinds of such proof: 1) the statement to be proven must be shown to be rationally and logically correct, i.e., it must be intellectually consistent; 2) there is also an emotional aspect which must be shown to be consistently correct; 3) the statement must meet the requirements of the logic of Solvitur Ambulando, i.e., it must be shown to work or, in other words, that it is true in a practical sense. When all of these aspects of proof have been summed up in the personal experience of the investigator, then—and only then—can verification be said to have been reached.

A little can also be said concerning the origin of the information here treated. This information comprises part of the Hidden Learning, which is passed on from generation to generation and from age to age by various means, the most successful of which is the establishment and maintenance of Schools or, as they are sometimes called, Esoteric Schools. Only infrequently are the existence or the names of these Schools known at all to the general public but the Pythagorean Institute at Cretona may be mentioned as one School of this kind which has come to public attention. Such Schools are quite different in character from ordinary schools of everyday life. They are concerned with instruction only in the sense of an accurate transmission of the information to be preserved and their primary function is the training—in a literal sense the "education," the "leading-out" or development—of a highly selected number of human beings, some of whom may succeed in coming to an individual realization of these truths and thus attain to a position of ability to transmit them without alteration or distortion. One purpose of such transmission is to preserve for mankind the correct information regarding the Universe and himself and the real relation between them, during those cyclic periods of regression when otherwise all such genuine information would be lost forever. These Schools are the possessors of the A-type knowledge mentioned shortly above.

Then why the secrecy? There are many, very numerous reasons for it but, here again, neither a love of mumbo-jumbo nor a pretense of exclusive self-importance is among them. The training of the postulants in such Schools must be both severe and at times dangerous; only a few persons are capable of undergoing such a discipline successfully and, since the Schools are not concerned with turning out maniacs or the hopelessly broken, great care is taken in the selection and acceptance of those who are permitted to enter. For this reason alone it will be seen why the present kind of information cannot be scattered indiscriminately before those who not only are incapable of understanding it but who, through their own misunderstanding, must inevitably injure both themselves and the aim of the Schools. Christianity is essentially the broadcasting of the teachings of the Essene School, of which Jesus the Christ was a high initiate; and those teachings, subjected to public distortion, have brought Christianity to an almost complete reversal of its origins. Contemporary Buddhism shows the same reversed distortion; the collapse and disintegration of the tremendous civilization of ancient Egypt is another instance of the consequences of the degression of genuine human truth when it becomes accessible to the ordinary or common man. The reasons for this unfortunate and deplorable state of affairs will become clearer when the formulations of the following chapter have been completed.

But if this be so, then one must naturally ask how this Version of the Hidden Learning could ever have been offered to the semi-public audience to which it was presented. Are its sponsors and formulators renegades and apostates of some contemporary School? Was Jesus Christ a renegade and apostate of the Essence School? It can scarcely be supposed so and thus the only alternative must be taken: that from time to time so serious and crucial straits are encountered by mankind that even the most doubtful and hazardous means must be accepted in the attempt to meet and deal with the crisis. Some crises can be truly desperate, of such a nature that their final outcome for mankind on this planet remains in genuine doubt even for the Schools. At such times it is said that the Hidden Learning is disclosed, much as one might hurl lifebelts indiscriminately into the sea among the struggling fugitives from a sinking ship. *Sauve qui peut.* At such times a rigorous selection is no longer possible; some lifebelt may be caught and used, out of many failures there may be a few successes when successes are most terribly needed.

It is just this sort of period which we have now encountered in the history of mankind upon this planet. That is the answer given in this Version to those who ask why such information is available at this time in this way.

But although the need is urgent, there can be no haste or carelessness in the exposition. First things come first and we must start at the beginning. We shall therefore leave these greater questions for the time being and consider what is closer to hand but perhaps not the less important upon that account. In the next chapter we shall consider some commanding features of the local Map.

II. THE LOCAL MAP

I.

The modern scientific investigation of the problems of human psychology has established no agreed position and no generally accepted viewpoint regarding the definitory nature of the human being. It sedulously avoids any serious consideration of the central and basic problem of the nature of consciousness and thus the so-called science of psychology presents the picture of an attempted construction lacking the necessary element of a foundation. Often it puts forward privately held and directly contradictory views of what human beings are and what their essentially human functions are; and generally speaking, it possesses no commonly held and central aim in its investigations. Yet, if we exclude the private cultists of psychoanalysis, the mental testers, the mere statisticians, the social workers and those whose real goal it is to adduce some sort of supports for their projects of social miscegenation—all of whom like to call themselves psychologists but whose relation to psychology as a science is both distant and obscure—then we can perhaps assemble the elements of a more or less consistent position from the results of the more legitimate researches and undertakings.

The neurological equipment (the nervous systems) of the human body puts it into contact with the world outside of the organism and this equipment also mediates the responses of the organism to the great volume of internal stimuli arising within the body itself. The action of the neurological equipment is not of a reflex, push-button type; primarily its activity is of an extremely complex, integrative kind, its chief and basic function being to coordinate and harmonize the external and internal stimuli constantly impinging upon the organism and thus to produce an adequate reaction balance consisting in the internal and external responses of the organism. The very rapid functioning of the neurological portions of the body permits the continual maintenance of these finely adjusted balances.

From conception until death the nervous systems are in control of the organism. From the moment when the sperm fertilizes the ovum and cell multiplication commences, the steady-state biological field of the organism lays down the human body-pattern and the first differentiation to appear in the developing embryo is thus determined and thereafter determining neurosis, i.e., the neurological organization from head to tail. It is the neurosis which controls the whole maturation process from the beginning of the embryo to the attainment of the adult form of the organism; and increasingly and wholly it then controls the complicated responses of the organism both to outside and to inside forces.

From very early on in their history these neurological structures are divided into three main sections: the central nervous system, comprising 1) the head brain (the originating source) and 2) the spinal cord; and 3) the autonomic system, originating in the basal ganglia portion of the head brain and including the sympathetic system comprising the nervous nodes scattered throughout the upper trunk of the body. A triplex division marks each of these primary sections in turn, the head brain consisting of the cerebrum, the cerebellum and the basal ganglia, and the cerebrum again comprising sensory, motor and correlation portions. The cerebellum is divided anatomically into two lateral lobes and a middle lobe and an interesting point to notice in respect of it is that, with the exception of a few minor reflexes related to equilibrium and posture, it is non-functional in human beings as they are now found: two-thirds of the enormous nerve-impulse output of the cerebrum disappears into the cerebellum *via* the cerebro-pontine-cerebellar tract but, with the exception just noted, nothing emerges.

These arrangements, accessible in the sense of information to any ordinary inquirer, account well enough for the behavior of the persons whom we meet. But what of their experiences? Surely a neural impulse received in the sensory zones of the cerebrum is not the same thing as the sensation of blue? Well, there are some psychologists who can be brought to the admission of the reality of consciousness, not as a neurological function but as a functioning element of the human being. Once this has been done, the situation is reasonably plain. It is similar to, though not identical with, Locke's analysis of the problem many years ago, an analysis which lies at the base of almost all scientific work since his time.

In accordance with this view the neurological end-products of the functioning nervous system not only account for the subsequent motor responses and thus for the behavior of the body but also provide the foundation or substratum of the subjective experience of the individual. It is the mediation of the factor of consciousness, the third or neutralizing factor in the economy of the human being, which transforms the factor of neuron phenomena into the factor of subjective experience, so that the events taking place along the calcarine fissure of the cerebral occipital lobe (specifically at Brodmann's area 17) are experienced by the subject as sensations of vision and color. The final neurological loci of various sensations have been fairly well mapped upon the cerebral cortex and certain regions of the frontal lobes have been reasonably well identified with some of the correlative mental functions of a subjective kind, such as recent memory, unitary experience of the organ-

41

ism, etc. Some psychologists suppose emotional experience to be associated with the neurological functioning of the basal gangliar portions of the head brain, others with the motor tracts and still others with the lower levels of the sympathetic system. A full mapping of the local neurological bases of differentiated subjective experience has not been completed and in many cases the views held are still tentative, but the general situation will appear from the above.

From a strict interpretation of this position it will be seen that subjective experience must here be *post facto* event. Neural phenomena take place within Brodmann's area 17 and *then* a sensation of blue, for example, occurs; whether the sensation is simultaneous with the neural event or arises later by a tiny fraction of duration, the nerve-impulse integration determines the sensation. In a similar fashion the neural phenomena of the frontal lobe must determine the mental experience which is based upon them and the emotional experiences must likewise be determined by the functioning of the apposite portions of the nervous systems. Thus, when a man thinks he thinks, his response is really a subjective awareness of an already determined neural event taking place within the limits of the frontal lobes. And the whole notion of subjective control, whether mental, emotional or practical, is in fact a delusion comparable to the case of the rationalization of an action performed previously to the rationalization. While no doubt all psychologists would not agree with this view, it is nevertheless the most respectable, rational and scientific position adopted by these workers and, as such, it has been selected as the best to represent the science. Moreover, it will be found that this view corresponds to the positions of physics and biology, for in psychology we again have the universal three forces represented, the negative force of neural end-products, the positive force of the subjective experience and the neutralizing factor of consciousness or the pure faculty of awareness irrespective of its particular or given object.

This view of the situation is also able to render an explanation of one of the most serious errors and of one of the most serious omissions in modern psychological opinion, such a criticism as, in connection with its own position, its rivals are in turn incapable of providing. For a denial of consciousness or a profession of ignorance concerning the meaning of the term has led to the behaviorist fallacy in which rats and apes become of more account to the science than do human beings; and this fallacy is obviously based upon the failure to recognize the third or neutralizing factor involved. Again, the omission from consideration of this same factor has led other psychologists into a failure to distinguish between consciousness and conscious content with the result that the neutralizing and positive forces are confused with each other. But a person unable to perceive the difference between the faculty of pure awareness and the separate subjective phenomena resulting when pure awareness is directed upon an object (some end-product of neural functioning), is plainly unable to furnish that defining description of the nature of a human being which it is one of the foremost requirements of any genuine psychology to provide. All this is only another instance of the absurd, though unrecognized, assumption that the human being is some sort of foreign or unnatural intruder in this Universe when in fact he is manifestly a part of it. For if he is part of it, then very certainly those same three forces which determine all other phenomena in this Universe, apply likewise to him.

We must therefore reach the conclusion that the human being finds himself in much the same position as that of Marathon. "Marathon looks on the mountains, the mountains look on the sea." That is, his access to the external world is indirect. His awareness is actually directed upon the end-products of the neural functioning of his body and everything is there included of which he can be directly aware. Many of these end-products in turn refer to phenomena of the external world, e.g., the patterns of visual and auditory nerve impulses along the calcarine fissure or at the gyri of Heschl, but it is at these latter that the subject's awareness must necessarily be directed and not at the outside landscape or tumult that there are indirectly represented. Other such neural end-products indirectly represent the current condition of the subject's own organism and thus "he" is in indirect contact with his body through the same relationship of consciousness to neurology, for a man's body, so far as concerns "him," is also a part of the external world. "He" is Marathon; the mountains are the end-product furnished by the operation of his body's nervous systems; the sea is the whole world external to "him," both his body itself and those further phenomena with which his organism is designed to place "him" in indirect contact. "Marathon looks on the mountains, the mountains look on the sea."

Another confusion (like that in regard to the three forces) which irks modern psychology, refers to the significance of the terms, normal and abnormal; but since certain psychologists have defined these terms in the same rigorous and technical senses employed in the present Version, we may consider the matter here. Normal means neither average nor ordinary; if it did, we should not need the term at all in our vocabulary. Average is a term referring to the result of mathematical computation dealing with two or more cases; ordinary is synonymous with usual. The meaning of normal is quite different and relates to the element of design. The etymological derivation of these terms is sufficient to inform us of the distinctions between them. Average derives from the Latin preposition, *ad* (= to or toward), and the Latin noun, *verum* (= truth); it signifies that which moves toward, or approaches, the truth, thus an approximation. Ordinary derives from the Latin adjective, *ordinarius* (= regular, usual, customary) and is in fact the same word with an English instead of a Latin ending. To the other hand normal comes from the

Latin noun, *norme* (= a mason's tool or square by means of which his work was guided and standardized); and thus its proper significance relates to the matter of standard or design.

Statisticians have misused and abused this word at least as inexcusably as others, specifically in the case of the so-called "normal" probability curve and in that of the term, norm, deriving from it. But there is nothing normal about a probability curve, it being simply a mathematical expression for what is usually found to take place, and so its correct designation would be either "ordinary probability curve" or "usual probability curve." To usurp a long-established and clearly defined term on a falsely technical sense is not an accomplishment of scientific work but instead it is a symptom of scientific deterioration.

For us in this treatise the term, normal, shall be a technical word, strictly and rigorously defined so as to have a single meaning and that alone. Here is the definition: the normal is that which functions in accordance with its inherent design.

There are certain implications of health or of fitness or of propriety contained here. A cart with a broken wheel is an abnormal cart; it cannot function in accordance with its inherent, and plainly observable, design. And a similar sense of the term is applicable to human beings. For the manifest design of the human organism, the character of the biological, electrodynamic field so closely associated with it, is such as to establish an harmoniously functioning and mutually reinforcing relationship between all its subordinate parts or subdivisions. This is also the primary role of the nervous systems, which integrate the body as a whole. When and only when, such harmonious functioning is present, can the organism be said to be normal; when it is absent, the organism is abnormal. It will be seen that this use of the term, normal, is just the opposite of its common abuse. For what is usually, ordinarily or on the average found to be the case with human beings, is that they are abnormal in one way or another; and thus the misuse of the term, normal, in the sense of average or ordinary, at once involves the user in the self-contradictory allegation that the normal is the abnormal. The reader must accustom himself to the correct, technical employment of this term; it makes no statement as to the nature of any given design but what it does mean clearly, is that function and inherent design correspond unequivocally whenever the term, normal, is applicable.

The matters so far discussed in this chapter do not, of course, constitute any part of that map of a new continent of knowledge to which we have referred. They are terms of information readily accessible to anyone in the ordinary course of events, they are not derived from any of the Schools previously mentioned and, especially, they give us opinions concerning the nature of the human being, i.e., of ourselves, which to the one hand are tentative and to the other not infrequently self-contradictory. To stay within our analogy, it may be said that such information does provide a map of sorts but it is a map of the continent we are leaving, not of the one in which our explorations lie; it is a chart of our port of departure, not of our port of arrival. Let us turn now to the latter chart, which will give us first of all a plan of the actual constitution of a man.

2.

The most obvious, and the primary, functions of man as he is now found on this planet are thinking, feeling and action. Alternatively, they may be called mental functions, emotional functions and moving functions; and all other specifically human operations which he performs, are either of the nature of subordinate details within one of these fields or else they consist in combinations of some one of these functions with another.

But all functions are functions *of* something; they do not exist *in vacuo* or, as it were, in a disembodied condition. And in the present case the mentioned functions are the operational aspects of three different structural subdivisions of the adult human organism. In the Oragean Version the technical names for these structural subdivisions are Centre #1, Centre #2 and Centre #3 and their respective convergences are at the base of the spinal column, the solar or celiac plexus and the forward portion of the head brain.

This employment of the term, centre or center, is somewhat broader than the customary scientific usage wherein centre is defined as "the ganglion or plexus whence issue the nerves controlling a function." In accordance with that definition the neuroanatomist may distinguish hundreds of "centres" within the nervous systems but of course they are centres referring to minor part-functions of the organism. When, as at present, we use the term, function, to designate a primary general function as, for instance, emotion, then the term centre is applied to the core or focus of the structural subdivision which mediates that general function. People are often wedded, by familiarity or by merely obstinate habit, to one use of some term, but since the word, centre, is a highly important one in the present Version, the reader should take care, from this first employment of it onward, that he understands its technical reference and significance as here used constantly.

A diagrammatic representation follows:

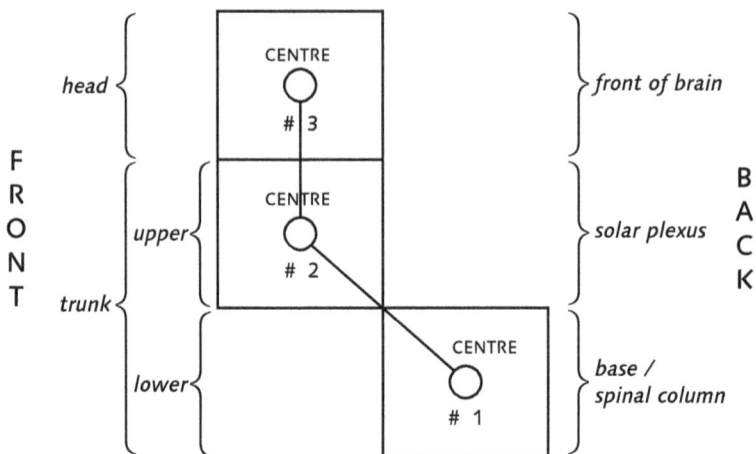

Figure 3. Cross-section of human organism (from left side).

It is plain to the briefest reflection that there is something different as between mental and emotional activity (we can distinguish between them without difficulty in our experience) and that physical action, either of an "instinctive" or of a practical sort, is again of a different kind. To think, to feel and to act are to be engaged in distinctly separate activities and these different functions are mediated by different structural subdivisions of the organism. The lower levels of the neurological mechanism of the body are concerned with the involuntary maintenance of the machine, with the processes of metabolism, of automatic food digestion, of breathing and with those reflex actions which respond to the stimuli from external environment that take place before, in fact, we think about them. This kind of activity originates in and is mediated by the spinal cord mechanisms.

Emotional responses, although affecting many portions of the organism, have their centre of gravity, as it were, in the nervous nodes of the upper trunk, i.e., in the sympathetic nervous system. This system, in man as we know him, is not so consolidated as the other two and the sympathetic ganglia are relatively scattered throughout their own region of the body; but the celiac plexus is the largest and most complicated of these and it is possible to consider this as the focus of emotional activity. The forward portions of the head brain, primarily the cerebral cortex, mediate not only speech and formulatory ability but many other functions such as memory, foresight, abstract conceptual processes, perceptions of relationship, recognition, and so on. These are what we call the mental faculties and their seat in the body constitutes Centre #3.

Such an analysis must not suggest, however, that these different general functions are actually independent of each other. That is not the case and in fact they are very closely connected together, so that the responses going forward in any one of them inevitably influence the current phenomena in the others and are in turn affected by what is happening elsewhere in the body at the same time, as well as by what has previously happened. Thus the organism reacts fundamentally as a whole, that circumstance being brought about by the sequence of its original growth: first, Centre #1 is formed and then there grow from it Centres #2 and #3, strong and permanent connections remaining between all of them as a matter of course, much as the branches of a tree remain joined to the parent trunk. At the conclusion of the process we have an organism composed of mutually interacting parts or divisions, in which the principle of integration is a manifestly important element of the design.

The above series of statements is, so far, only a partial and incomplete formulation of the full position, such as we have discussed earlier when using as an illustration the articulation of the numeral, 124—and the reader will only much later appreciate it in its entire and proper significance. Meanwhile, however, there is no necessity for needless confusion and the reader with some biological knowledge may view the situation as follows. As to ontogeny, at the instant when the respective male and female germ cells coalesce into a single cell, Centre #1 may be said to originate. This single conceptual cell contains within itself, of course, the steady-state biological electrodynamic field previously associated with the ovum and within which there exists, as a real potentiality, the fully developed form of the adult organism. The multiplication and segmentation of this original conceptual cell eventually result in the formation of the differentiated Centres #1, #2, and #3 in the forms in which we find them operating in the adult body. There is thus only an apparent, but not a genuine, discrepancy between the statement that Centres #2 and #3 derive from Centre #1 and the known course of ontogenetic development in which the neurosis of the organism is laid down first.

The next point to be considered is that these three centres are not to be thought of as merely empty structures or sieves through which impulses pass once and for all, leaving no traces behind. Whether such modifications consist in a deepening, as it were, of certain pathways or in a facilitation of synaptic integration where nerves or nerve trunks meet, any impulse received within any centre effects some greater or lesser alteration in its future condition. This effect is the basis of memory, which of course is of three chief kinds, sensori-motor, emotional and mental, it being only the last which, when we become introspectively aware of it, we ordinarily call memory proper. The main consideration here, however, is that these operations furnish the three centres with content.

This content makes a difference, if we consider the centre not simply as an empty structure but as structure-plus-content. A freight train, a passenger train and a circus train may all pass through the same railway yard and even over the same switches; but a railway yard through which all three are passing at the same time is in a different condition than one through which only a single train, or none at all, is passing. Both the switchmen and the men who may be working upon the tracks are well aware of such a difference. In the same way a centre with content is not at all the same as one without content and, moreover, it makes a difference what sort and how much content the centre has absorbed.

From the moment that the three centres are first formed—and this considerably before birth—content begins to pour into their neurological structures and the process continues up to the moment of the organism's death. And a moment's reflection will assure us that neither the given human being nor the centres themselves have any control or decision over the nature or the sequence of this content. Their condition is due in the first place to heredity and in the second place to environment.

The forces which we call heredity, including of course the biological steady-state field of the organism, completely and finally control the formation of the three chief brain-systems and they also completely and finally determine the degree of efficiency or normality which the given centres must possess as regards their functioning structures. From this element there is no appeal whatsoever; neither ignorance nor sentimentality nor the most competent later knowledge can alter the hereditary contribution to any degree at all. But after the organism has been laid down and is developing, environment at once commences to bring to bear its own distinct influence and, in the usual case, this is incorporated in the external stimuli furnishing control to the centres. Such content cannot, and does not, alter the structural characteristics of the centres nor does it affect their general responsive capabilities which by heredity may be adequate or inadequate *vis-à-vis* the general range of stimuli usual for a human organism upon the surface of this planet. This is why it is totally impossible to transform "a sow's ear" into "a silk purse," no matter how many social workers emit their shrill cries of affirmation.

All properly controlled researches have shown that slums occasionally produce able men and women and that palaces sometimes produce the incompetent and the ill-disposed. It has also been shown that the average slum-dweller, transferred to a "better" environment, remains a slum-dweller (i.e., one whose characteristics are such as create slums) all his life, as well as that the able man who through some fortuitous circumstance has lost his economic position, retains his abilities unimpaired.

Another factor in weighing the respective influences of heredity and en-

48

vironment eventuates to the advantage of the former. If we state that the contribution of environment is in the form of centre-content and that this in turn originates from the stimuli affecting the organism, then we must remember that many of the most important of these stimuli originate internally. In other words, the body manufactures a great many of its own stimuli within its own mechanisms—reinforcing, inhibitory, integrative and also primarily causative stimuli. Thus only a part of the content-producing stimuli are referable to environment per se; and if we denote structure by A, externally originating content by B and internally originating content by C, then hereditary influences will comprise A + C, while environmental influences will be composed by B alone.

Nevertheless, environment may be a potent factor in the development of a particular person since, although it can never alter the abilities a man may possess, it either permits or denies their exercise. Thus a man may have inherited a constitution such as would give him the opportunity of becoming a championship runner but if environment breaks his leg, he cannot exercise his ability for the time being; if environment so injures his leg that amputation becomes necessary, then he can never do so. The environmental effect is brought to bear not upon the abilities but upon their manifestation; in general any ability will be manifested when this is possible but, if the impediments imposed by environment are sufficient, then it will not be manifested because, after a certain degree of obstruction has been encountered, it cannot be manifested.

The whole, often deliberately entangled, position regarding heredity and environment comes down to no more than this: that heredity provides the equipment and that environment determines its use. These two great categories of forces, the one hereditary and the other environmental, are both important; and either the one or the other may often be decisive. But from the point of view of the given human being their most momentous aspect is yet to be cited. No one claims that he has controlled his own heredity; and it is equally plain to the unprejudiced that the course of their lives consists in what has happened to them accidentally and by chance, i.e., that in any really valid sense no ordinary man controls his environment. How many of our outstanding successes have been due to a lucky break at the crucial moment, how many of our failures have been occasioned by the opposite? Did a man like Hitler create his commanding position himself? Of course he did not; in the basic sense he was automatically selected for the role of impersonating the forces of his time by those very forces and had no more choice in the matter than had those other people who automatically opposed him. The same may be said with equal justification of characters like Washington, whom we are subjectively inclined to estimate as more admirable.

The situation, then, turns out to be anything but fortunate. For after we have finished debating the respective influences of heredity and environment (and naturally have ended by holding the same prejudices with which we began), we find that in fact we have no control over either one of them. We do not determine them, they determine us. The crucial fact about these two sets of forces is that the ordinary man is molded by them into what he is today.

Thus we find that the organism consists of three interacting systems or Centres whose current condition has been brought about by a multitude of specific forces and events, all of which may be denominated as deriving either from heredity or from an environment external to the organism. With this organism the man, *qua* human being, is associated in some intimate and peculiar way not readily formulable by him.

His body is predominantly a self-contained and self-activating unit, due to the close association of its three main subordinate systems. Although the external environment is far larger and in its totality more powerful than the organism, nevertheless at the focusing point where the two make contact, the organism itself almost always represents the much more powerful set of forces involved; this is due to the fact that, of the items which are constantly being integrated by the action of the nervous systems, a great many are contributed by the self-activity of the organism and that, in addition, the very mechanisms which are called into play in order to effect the integrations and thus their result, are the organism's own mechanisms and correspond to its own nature, not to that of the external environment. Therefore in the usual case the organism is the preponderant element in the relation, organism-environment; which is the reason both for the circumstance that men have been able so greatly to change their "natural" environments and for the other circumstance that an altered environment (despite the claims of reformers) never transforms the essential characteristics of those persons subjected to it.

Now the design of such a body possess very clear implications in respect of function. If in a wilderness we should come across a machine having two wheels one in front of the other and connected by a structure supporting a seat, made moreover in such a way that the front wheel could be steered by bars and the rear wheel propelled by pedals, we would recognize that we had found a bicycle. Even had we never before in our lives seen a machine of this kind, it would take us no long time to work out for ourselves its use and its usefulness. Because structure and function are always indissociable aspects of the same entity. For that reason the definitory nature of the human organism presents us with a triply integrated mechanism for response to environment. Such a mechanism is obviously designed to manifest the maximum reinforcement and mutual cooperation between and among its three chief subdivisions in its total response-patterns of behavior; and when this type of harmonious functioning takes place, the whole mechanism will operate at its highest efficiency. Under these conditions it may be said to be normal in the full and technical sense. When functioning thus normally, there are almost no conditions or circumstances on the surface of this planet which it cannot meet and successfully overcome. One necessary requirement, of course, is that its three Centres should cooperate instead of interfering with each other; but that is implicit in its design and constitutes one of its own chief standards of normality.

Within the three primary Centres there exist a great number of subdivisions but of all these only one is so significant that it needs mention now. This subdivision is formed, again by heredity and environmental forces, in Centre #3 and in the present Version its technical designation is Magnetic Centre. Roughly its function corresponds to what is ordinarily called intellectual curiosity, but to curiosity of a particular kind defined by the objects toward which the curiosity is manifested. Its activity is closely associated with certain emotions and the objects of its inquisitiveness are the strange, the bizarre and the wonderful; especially does it respond to the challenge of the more profound questions which have always intrigued and fascinated the reflective portion of mankind, viz., for what purpose do human beings exist, what is the true nature of this complex and astounding universe in which we find ourselves, whence came we and whither do we go, is there such a reality as destiny and, if so, what may our own be?

The possession of a strong Magnetic Centre is at the same time both a dangerous and a precious attribute. In the absence of its owner's meeting with the source of any genuine information it may render him the victim of false prophets, of charlatans, of sincere self-deceivers, of imposters and of spurious teachers whose ignorance exceeds even his own. Though half-suspecting the fallacies he swallows, an insatiable interest may force him to deny his own intellectual integrity and he may end as an abnormal and credulous dupe. But the same Magnetic Centre may also, if chance favors him, open to him the unique opportunity of a genuine version of the Hidden Learning, for it attracts to itself and there preserves stray hints and suggestions of the existence of Magnetic Centre and of both the dangers and the boons of its possession. By all means permit it to function; but let its functioning be controlled by common sense and by that skepticism which is an attribute of reason itself. Let the reader do this in his own case and specifically in respect of the Version here presented.

In doing so it will be of advantage to reflect upon the difference between the present section of this chapter and the preceding section; for now we have left our former shores and are here considering part of the map of the new continent to be explored. This new map is in many respects the reversed counterpart of our old and accustomed map and two major points, in which this is so, may be remarked.

The usual scientific view held by most persons—at the port of departure on the continent we have left—identifies the steady-state biological field of the organism with the factor of design in the human economy. It is this field factor which accounts for the phenomenon of biological organization, that is, the gross and the minute form of the organism; but no detailed description of definitory human design is offered by any branch of science, it being merely asserted that, whatever the design may be, biological field forces account for it. Here, as contrasted to so unresolved a position, we have defined, three-centred design of the human being presented as a datum given, as an asserted fact which has been discovered and confirmed. It may, and should, be doubted and it may be investigated; but there it is, once and for all, no longer subject to tentative equivocation, the design which defines what a human being actually is.

And as regards the contrast between the scientific position and that of this Version, that, too, is evident. The agreed statements of science are presented to the reader as correct statements, the only qualification being that they may be subject to later addition or expansion. But in fact no single statement of science may legitimately be so presented; every one of them remains essentially hypothetical due to the circumstance that the Fallacy of Affirming the Consequent, implicit in scientific methods, prevents a final, valid proof and thus the best of such scientific statements continue only as statements of likelihood in a greater or lesser degree of probability. Assertedly they are facts, actually they remain hypotheses.

Here the position is reversed. The statements of this Version actually are facts but assertedly they constitute hypotheses for the reader. He is urged to consider them, not as facts to be accepted but as hypotheses to be investigated. That is not the case when chemistry tells us that water $= H_2O$, we are expected to accept the statement without further debate, although it is very doubtful indeed that the expression, water $= H_2O$, is a valid one in any real and final sense. But when we say here that man is a three-centred creature, we neither ask nor permit anyone to accept that statement on faith; to the contrary we assert that no one is properly entitled to put forward the statement as being correct until for himself he has realized its truth and confirmed its correctness in his own personal experience, checked and counterchecked. Because at the beginning no one can properly do so, we insist that the position remain hypothetical for the reader, since that is his situation in fact. The contrast, then, is this: for the reader scientific assertions are claimed to be facts but actually they are hypotheses; for the reader *these* assertions are claimed to be hypotheses but actually are facts.

We shall now explore the Local Map a little further and discover how the reader comes to be in his present position of being for the moment incompetent to verify facts. We have been considering the nature of human beings only insofar as they are actually found to be (in their present condition) but we have by no means completed even a brief survey of the situation. We have laid down the fundamental human design but we have yet to explore the currently functioning state in which this design is found to be operating. That shall be our next inquiry.

3.

Such an exploration may be begun by a consideration of functional types. As is obvious from the words themselves, functional types are distinguished from each other by reason of the different predominant functions which they manifest. Thus one man may be a practical type, another of emotional type, and a third intellectual in type. The athlete and the businessman are examples of the first type; Babe Ruth or an Andrew Carnegie. Artists and religionists are of the second type, a Rodin, a Calvin. Plato, a philosopher, or Compton, a scientist, furnishes an instance of the third type. These types are taken from the actual manifestations of human life which in fact we see about us but it will be evident without discussion that, in their behavior, they correspond to the three centres previously described. It is as if the scientist were the objectification of one centre only, the artist that of another single centre, and so on.

Our ordinary observation, however, assures us that this is not so. We know that the scientist is capable of experiencing emotion, and frequently does; we also know that he can perform practical acts, such as eating and providing himself shelter, for example. So also with the other chief functional types; they can, and do, engage in activities characteristic of other types than their own. The distinction rests upon their *predominant* mode of behavior, upon the ways in which they manifest themselves most of the time. These typical ways of behaving, usually associated with a life-occupation, in almost all cases present us with the possibility of a classification sufficiently accurate to be called correct. Of course it is not necessary that a man be an outstanding philosopher or an extremely successful businessman in order that he be classed with the relevant type; it is not the degree of competence that determines functional type but simply the sort of predominant activity or the kind of ability usually exercised, whatever its degree.

In a very small number of cases, especially in the instance of a person of leisure where gainful occupation offers no criterion, the application of this classification may not at once be apparent. But even here a more detailed inquiry will almost always soon disclose the subject's type, for if his interests, his abilities and his activities should indeed be divided among the typical human functions in approximately equal amount, such a person would show himself, on his own level of being, to be relatively normal. It is unlikely that any reader has ever encountered such a person, if outwardly it may seem so, that was only for want of an adequately searching investigation. For though these three main types may be further classified into many subdivisions, all of us fall really into one or another of them.

There have been innumerable attempts, on the part of scientists and others, to classify mankind into various types by means of specially selected criteria, some of which have been shrewd and observant while others have displayed no more than phantasy. In recent times there have been advanced the so-called somatotypes of Sheldon—endomorphs, mesomorphs, ectomorphs—deriving from the gross morphological distinctions of Kretschmer and, at the opposite extreme, the purely subjective categories of introverts and extroverts pleasing to psychoanalysts. Glandular function has been accepted by some as the basis of human types, by others some special and temporary sort of environmental behavior and by still others the various degrees of practical competence or of emotional competence alone, as in the cases of reaction times to different sensory stimulus or of the distinctions that may be made between different kinds of liars. By these means there soon arises a hodgepodge of contradiction, confronting the inquirer with an impossible variety of incompatible data, a situation characteristic of modern psychology in all its subdivisions.

The evident fault with even the best of these attempts is that the criteria selected are not fundamentally characteristic of man. This may be either because they refer to part-functions or to structural subdivisions which in themselves are not solely or essentially human, or else it may be because the selected criteria are merely subjectively plausible or sometimes outrightly phantastic. The three main functional types here described do not suffer from either of the foregoing limitations. Since their criteria comprise exactly the three chief functions by which man himself is defined, to the one hand they are easily and speedily recognizable in subjective experience and to the other they are based firmly upon the objective structural and functional primary divisions of the human organism.

This brief excursus into the question of types is not only justified, but demanded, by the requirements of the present Version, since one of its leading principles is that no formulation can be an acceptable one—even though it may be fully adequate in a positive sense—unless it is prepared also, in a negative sense, to show inadequacies of all rival positions.

The first point to strike us about these three main functional types is conflict. The scientist's emotions do not assist his formulations but, instead, interfere with them. The businessman, disdaining speculative thought, soon comes to fear it as an intruding influence upon his efforts; and the artist or the genuine religionist must not (he supposes) allow himself to be diverted from the pursuits which fascinate him, by any consideration of mundane practicality. These oppositions between the centres functioning within the man are mirrored accurately in external hostilities. The symphonic composer looks with scorn upon the mere financier, the latter (with nowadays a single reservation as to possible practical upshots) considers the theoretical scientist to be an involved and dreamy nonentity; and the philosopher looks down from what he imagines to be his intellectual heights upon activities of other kinds. All this is quite different from the inevitable jealousies and envies experienced by the less competent toward the more competent in any given field; men of equal competence in different primary fields often object to each other, not at all because of any personal envy but rather as a result of their hidden convictions that the other's ability is not as genuinely or as typically human as his own.

From any social point of view nothing could be more preposterous; it is evident that mutual respect and cooperation are a desideratum here, not on behalf of some abstraction called society but in the interests of the men themselves. Indeed this conflict among men of different types is one of the chief reliances of the self-serving politicians of the democratic and socialistic stages of society who seek unceasingly to set one class against another to the end of profiting personally from ensuing turmoil. But for us it is necessary to understand that such external hostilities are testimony in the interior conflict between centres within the men themselves, that they present evidence of a mutual interference taking place as between and among the three primary subdivisions of the human being's own economy.

Here is a puzzle indeed! The very term, organism, is applied to a living body whose parts by definition make up a congruous whole; and in the instance of the human organism (so obviously designed as a machine whose parts should act in an harmonious cooperation) what explanation can there be for precisely the opposite phenomenon?

The manifest fact is that the organic behavior of the human being is not in accordance with his designed functioning, in other words that is not functioning but, instead, is malfunctioning. By definition he is, in fact, abnormal. And the explanation is that there exists no control.

Even in so simple a machine as an electrical generator, designed to supply power to lighting and heating systems, it is necessary to include a governor so that, as the operating load to be drawn from the machine varies with the cutting-in and cutting-out of different appliances and lights, the motor will speed up or slow down to maintain a comparable output. In the case of the three-centred human organism it is necessary that a much more complicated governor should act in order to keep its triple functions balanced. It is not sufficient that the centres be merely connected with each other so that the possibility of interactions be present, it is required further that this interaction, inevitable because of the designed interconnection, be of an harmonious and mutually reinforcing sort, and for this a special kind of governor is needed. Now from the objective point of view such a governor is included in the organic human design and it is in fact present within the human organism. The difficulty resides exactly in the circumstance that it does not function, with the result that all the other functions it is designed to coordinate, manifest a jangling maladjustment and disrupt the proper operation of the machine. It will be seen later that this nonfunctional regulator or governor is associated with that other predominantly nonfunctional division of the head-brain, the cerebellum.

On the subjective side of the discussion this brings us to the enigmatic word, "I," and to a preliminary consideration of some of the levels or degrees of consciousness.

What do we mean when we say "I"? Do we really mean anything? Many persons assume this but the position cannot be maintained. Obviously it can happen that Mr. So-and-so becomes Dr. So-and-so and continues to say "I" as before, not recognizing a distinction in identity any more than does the tax collector. And far more drastic alterations than that can occur, the address can change, and frequently, and the name itself can be transformed legally and practically out of any resemblance to its previous counterpart. Yet one still says "I." Then surely the name-and-address fallacy may be dismissed.

Who, then, is the real subject of these various conversions? Do we in fact identify ourselves simply with specific (and essentially nameless) physical organisms, the bodies with which we assume ourselves to be dichotomously associated? Or *are* we in fact those bodies? But one can be aware of one's body as something separate from oneself, as every person with a dental history knows. And between "something" and the organism there exists an experiential distinction, this "something" is what we call "I."

But plainly enough "I" am always identifying myself with something else. When "I" do so simply with a name and address—in general with any combination of life-circumstances—an error is involved, since even my wife may elope with the chauffeur and my children fatally be stricken by the plague. Shall we say, then, that "I" may identify myself with an optimistic frame of mind or an affectionate mood? But these are precisely those attributes which are in constant flux and change, and the abilities (even were they as great as my own opinion of them) can be, and sometimes are lost without any interruption of that continuing assertion, "I."

In general it would seem that what I customarily identify myself with— what I ordinarily call "I"—is not some separate aspect of my organism's activity, but rather a general balance of closely interrelated activities, comprising an integration of mental, emotional and sensory components simultaneously. It is then but a short step to the error that such an integration may properly be considered as at least a semi-permanent unity. Unfortunately it is not so. We cannot sit down to think without all sorts of unnecessary muscular strains interfering with our thoughts, even more uselessly some mental segment arouses an incongruent emotion by automatic association, and our train of thought is destroyed. In the same way, let us set about some complex physical activity, perhaps a golf or tennis match, and not only do fears and hopes interfere with our required movements but irrelevant thoughts likewise intrude to upset our coordinations. So that such an imagined unity is not a unity at all; these integrated states with which we identify are a) not harmoniously integrated but instead are only temporarily existing imbalances and b) for that very reason must be impermanent and constantly altering to entirely different imbalances, temporarily integrated in turn. Such a succession of contrasting imbalances can hardly serve as the valid foundation for a supervading identification any less impermanent than are the integrations themselves.

The point to be brought out, is that the assumption of a permanent and steadfast "I" is in fact without current basis, and whatever may be said about it later on, in contemporary actuality "I" is a genuine delusion.

The ordinary man or woman, you or I, is not a permanently integrated individual but a clear case of multiple personality. Do we not often go to bed with the firm intention of rising earlier than usual the next day, perhaps in order to accomplish some extra chore that seems to us to be desirable? Yet in the morning the matter presents an entirely different aspect, and what so little previously had seemed called for, and even necessary, now takes on the appearance of a rather foolish triviality and we are easily able to assure ourselves that the really reasonable thing to do is to stay in bed a bit longer and thus the better fortify ourselves against the coming day. But surely these are two separate personalities that view the very same question in such contrary ways. Both of them speak of themselves as "I" without hesitation but they are much too far apart both in their opinions and their behaviors for us to assume that they are merely somewhat different aspects of the same "I"; indeed they present between them all the stigmata commonly associated with multiple personality, even to a lesser degree than do the more sensational cases.

Hence arises the suspicion that the evening "I" and the morning "I" constitute two separate entities, since in the first case the identification is with a certain set of feelings, thoughts and intentions and in the second with an entirely different and opposite set. Moreover, throughout the whole day these varying and frequently contradictory misidentifications take place, one following another without interruption as external situations alter and also the internal conditions wax and wane. Instead of the delusionally permanent and unchanging "I" a whole troupe or multiplicity of "I's" holds the stage in turn. It's often happening that one of these "I's" undertakes obligations on behalf of the organism only later demanding discharge painfully and embarrassingly by quite another "I."

And provided the reader will consent to examine his own experience without *a priori* assumption, he will perhaps find something still more disquieting, viz., that some of these personalities of his approximate to being unconscious of certain others. Here we approach the classic instance of multiple personality wherein one "I" is totally unconscious of another and the subject assumes an altogether different character alternately without any intercognition as between them. That is the alleged mark of the various "schizoid" types. That in ordinary life most people come close to it, is evident from a consideration of behaviors while in the transports of romantic love; these are often unbelievable to the victim following recovery. Occasional states of rage, in which opinions and intentions are held which afterwards seem unrecognizable to the subject, are another case in point. "But I *couldn't* have said such a thing, no matter how angry I was!"

One fears that in one's own case, as well as in those of others, he can observe quite clearly this astonishing procession of discordant "I's." It must be confessed that this causes small concern, for among everyone else whom he knows, one can easily recognize very different personalities manifesting themselves, for instance in discussions with the banker, when relaxing among intimates, at some formal affair, when exercising some talent in which the person is unusually proficient, or simply on different days even under generally similar circumstances.

To call these differing manifestations "automatic roles" (as presently we shall) cannot alter the question at all. If we grant that in each of us such multiplicities of "I's" are continually elbowing one another aside to hold power briefly until in turn they are shown the exit, then certainly the situation is not normal in any proper sense. It is quite impossible to assume that such an incongruous parade of the honest, the unscrupulous, the clownish, the sober, the inept and the competent constitutes the properly functioning design of the human being. Assuredly his organic design is not constructed upon so haphazard and indiscriminant a principle.

And that is just the point. The organic apparatus contains everything required in order to obviate all this injurious jangling and conflict; and the trouble lies not in the organic factor but in the factor of consciousness. Let us return for a moment to the threefold analysis of the nature of the human being, in which the three basic elements appeared as content of experience, end-products of neural functioning and the third-force factor of consciousness *per se* or the mediating factor irrespective of what neural end-product it might be mediating. In this analysis, as in any other, it is all too easy to make the erroneous assumption that the independent factors are existing separately from each other. Theoretically, of course, they may but in that case no human being is given; whenever a human being is found, the independence of the three contributory factors consists in the incommensurability of their respective contributions to the whole but not at all in any supposed mutual disassociation as among them. Thus the factor of consciousness may be considered by itself in an abstract way but, *so far as concerns a human being,* it is a factor or aspect of his total being and not some separate entity which may or may not be present in the presence of the other two factors. It is necessary to emphasize this because, although analysis is a valuable intellectual tool, it usually brings with it the fallacy that what is analyzed out can therefore be dropped from the totality of the phenomenon and either itself be considered as separate or the residue be considered as separate. This is not so and in the case of the human being neither consciousness nor any other of the three basic factors can be dropped without destroying the human being as such. Without organic end-products or without experiential content or without consciousness there can be no human being; it is precisely the amalgamation of all these three independent elements which comprises and defines him. Thus "I" cannot be identified simply with consciousness alone but only with the totality of which consciousness is an independent but necessarily associated factor. Although there must be a later distinction, for the moment we can consider that the proper employment of the term, "I," refers to that totality.

Nevertheless, when we discover something seriously wrong about the situation, our analysis proves valuable in pointing to the seat of the trouble, in showing for instance that it resides primarily not in the organic factor and is related to the mechanical automatism of human beings previously discussed.

We have already seen that, as the human economy actually operates, its neural end-products determine the content of experience likewise. If one admits the undeniable fact that neurological phenomena along the calcarine fissure of the occipital lobe determine visual experience, then it is quite impossible to deny that frontal lobe phenomena determine intellectual experience and basal ganglia (or other apposite) phenomena determine emotional experience. In the absence of such phenomena there can be no experience at all; and since the experience originates at these locations; the corollary that it is determined there, is inescapable. Phantasies and delusions about Free Will are comfortable phantasies and delusions but they are also irrational and abnormal; that is why they are termed phantasies and delusions. If one's aim is delusional comfort, well and good; but if one aspires to some degree of human normality, these facts must be faced. As regards the actual situation they establish an important formulation: in the case of the ordinary human being consciousness is a purely *passive* factor; it suffices for the transformation of neurological phenomena into experiential phenomena, and it suffices for no more. What is transformed is determined by neurological laws acting through neurological structures and the delusion of voluntarism arises from the erroneous assumption that the conscious factor interferes in such processes in some inexplicable way, when in fact the actual role of consciousness is simply and solely the translation of neurology into the terms of subjective experience.

It is necessary only to state that real situation clearly and definitely in order to be assailed from all sides by the Pauper's Denial. "Of course we have Free Will," cry these voices, some shrill and angry, others merely astonished that so obvious a matter can be called into question. And so it is, until they look at it; indeed they are the very protagonists of the Pauper's Parable. . . . Once there lived a man so disreputably clad and starving that others came to him saying, "Alas, that thou art bereft of all wealth to this extent! For thy bones stick through thy skin and thy cloak is more holes and patches than good wool. Behold now, bestir thyself, for coin is to be had through the efforts thou canst make and with that coin thy dire needs may be remedied." To which the pauper answered: "Begone, ye fools! Are ye so dull of wit ye cannot see one of great possessions before ye, who needeth not to make an undignified scrambling after thy petty coins? Begone, for here small patience shall reward sophistries and thy twistings of words!" So then those others left him; and not long later his emaciated body was found beside the roadway, a testimony to the starvation he had denied. . . . By this story it is intended to be shown that no poor man can become wealthy, if, in advance of his efforts to do so, he is deluded by the notion that he is already a millionaire. It is the same with Will. Arguments regarding its possible attainment are bootless in the cases of those who confuse it with the delusion of voluntarism; and since they imagine that they already possess it, *ipso facto* they are prevented from taking the first step toward it. A recognition of importance is the obligatory first step toward strength.

Such a recognition, however, is by no means enough, for invariably it is followed by the fallacy of reform. And from the above description of the mechanical automatism in which we live, it can be seen how empty and hopeless are all projects of reform. What is reform? It is the increase of activity of one subdivision of the organism and its predominantly effective interference in the functioning of other subdivisions. Let us suppose a well-reasoned decision to overcome some emotional unpleasantness, say an habitual behavior of deception. Of course it can be done, but it is always done by force; a "determined intention" is brought into play, the lying behavior is carefully noted and, whenever it is noticed, it is suppressed. Unquestionably a change is produced. Yes, but what change? Just the desired one and no more? Substitution is thus achieved but never only destruction. Centre #2 is not abolished because certain of its manifestations have been repressed. Perhaps the man now lies to himself instead of, as formerly, to others; perhaps the lying has been suppressed entirely and the emotional energy, hitherto thus used, now expends itself in some other direction, the man suddenly finding himself the victim of unaccustomed timidity and fears; or perhaps the action has been still more drastic and digestive disorders ensue, superficially quite unrelated to anything that has occurred but actually the result of it. This is the characteristic pattern of all reform, in which some end is attained but always at an unknown expense. Expense there always is, for nothing is accomplished at no expense; and when the expense is unknown, it may be very harmful indeed. In social reform a false façade of virtue is presented to the public at large; in private reform it is presented to the man himself. And underneath it in both instances the former vices seethe with their bottled-up energies now channeled in unsuspected ways. Reform always results in something worse than it cures.

It is therefore of no value to admit that we are deplorably automatic and mechanical in our functions and then to assert that we shall change all this, develop our "wills" and become what we obscurely but essentially realize that we ought to be. At bottom such a reform is no different from all the rest; all of them reflect only the meddling and tyranny of one centre over the others and the result is always discord, conflict and interior disruption, jostling our organic equipment into further maladjustments. One centre does not understand another, its sustenance and operation are different, it is not entitled on any grounds to prescribe its own remedies for another's faults, because it is unable successfully to do so by the very nature of the case.

The problem we confront here—the problem of our mechanical automatism—is profound and fundamental. It is also an extremely subtle problem. Scores of fallacious solutions have been offered for it, some merely absurd but some of so cleverly plausible a kind as to have deceived all except the extraordinarily competent. It is one of the objects of the present Version to solve this question correctly, but as yet we have not proceeded far enough for a direct attack upon it. At present we are concerned with formulating Actuality, we are engaged upon describing man as he is.

There is a simile employed in the body of the Gurdjieffian ideas to furnish an image of the nature of man. This simile is called the Equipage; and it consists of a horse, a carriage, a driver or coachman, and a passenger. The driver is Centre #3, or mind; the horse is Centre #2, or the emotions; the carriage is Centre #1, or what is usually called the body; the passenger within is "I." Between these various parts of the Equipage there are to be found the necessary connections: the horse is attached to the carriage by means of shafts, enabling him to pull it about, and the driver is related to the horse by means of the reins, thus being in a position to guide the latter. The passenger communicates with the driver through the agency of speech, telling him where to proceed. In proper conditions this is a workable contrivance, for the passenger informs the driver of the destination, the driver starts off the horse and thereafter guides him by reason of his coachmanlike acquaintance with the locality and the horse then pulls the adequately greased carriage along to the goal. All this, of course, in proper conditions.

The actual picture is somewhat different. Here we find the passenger unconscious within his vehicle, the coachman drunk upon the box, the horse rampaging about in terror-stricken hysteria or vicious rage and the carriage, equipped with a cleverly designed self-greasing mechanism which only rough roads will activate, creaking with burned-out axles along the artificially smooth streets of the city's amusement centre. This picture is asserted to be a true one; the rational thing to do, is not to deny it but to investigate it.

Another simile of the Oragean Version likens the empty word, "I," to an exiled Prince instead of to the unconscious passenger. Deprived of his birthright he spends his existence outlawed from his land (the organism) while a succession of usurpers arrogates his duties to itself. Now Centre #3 seizes control, now Centre #1 and now Centre #2; and even their subordinates ape them in usurpation, for the members of that whole train of multiple personalities play out their automatic roles in a degraded succession upon the ravished throne. When shall that Prince awake? When and how will he gather his forces, eject his miserable counterfeits and regain his rightful place as the legitimate ruler of his own domains? Indeed he needs a Merlin, and sorely. His Merlin is the A-type knowledge possessed only by the Schools.

Do these similes apply to us in person? It is said here that they do, to all of us. Let the reader gather the last ounce of sincerity he possesses, and then let him ask himself. Let him catch a glimpse, if only a short one, of himself as others actually see him; let him achieve even a partially objective answer to this question, and he shall no longer doubt.

Assuredly a change is demanded, a very drastic change, but not any change nor the first one suggested by desperation or despair, either. Mere change in itself will not avail; reform and "improvement" will effect the opposite of the intended purpose and he will be more closely beset than before. His problem is to be solved neither quickly nor easily, for let him know, too, that this dilemma is his alone. The Universe, or any of it, is not interested in his quandary; just as he is—mechanical, disrupted, impotent, automatic—he is serving his allotted function in the Universe well enough right now.

4.

Men, as we find them, are only partially conscious. Modern psychology, dealing with Actuality, recognizes two chief levels of consciousness, sleep and waking. As regards the sleeping state psychology has developed its own varieties of the age-old practice of dream-interpretation, the most widely publicized of which is the psychoanalytic technique. This is almost an exact analogue (of an intellectual kind) of the various similar emotional formulations at the present time known as Voodoo. The latter, having had a considerably longer history, have achieved a greater complication, with their mamolois and papalois, their many unfragrant "gods," the undead and a great number of twisted "rites"; in the former the hobgoblins are of a mentally verbalistic (but still entirely subjective) kind—complexes, ids, repressions, egos, Oedipus nodes, latent contents, strangely unreal distinctions between foreconscious, unconscious, subconscious, and so on. In both cases there is an underlying substratum of reality, for both are dealing with real phenomena; also in both cases a distorting ignorance is employed, the one emotional, the other mentalistic.

With regard to the waking state, psychology confuses mental introspection with consciousness, a direct outcome of two elements in its treatment of the problem: 1) a lack of knowledge concerning the basic levels or degrees of consciousness natural to human beings, both actually and potentially; and 2) a failure to analyze properly the nature of the human being as such and to recognize the specific character of the three primary forces which contribute to his being.

Thus it is not surprising, as man wanders in his maze of automatism conditioned by the purely passive waking consciousness whose role is only a lethargic registration of neurological events, that man's mechanical efforts, intellectual as well as others, lead him merely in widening or contracting circles to the same destination from which he always sets out. But despite this "magic circle" hemming him in on all sides, man still serves quite well a natural function in the Universe. That that purpose is Nature's rather than his own, does not alter the fact that it is a purpose.

His own purposes semiconscious man does not accomplish. In recent times the United States has entered two world wars, both times after delay and full debate. On the first occasion the nation's alleged purpose was to make the world safe for Democracy; and it is an undoubted fact that for many millions of people the aim was sincere and deliberate, whatever reservations their cynical political leaders may have cherished. As a result of that war the United States itself presently collapsed from Democracy into Socialism and the realms of its former enemies and allies were transformed into Dictatorships.

In the secondly mentioned war the aim was to liberate mankind and to restore human freedom; and here again the acquiescence of the people was involved, even though on this occasion their political leaders showed themselves to be more cynical and treacherous than before. The outcome of this second conflict has been that more than half the human race has become slaves in the most literal sense, while in the United States itself an accelerating social decline has cramped the freedom of the individual into the vise of a hardening Socialism.

These instances have been taken only because of their contemporary familiarity, for throughout all known history the same has been repeated over and over again. Man never accomplishes what he sets out to do; indeed he is fortunate if a failure is his only reward and if he does not conclude by producing an exactly opposite effect to that intended.

But though his own purposes plainly enough are not served, it is impossible to deny that mankind serves other functions whose shape is unknown to him. Surely no one any longer supposes that man is a special creation in this Universe, that he is some sort of "unnatural" creature, an incredibly exceptional intruder in the immensity of all created things. The only rational ground for such a superstition was the assertion that man alone possessed consciousness whereas nothing else did; and we have just seen that the most astute adherents of this dogma know little or nothing about the nature of consciousness themselves. In an opposite sense we have already recognized that man is an integral part of the Universe and we have even identified which part he is: he is an important part of the organic kingdom upon the planet, Earth. As such he manifestly serves a natural function in the universal economy.

Beyond the limits of present historical memory there have always been stories and fables hinting at the existence of such a situation for mankind; fables and allegories are one of the many means adopted by Schools for passing on a concealed knowledge which may yet become available to those in a position to interpret them correctly.

An acquaintance with one of these tales is not unusual today; it is the Myth of the Black Sheep. This story is a genuine myth; it is, not, as many naïvely suppose, merely a little fairy-tale for the entertainment of children. It contains many authentic elements of A-type knowledge and those elements, moreover, are concealed only to the extent that we are not directly told to whom the story really refers.

Ostensibly the tale related to a shepherd and his flock of sheep. To the latter the shepherd takes on the aspect of a beneficent being, indeed of a beneficent god. He continually addresses himself to their welfare and he employs what can seem to them to be only supernatural and unimaginable means to assure their safety and to rescue any of their number who may have the misfortune to wander away and become lost or to fall into some other jeopardy. He leads them to shelter against the cold and he provides them with the food and other requirements necessary for their existence. He takes very good care of them, much better care indeed than they could assure for themselves. It is therefore no source of wonder that they should look upon him as genuinely concerned with their welfare and entertain toward him feelings of grateful awe.

The shepherd himself, however, has purposes in relation to these sheep of which they are unaware. These purposes would much astonish the sheep if the latter were to know of them; they are concerned first with a supply of wool, and later with a supply of mutton. In fact the sheep have somewhat seriously mistaken the shepherd's motives, for his care of them is occasioned primarily by considerations that the wool should be thick and useful for human (not animal) protection and that the meat should be well-nourished and tender when it is finally brought to market. These values, held by the shepherd and the real causes of his behavior, relate to matters entirely beyond either the knowledge or the comprehension of the ordinary sheep.

The ordinary sheep, as can be seen at a glance, is white. He and his fellows, as alike as so many peas in a pod, make up the vast majority of the sheep population. But very occasionally at long intervals there appears an unusual sort of sheep whose presence can also be noted at a glance; for this is a black sheep. The black sheep is both more skeptical and far cleverer than the ordinary member of the flock and while taking care to present an appearance of conformity in his daily sheeplike behavior, he is all the time directing his attention toward little anomalies which seem to contradict the general views held by his companions. The annual shearing, for instance, is certainly done at a time of year when the sheep will be least discommoded by it; yet it really seems a strange proceeding and, upon serious reflection, one that can scarcely be thought of as motivated primarily by a concern for the sheeps' comfort. The black sheep also speculates upon the problem raised by the unaccounted-for disappearances of his compatriots just when they have reached their manifest prime; and he explores various hypotheses in an endeavor to explain to himself these peculiar happenings. Many a black sheep never arrives at any satisfactory conclusions upon these questions before his own turn at the butcher's comes around but very, very occasionally some unusually clever specimen contrives to see what he should not see or to overhear a conversation at which he is not presumed to be present. And thus he learns the secret.

We may imagine his consternation as the truth becomes known to him. The situation is not only a shocking surprise, it is also so contrary to established opinions and convictions as to overturn them completely. Every seriously held life-view concerning sheephood is destroyed at a stroke. And supposing the sheep to experience some feeling of solidarity with his paler brothers, we may next imagine his concern to share with them the information he has discovered regarding their desperate circumstances. A large proportion of the black sheep who have by some chance reached this position, do not proceed beyond it, for hastily to blurt out the dreadful news not only arouses the disapproving incredulity of the other sheep but is calculated likewise to bring matters to the attention of the shepherd. There is a ready means at hand to quash such subversive activity; it consists in a premature trip to the slaughterhouse, inevitable later in any case for this remarkable fellow who is both too clever and yet not quite clever enough.

Still, at very long intervals indeed, there does occur a black sheep of such outstanding acumen that he avoids this pitfall, too, and is thrown back upon the most sober consideration of what to do for the best. Such a sheep has lost his peace of mind once and for all; and he soon comes to realize that in his extremity nothing will suffice except to add an equal degree of courage to the intelligence which has brought him to his present pass. To remain where he is, is certain death, even (in his own conditions) a sort of deliberate suicide. But what then is he to do? It would be difficult enough to escape the watchful eye of the shepherd and, even if such a miracle were accomplished, where could he find fodder to keep himself alive or shelter from the winter which he likewise knows will surely come? All these necessities have always been provided for him; he lacks any knowledge himself as to how to go about obtaining them. Would it perhaps be better to forget the whole thing, to enjoy a life in many respects obviously suited to sheephood and to resign himself to the fate which will overtake him only a little sooner than properly, in any case? And so, finally, we may imagine in what straits our sheep struggles with these alternatives.

At the end of the fable we are told of the black sheep which came to a final decision. Having waited interminably for a possible opportunity, that black sheep disappeared one dark night from the fold and could not thereafter be found. It had escaped. We are not told what happened to it after that.

This Myth, incidentally, is said to have been put into public circulation originally by that School which flourished for a time in medieval Europe and two other of whose productions were the earlier Gothic cathedrals and the Orders of Chivalry. The true name of the School, which itself stood behind these different activities and directed them, is not disclosed.

Certain points about the allegory are evident enough. The sheep, of course, correspond to the human race of which we are members. And the black sheep is that extraordinary person whose pronouncements are too difficult or too unpleasant to our tastes to be acceptable to investigation, even if we experience the profound unlikelihood of ever meeting with him. But what is the hidden horror he is endeavoring to communicate to us? What, in our case, is the wool and mutton of the fable? Who is the ambiguous shepherd?

These are the questions, specifically, which the Myth is designed to arouse in those whom it reaches and who also by chance possess a Magnetic Centre. And it does indeed stimulate those queries; but it does not answer them. Here we are concerned with the answers, no longer veiled or speculative. And first we shall give the answers, which are both literal and part of the Local Map; then for their explanation we shall have to take a further glance at the Greater Map, for it is there that their reason lies.

The black sheep's secret is this: that our lives have nothing to do with our personal aspirations or desires; that we are born and live because death must follow life; and that in death we provide a kind of food required in the economy of the Universe, which nothing else can provide. The wool and mutton of the Myth are our literal physical bodies, in which during life certain purely physical substances are accumulated, quite unconsciously upon our part, substances that, when automatically released at our deaths, will furnish ingredients required by the cosmic machine. These substances are altogether physical in character but they belong to the realm of physics rather than to that of chemistry; their nature is electromagnetic.

We have already seen that the third factor comprising the human organism is the steady-state DC organic field which accounts for the biological organization of the specific man. This is no verbal abstraction; it is a physical field and it is a force-field. In combining as the organizing or patterning factor with the other two factors comprising the human organism it furnishes the phenomenon of human life and, by the reciprocal action of life-behavior and of life-experience back upon itself (cf. the reciprocal action between site and constructions in the case of the city), it is further enriched in the sense of complexity, during the life-process. When a man dies, his steady-state DC organic field simultaneously vanishes. This is really the only reliable criterion of physical death. One may guess that the organic field corresponds to the prana of Buddhism; consciousness does not accompany it and it will be of no further use to "you" or "I," for consciousness has never had any contact with it. But we must remember that it is a force-field, literally, and having in mind the principle of the Conservation of Energy, it cannot simply disappear into non-existence and it must go somewhere. We shall see in a moment where this now extremely complex concatenation of force is drawn when it is no longer associated with a physical body, i.e., when we die. For plainly enough, it remains an element among all the other physical elements of Nature and at once establishes a new relation with the operation of the physical universe.

But what of the shepherd? Who is he? In the Myth he did not stand for mankind in general in relation to the sheep; instead, he was a specific man. In the same way, the tale dealt not with all sheep but with a specific flock of sheep. Mankind on this planet is not the entire human race for, if so, we could never have known a Buddha or a Christ, by their own original accounts messengers not from heaven but from elsewhere in this universe. And just as the sheep could see the shepherd well enough but did not understand at all what he was, so we can, and do, see our shepherd almost every day without the slightest recognition of his real role in our lives. He is not an abstraction nor is he a generality; he is no such thing as Nature in general or Nature with a capital N, he is a specific and concrete part of Nature. For men on this planet their shepherd is the Moon. And because the Moon is specific to this planet, the black sheep's secret is specific to this planet, too.

It will not do, however, to consider the Moon as a kind of devil. Devils are no more than the inventions of romanticists and there are no authentic devils in this universe, although it is true that Nature may properly be called our Evil Stepmother. In a perfectly proper sense it is Nature which exiles man from his high destiny and keeps him in his exile. Nature here is to be considered in her most general aspects, not only in those aspects of man's own nature which continually prevent his awakening from his usual semiconscious state but also in those aspects of the mechanicality and automatism.

The immediate manifestation of the latter aspects for us upon the Earth is man's Bad Shepherd, the Moon.

For further explanation it will now be necessary to approach the field of cosmogony, to consult the Greater Map and to consider a large view of the operation of the cosmic machine. As to this cosmogony one would not expect, or hope, it to be of the usual philosophic kind. In the latter very numerous hypotheses exist, all of them mechanical, which seek to account in different ways for the formation of nebulae, of galaxies, or solar systems, and so on; in most of them an attempt is made to construct this enormous instrument or tool (for that is what the Universe is) from the bottom upwards as it were, by deriving it from undifferentiated elements which are supposed by some means to have coagulated into atoms, to have coalesced into burning masses of vapor which, in turn have condensed into planets and suns and eventually into the whole arrangement as now partially seen. All this, of course, entirely without any accompanying element of consciousness, for modern rationalists, both scientists and philosophers, are afraid of consciousness, very much afraid of it.

But the facts are somewhat different than as seen by them. As to the creation of the external universe an account of it will be given much later but it may be said at once that it is no mirage à la Christian Science, that it is completely and finally physical in the usual meaning of that term and that everything in it—including human thoughts, "ideals," and emotions—is also physical without any exceptions or loopholes. But equally the Universe is an integration of the same three fundamental forces which comprise a human being, and among those forces the factor of consciousness is included as the third of the forces involved. Naturally this does not mean that you can carry on an intelligible conversation with a stone or even with a tree but it does mean that any purely mechanical interpretation of cosmology is mistaken.

The point now to be considered is a specific derivation of this general view. The usual modern cosmogonist looks upon the Universe as dying, and for a time attempted to support his position by references to the Second Law of Thermodynamics. The Moon is dead, the Earth is dying, the Sun itself is gradually losing its heat-energy and some time will cool to the present temperature of the Earth. Although the time is far distant, and we need not worry about it personally, the final upshot must be a dead level state in which the smallest energy-transfer becomes a self-contradiction and all differentiated forms of matter have been reduced to homogeneous uniformity.

It is not without significance that this democratic-socialistic view of Nature has appeared exactly within those social systems which themselves are undergoing a democratic-socialistic decline.

The statement of this Version is opposite in meaning. The derivation is from above to below, from the top to the bottom, from the complex to the simple. At this point we need consider it only in brief outline. We begin with the Universe-as-a-whole. Then from the Universe are derived the galaxies, the various Milky Ways, within these in turn suns and solar systems are differentiated. From suns planets are derived, from planets their satellites or moons. The direction of energy-transformation, more and more diluted in the sense of progressively slower vibration-rates as the process continues, is from the Sun-Absolute to the satellites.

But such degression is not uniform; it proceeds through octavic intervals. A single succession of this kind would comprise the line from Sun-Absolute to Galaxies (or universe) to Milky Way to Sun to Planetary System to Earth to Moon. This succession is an octave and furthermore each separate stage or note in it is also an octave within itself; the entire series of energy-transformations comprises a tremendously complicated train of octavic phenomena but here we deal only with the great, fundamental octave of the whole universe. In this immense extension a special term is attached to the path from Sun-Absolute to any given individual satellite or moon; such a specific energy-path is called a Cosmic Ray.

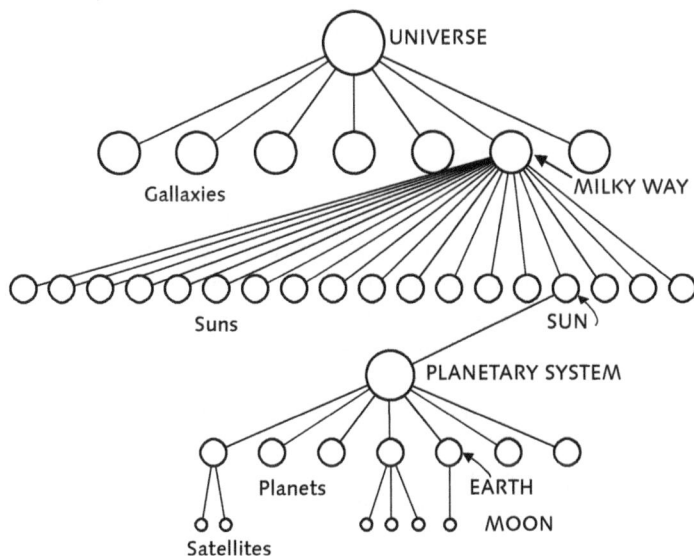

Figure 4. Diagrammatic Representation of a Cosmic Ray.

Each of these countless Cosmic Rays is considered not only as a path of energy transformation but as a line of *growth*. They represent the more and more intricate branchings of the limbs from the parent trunk the farther they recede from the point of origin. The one in which we find ourselves concludes with the present Moon; and that satellite is the growing end of our own Cosmic Ray. It will be seen that this view presents a reversal of the academic cosmological picture; according to the present formulation the Moon some time shall become a planet of similar status to that of the present Earth and the latter will eventually attain the position of a sun, the centre of numerous surrounding planets developed from satellites yet to exist, of which the Moon will be one. These satellites-become-planets will in turn develop other satellites of their own and thus the growth process will be carried on. It is therefore shown that an immense energy output is required along the path of the Cosmic Ray, since growth also must be provided for in addition to the maintenance of what has already grown; and in the relevant transformation of that energy human beings quite unconsciously play a large part.

So large a part indeed that their involuntary contribution to the process becomes of relative importance and its failure might threaten seriously to disrupt the arrangement, as we shall see shortly when the function they fulfill is identified. For, although the above destiny is the normal and proper one for satellites and planets, its successful outcome is not guaranteed. All life and growth is in part an unpredictable adventure and if, for instance, the human portion of the Organic Kingdom upon the planet, Earth, should succeed in destroying itself in the prosecution of its blind antagonisms, the supply of that particular energy which it furnishes to the natural economy of the Moon, would be cut off. This circumstance provides the human race with a certain importance, although not precisely of the kind which it customarily supposes itself to possess.

The energy-transformations along Cosmic Rays will be dealt with in a later chapter; it is here necessary to remark only upon one characteristic of their large octavic design. In this again the two inherent intervals are encountered, at which points a novel, foreign or extraneous influence must be introduced in order that the required energy-transformation may take place. We shall not now discuss the first interval between the superior 'do' and the 'si' immediately below it, the interval, that is to say, between the Absolute and the galaxies considered as a whole or the Universe. It is the interval at the neighborhood of the note, 'fa,' which bears upon the present point. To make this clear we set out the full cosmic octave, although very many of its relations will not be understood as yet:

DO	Positive Absolute
SI	Galaxies
LA	Milky Way
SOL	Sun
FA	Planetary System
MI	Earth
RE	Moon
DO	Negative Absolute

The position, 'fa,' locates the question at issue now. Between 'fa' and the 'mi' below exists the gap or interval which must be bridged if the energy-transformations originating from the Positive Absolute are to be carried below the phenomena of planetary systems and to permit of the further phenomena which, when established, will constitute the growing end of the Cosmic Ray. The cosmic device adopted to this end consists in the existence of Organic Kingdoms on the surfaces of planets. Through the operations of an entire organic kingdom the energies received at the Earth's surface from the Milky Way, from the Sun and from the combined influences of the other planets of our system are absorbed, transformed and again passed on in changed form to the Moon, for its demanded nourishment and growth. We have already remarked upon what the contribution of the human portion of our Organic Kingdom may be.

This interposition of Organic Kingdoms between the given constituent elements or given successive cosmic levels of the Universe is also necessary to the universal feeding process of the whole. For there is a reciprocal, very complicated process of that kind which continually goes forward throughout the entire Universe, keeping it in a perpetual balance and activity; it applies not only within the limits of an Organic Kingdom, within which a delicate balance is maintained among the various species which are the naturally respective prey of each other, but a comparable sort of reciprocal feeding is instituted throughout the whole manifested Reality. The Earth, as we know, is not overrun by certain insects for this very reason; in Bermuda, for instance, the ants are eaten by the cockroaches and the cockroaches are eaten by the spiders; and in any locality, when these balances are upset (usually by some artifice of the ignorance or of the meddling of semiconscious man), very serious results ensue, such as crop failures due to a sudden outbreak of pest propagation or to some unexpected increase in soil erosion, and so on. Such balances, however, are not confined only to the phenomena of Organic Kingdoms and they pervade and maintain the operation of the full universal economy. Often we do not see the ends of these trains of reciprocal feeding in either direction and assume erroneously that they are both more circumscribed and local than they are. In our own case much of the Earth's Organic Kingdom feeds man directly or indirectly. Man in turn feeds the Moon, as well as enriching the planet's soil by his body's inevitable decay.

These are the real, objective functions which man serves in the economy of Nature whether he knows it or not, these transformations of cosmic energies through his own life-process and, at its conclusion, the passing on of such accumulated and transformed energies, which are drawn toward the Moon automatically at his death. There is nothing too astounding in the situation, for is has long been known, by perfectly ordinary means, that the human organism is primarily a device for the transformation of what are called electrical energies. The fuller information, however, cannot but effect a radical alteration in our customary values, especially as concerns those extraordinary persons often called geniuses, psychics, and those endowed with what are supposed to be great and remarkable talents. For the more extraordinary such persons may be considered, the more are they *ipso facto* the more valuable slaves of the Moon, it being plain that the greater the amount of energies down-graded in these more complex nervous systems during lifetime the richer is the energy-supply projected toward the satellite at their deaths, as compared with the cases of ordinary people. This is one—but only one—of the reasons for which it is said in this Version that the path to development is from the extraordinary through the ordinary to the normal. If one has the misfortune to be "an extraordinary man," then first he must become ordinary before an opportunity is at all open to him to become normal. It is neither mere superstition nor mere ignorance which has given the Moon's name, in an objective sense, to lunatics.

For the Moon is the real mainspring of human activity on this planet, it is the great pendulum imparting motion to all the doings of semiconscious men. Their greatest heroisms and their greatest crimes are equally the outcome of their lunar-motivated sleep. That they are asleep is yet to be shown, and literally so; but that shall come at its proper place in the narrative. This is the Actual about men as regards Cosmogony, that though unwittingly they are nonetheless objectively the mechanical slaves of the Moon. Not only so but the more powerful the dictator, the more fanatic and successful the religionist, the more renowned the philosopher, the more celebrated the mathematical genius; by this very token the more is he the Moon's slave.

The Potential concerning man is of course another matter.

5.

But first it must be understood that under no conditions at any time or at any place can man escape serving the Universe; that is, he can never, even potentially, avoid fulfilling some cosmological function. His potentiality here consists only in the remote possibility of a choice. For in serving the Moon, as he actually does, there is no purpose of his own that is likewise

served. Willy-nilly he provides the wool and the mutton of the Moon's nourishment and in doing so he provides no by-product for his own use, too; no
matter how shrewd his glance may appear to the casual observer, his face is
the blank and bleating countenance of the empty-eyed white sheep.

It will be worthwhile just here to notice a few of the many mechanisms
that are employed in order to keep man in his impotent bondage. That these
means are attributed elsewhere to have originated from a higher type of
intelligence than his own, will be remarked upon later but now it is of more
importance to see what they are. The first and the greatest of them is man's
inability to see reality other than upside down. If a thing is objectively large,
he must see it as apparently small; if indeed it is high, to him it must look
low; if any matter has a genuine, and even a final, importance to him in
objective fact, then he is constrained to view it as a passing and trivial consideration, if not as the outright nonsense of a fool. This circumstance is not
due to caprice or to chance but instead it is occasioned by contemporary
man's possession of a certain psychological faculty whose specific operation
is the reversal of any observed truth.

*As one instance of such operation let us take the Scientific Fallacy already
mentioned. Other than scientists no other group of men so pride themselves
upon the rigor and rationality of their procedures and of their techniques.
The most extreme and ingenious safeguards are provided in their experiments against the intrusion in the results of unpredictable variables, against
the mutual interferences, distortions or back-effects of the instrumentation
employed; even the "personnel error" has been meticulously worked out and
the necessary corrections made for it. The method is based squarely upon
reason, no prejudicial influences are permitted to intrude and the whole
progress from the first step of the hypothesis to the final item of so-called
proof is subjected to the strictness and most painstaking criticism. And at
the heart of this entire proceeding lies a logical fallacy, an error of reasoning
itself, so obvious as to have been known to men ever since they first had the
concepts either of logic or of reason. That any sincere scientist (and there
are many) could rest content to beg this question—and all of them do—is
indeed inexplicable. It is inexplicable, that is, until we take account of the
reality reversing faculty implicit in the semiconscious human brain. Few better evidences exist of the presence and mode of operation of that faculty.*

As a further illustration and as an exemplification of this very faculty we
take a term long famous among occultists of the Eastern persuasion and
students of mistaken Buddhistic lore. The word is Kundalini and by such
persons it is considered to denote a priceless faculty whose least result is
great inspiration and which may even lead to flashes of cosmic consciousness or, when developed to longer periods of the same, during which states

tremendous objective truths may be known to the subject. The physical manifestation of this faculty is alleged to consist in a sort of fire originating at the base of the spinal column and then rising in a kind of tide of illumination to invade the higher levels of the nervous system; and there are frequent attempts to clothe its precise operation in mystery.

In fact, Kundalini is nearly the reverse of all this. It is that attribute in man which provides and enforces his seeing of everything upside down and in inverse relationships. Man thus perceives the elephant as the flea and the flea as the elephant, i.e., he supposes the large to be small and the small large, most especially in the realm of values.

In one of the genuine (non-occult) traditions we are told that this attribute was first forced upon man from outside and that the method of doing so was purely physiological: due to the sort of air he breathed, an actual organic change took place near the base of the spine of such a kind as to affect the neurological functioning of the organism in the mentioned sense. The purpose was so to distort his perception of reality as to prevent one otherwise inevitable result of man's developing mechanical reason, viz., his premature realization of the fact that his existence primarily was of use to something foreign to his nature and his resulting efforts to frustrate or to escape from such use of himself. Later the necessity for this distortion disappeared; and by means similar to its formation the organic alteration was made to atrophy.

Man is born fully normal. But the *effects* of the occultists' Kundalini are carried forward from generation to generation by the mechanism of social inheritance, that is, by the training of successive generations by their own parents in this abnormality, an abnormality which the parents inevitably have received, in the same subjective fashion, from their own progenitors.

Now what is Kundalini, actually? It is a real faculty, true enough, and its correct name, as used in this Version, is Kundabuffer; it is one part, the diseased part, of the general psychological faculty of Imagination. This brings us to an analysis of that function and to a distinction related to the one previously made between Reality and Unreality.

Imagination may be divided into two separate faculties, Real Imagination and Phantasy. Real Imagination is imagination about, or concerned with, real things. One is exercising the faculty of Real Imagination if in considering a standing lamp, for example, one reflects upon the real nature of the materials composing it, upon the actual methods by which those materials have been obtained from mines and processed in factories, upon the theories of vision and the deduced purposes for which the lamp has been constructed, upon its various potential uses, upon its place in economics as an article of merchandise and in relation to the persons employed in the manufacture and sale and their recompense for these labors, and upon further aspects of the real lamp too many to be enumerated here. Not only in moments of idleness but during the homeliest of tasks Real Imagination may be exercised; when washing the dinner dishes one may be considering the nature of dishes in human life, the reasons for their invention and the same aspects of these particular dishes as have been suggested in connection with the lamp.

But does one? One does not. Instead, the washing proceeds almost in the absence of any consciousness at all, what little there may be being concerned with a hazy succession of daydreams; if there be any connection at all with the dishes, these daydreams deal with the impressions, good or bad, which the dishes might make upon persons who in fact will never see them, and more usually the imagination roams haphazardly, creating images relating to self-importance or vanity, to the injustice of having to engage in so menial a chore at all and to all the desirable, though quite impossible, things that one might otherwise be doing instead. This sort of performance is the kernel from which "creative imagination" grows and which, when more fully developed, is supposed to eventuate in most of our contemporary bogus art in fields from writing to painting and music; but as to its being Imagination of a creative type, it is no such thing. It is pure and simple Phantasy, the misuse and abuse of the function of Real Imagination.

Kundabuffer is the term used in this Version to apply to that actual function of a diseased kind so prevalent among all of us and of which some of us phantastically boast. It is the real name of the faculty more superstitiously called Kundalini.

But of course, objectively, Kundabuffer fulfills a certain purpose in human life and produces an effect more easily to be appreciated in the cases of others than of ourselves. It engenders and serves the process called Self-Calming. For no man's life is especially easy upon this planet (even though you or you may suppose someone else's to be) and thus everyone encounters a succession of difficulties, problems and obstacles as he proceeds upon his way. It is not customary to look upon them as opportunities for anything, rather are they viewed as unmerited misfortunes: why should this happen to me? In such conditions escape or avoidance becomes preferable to an authentic solution which may involve efforts of some considerable degree; and in Phantasy a remedy is at hand. Instead of the unpleasant trouble of obtaining a real solution and thereafter of carrying it into effect, there is a departure into fancied solutions and imaginary events which will serve to obviate the difficulty without any efforts of one's own whatever. Although nothing at all is effected in respect of Reality by these ineffectual phantasies and irrelevant daydreams, they nevertheless serve to relieve the uncomfortable tensions whose normal purpose is to stimulate exertions likely to overcome the real obstacle. They instate an artificial easiness, based upon Unreality but pleasant to the subject; and this is one of the ways in which Phantasy promotes the abnormal process of Self-Calming in the ordinary man.

Moreover, being rooted in Unreality itself, Phantasy renders man more and more subject to an upside down or reversed view of Reality, the more often he indulges it. It panders to all manner of abnormal weaknesses of his, such as vanity, self-love, self-importance and the like, which could scarcely survive for five minutes without the demanded reinforcement they continually receive from the Phantastic Imagination.

But all these matters that we have just noticed will be said to be natural enough. And in fact they are. They are part of Nature's stratagems for keeping us in line, for preventing us from waking up and seeing any item of Reality as it is, and for assuring that we shall compliantly continue furnishing the wool and mutton required by Nature's young child, the Moon. As for us, the phrase, Mother Nature, is a lying misnomer, and originally a calculated one. Toward us the role of Nature is not that of an affectionate mother but instead it is that of the ill-disposed stepmother who from her more powerful position forces us by guile and deceptions to serve her purposes against our own. Nature's trickeries and deceits are entirely beyond the conception of the ordinary man; it is just when he phantasies that he is overcoming her that he is performing as her most abject slave and engorging her offspring, the Moon.

Now manifestly this matter is not one in which a simple defiance will avail; directing curses at the Moon and vowing not to be her slave are only other ways of serving her, a little different from regarding her as the symbol of an abnormal sentimentality and a convenient rhyme for "spoon" or "croon"; but they are still ways. The Black Sheep must be extremely clever in order to circumvent a situation in which everything he does is arranged to lead to a single unpromising conclusion. It is just here that the real, rather than the phantastic, Potential for man becomes of interest.

In this connection the real human Potential is that man, if he can succeed in learning how to do so, may be able to serve the Sun instead of the Moon, may be able, that is, to direct his energies toward a level of the Universe higher than that on which he finds himself instead of toward a lower one. In such a case not only does he continue to fulfill a natural function in the universal economy but in addition he commences to manufacture by-products of that service which are of great value to himself individually. Not only Nature's aims but his own begin to be accomplished. The so-called "cult" of the Sun at On in ancient Egypt was not the superstitious nonsense it is phantasied to have been by those who do not even suspect that they themselves are involuntary Moon-servants; whatever it became later, originally it was a very serious and practical attempt to effect a remedy for man's dilemma.

The situation, then, is this. Actually we serve Nature's lower forces—the Moon; we have nothing to gain for ourselves by this, we are merely automatically used and with our deaths we cease forever, having served a purpose we have never even understood. Potentially, however, we may serve Nature's higher forces, represented for us by the Sun; and in this case we have something very valuable to gain for ourselves also, specifically the development of some of our real Potentialities as human beings and the acquisition of certain abilities now unguessed but genuinely possible for us. The Moon is served automatically and unconsciously but only conscious men can serve the Sun. So great an alteration in ourselves is very difficult to understand, let alone to achieve, and in order to take a first step in that direction let us investigate further some of the real potentialities now inherent in man although at present unactualized by him.

6.

We have described man as a three-centred or three-brained being and we have earlier located and identified his three Centres. These, since they are in functional operation, are actualities for him. But in addition he possesses three further potential Centres which are physically present in his organism just as it now is. These Centres are potential, not because they are absent but because at present they are non-functional, that is, their operations are not included within his field of consciousness nor do they furnish any part of his present content of experience. He possesses them because they are parts of his organic body but for all practical purposes he might as well not possess them so long as they do not function. Before confronting the problem as to how they may be brought into function, it will be well to see where and what they are.

CORTICO-PONTINE-CEREBELLAR TRACT

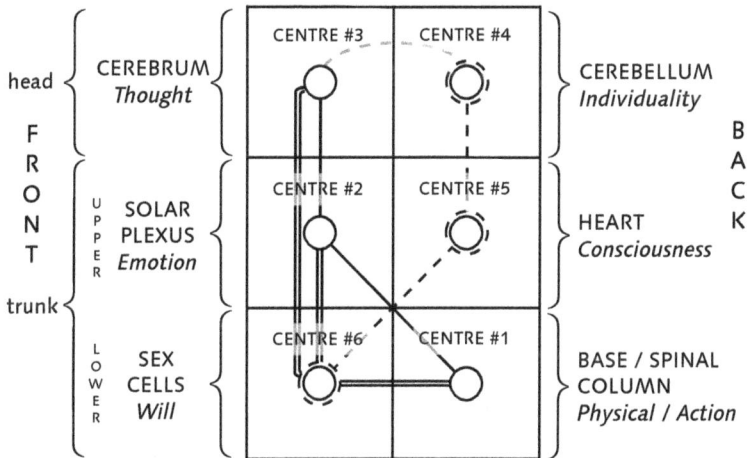

Figure 5. Cross-section of human organism (from left side).

This completes the partial picture presented in Figure 3 and represents the conditions as they now exist. The dotted Centres portray what exists physically but not functionally and the dotted lines indicate the organic connections now present in the body but also non-functional because they are not operating. In this actual situation distortions are inevitable; and the double lines show us certain abnormal interconnections which have developed for the very reason that the proper and normal connections are non-operative.

It will be seen also that a full octave* is represented here in outline, including the obstacle-note, fa, between Centres #3 and #4, which corresponds organically to the very large cerebral output which vanishes non-functionally into the cerebellum. Man is in this sense a miniature replica of the Universe but he is an incomplete replica in Actuality, that is, within himself he is an as yet undeveloped universe. The following diagrams represent the case as it is.

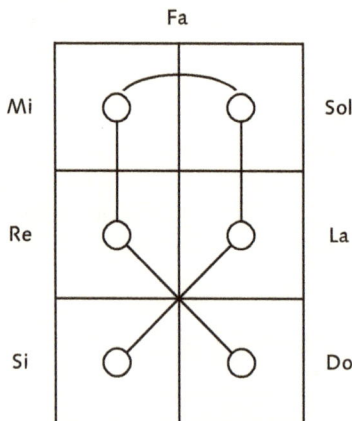

Figure 6. Universal Octave.

* For those with some acquaintance with the Gurdjieff System it will be noted that there exists here a discrepancy between the Oragean and the Ouspenskian Versions.

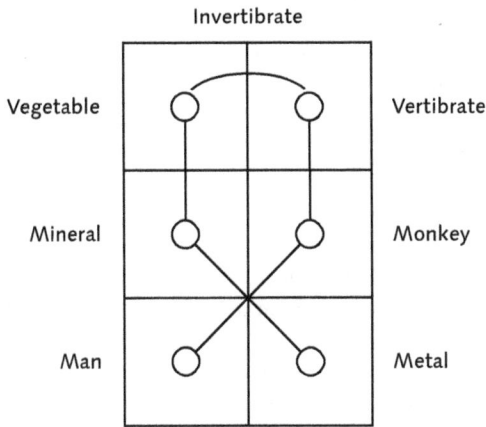

Figure 7. Organic Kingdom.

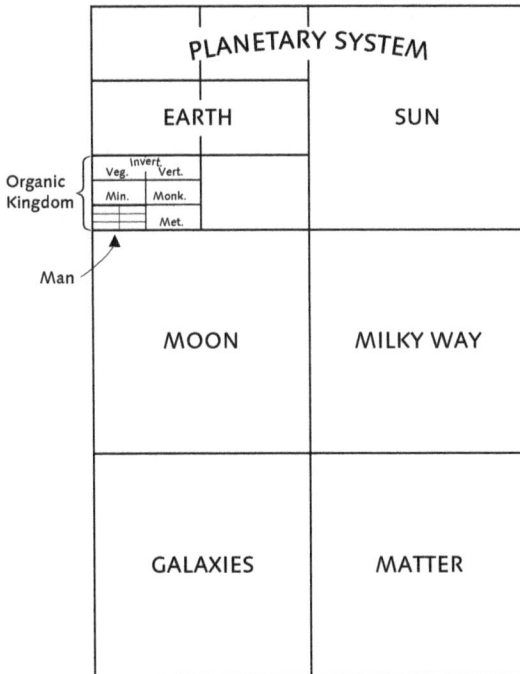

Figure 8. Diagrammatic Representation of the Universe
from the point of view of the Cosmic Ray.

79

Returning now to Figure 5 (page 77) let us distinguish some of the technical terms referring to this diagram. Centres #1, #2, and #3 are called the Lower Centres, #4, #5, and #6 the Higher Centres; thus #3 is the lower intellectual centre and #4 the higher intellectual, #2 the lower emotional centre and #5 the higher emotional centre, #1 the lower physical centre and #6 the higher physical centre. All of them of course are, properly speaking, completely physical in a physiological sense. In this Version the term, Intuition, is applied technically to any one of the three following momentary integrations: between #1 and #3, between #1 and #2, or between #2 and #3. The term, Understanding, denotes only an integration between #4 and #5, for we know that a genuine understanding of any matter simultaneously involves an intellectual component and an emotional component in agreement with each other, whose fusion gives the characteristic flavor to the experience really denoted by understanding. The above terms will always have those exact meanings whenever used in this treatise.

We have already defined the functions of the first three centres in general terms but may add to those descriptions now. Centre #1 contains two large functional subdivisions, called the Moving Centre and the Instinctive Centre. The former is concerned primarily with striped muscle response, with the movements of the external musculature and all those reflexes usually stimulated environmentally which evoke the relevant and adequate responses of movement by the organism, either locally or as a whole. The Instinctive Centre is chiefly concerned with the interior balances and maintenance of the organism and involves the smooth musculature; it mediates the multifarious activities of blood circulation, digestive processes and alimentary tract phenomena, water and sugar balances within the organism and in general all the processes comprised within the term, homeostasis. In ordinary men the Moving and Instinctive Centres are accompanied by consciousness very fragmentary or not at all.

Centre #2 manifests physically all the emotional states experienced by ordinary men. The subjective names for these states are many; hate, fear, affection, anger, sentimentality, dominance, compliance, submission, inducement, desire, satisfaction, and many more. Some of these are called Negative Emotions and some are termed Positive Emotions, a distinction too obvious to demand lengthy discussion, especially since the last two titles are not peculiar to this Version alone. The repertoire here seems large because it includes all manner of compound and of complex emotions, all of which are built up either as immediate successions or as simultaneous integrations of only four fundamental and primary emotions in their active or passive phases; actually the range of emotional phenomena possible to the Lower Emotional Centre is basically very limited.

In figure 5, above, the functions of Centres #4, #5, and #6 are respectively designated as Individuality, Consciousness and Will. But at the present point in our discussion those terms cannot be explained satisfactorily in their full technical meanings and a preliminary statement becomes required.

The Higher Intellectual Centre mediates a different kind of thought-process than does the Lower; but since we do not now experience this type of mental activity, it is difficult to do more than to point toward it by means of defined terms. In the Gurdjieffian System itself the general term for its function is Constatation. In the Oragean Version the term is Realizations, which is selected to indicate that Centre #4 deals intellectually with Reality, either with real things or with the real relations between real things. Also, in contrast to the Verbal Logic employed almost entirely by Centre #3, Centre #4 contains the potentialities of a fully developed Formal Logic, only partially capable of being manifested though #3, and of Objective Logic, which is not a potentiality of Centre #3 at all.

With Centre #5 we meet the same difficulty, that we do not at present experience its activity. Here again we have in our ordinary vocabulary words which denote certain of the higher emotions and some persons even imagine that they have experienced the corresponding states. But actually such suppositions are Phantasy; the authentic experience of them is utterly different from the pseudo-states with which the terms are identified customarily. Some of these terms are Ecstasy, Awe, Reverence, and the like. Their faint reflections do sometimes exist within our experience and that is about all that can be said of them intelligibly just now.

Even less may be said about Centre #6. Its Potential is the ability To Do. Of course, if we adopt the fallacy of the Pauper's Parable and fancy that even now we possess any such ability, then we shall never even remotely comprehend what real Doing is, much less ever experience it. It does not resemble the imaginary actions which are actually no more than the reactions we perform in our half-asleep condition. Genuine Action is a real human Potential but for us it is a very far one, at present the farthest of them all. It is necessary, however, that its possibility be stated now, and that the locus of its mediation be indicated.

At this point it will be said that the organic structures connoted as Centres #4, #5 and #6 do in fact contemporaneously function. It is true that they do, but only in very minor and partial ways. Let us consider this question.

Centre #4, organically the cerebellum: this structure now mediates certain postural reflexes and the responses related to equilibrium. So far as is known, that is all it does; for the rest it is what is neurologically called a "silent" area or in other words a non-functional area.

Now let us recall the functions of the cerebrum, occupying the front of the head-brain as the cerebellum occupies the rear. One-third of the neural output of the cerebrum controls, balances, integrates and activates the operations of all the rest of the organism, it is the operational headquarters of the complete entity. Twice as much (specifically, two-thirds) of the same neural output proceeds into the cerebellum and there vanishes. Is it tenable to reason that this enormous neurological activity is designed to eventuate only in a few postural and equilibratory reflexes? The single neurological ascertainment just mentioned is fully adequate to demonstrate that potential cerebellar functions exist of impressive degree and scope, on the present basis let us say merely to twice the amount of cerebral functions. In relation to these potentialities the operations presently performed are slight and minor indeed.

The structure comprising the core of Centre #5 is the heart, which now acts either as a vascular pump or simply as a large valve, depending upon which medical view one prefers to take. It also maintains reflex connections with Centre#2 and its action is automatically increased or decreased as an accompaniment of the lower emotional states; in the latter sense it contributes directly and indirectly to the total number of physiological symptoms of the lower emotions. The statement is made here that the centre of gravity of emotional mediation can, and should, shift from the solar plexus to the heart complex, that the organism is designed neurologically with the latter as the authentic structural centre of emotional function and that only when this is the case, is the organism functioning normally. When functioning normally, the emotional experience of the human being is naturally of a sort different than when functioning abnormally.

The contemporary function of sexual organization, whether active and male or passive and female, is procreation, the physical reproduction of the species. This function is very closely associated with the emotional centres, its tentative but broken connection with Centre #5 arousing genuine love, its substitute connection with Centre #2 stimulating the appetitive and abnormal emotions of sexual lust, jealousy, greed, desire and satisfaction. In the absence of the properly formed connections between Centre #6 and Centres #4 and #5, the substitute and abnormal connections have grown with Centres #2 and #3 and these are very serious for human beings, since they permit the latter centres to steal sex energy, as it were, and to operate upon a much more intense form of energy supply than is suitable for them or adaptable to their proper functions. Abnormal as sexual excesses and perversions are, they do not constitute the real abuse of sex in ordinary men and women; that real abuse is the misuse of sex energies through the second and third centres, which is the actual basis for the other distortions which are only secondary in derivation, and for much further harm to the organism. The normal functions of sex energy comprise a whole octave, of which procreation is but the first and lowest note; and when we realize how momentous that first of its functions is, we may well suppose that its highest is beyond our present apprehension.

In brief, then, such are the general functions of the Higher Centres in man, as delineated in the relevant area of this Version's Local Map. We do not as yet know that these statements are so, for we are not yet in a position either to confirm or to refute them. They are statements for our future guidance which may come in very valuably at the proper time, when new experiences confuse us and some framework for their organization and recognition will be urgently needed.

Before leaving our first view of the Potential for man, another topic must demand our attention. This is the mundane question of Food, to the ordinary information about which some surprising items are to be added. The subject likewise makes up a part of the Local Map.

For most people ordinary food and drink are thought to compose the totality of man's nutritive supply. A little reflection will convince us that the view is both hasty and incorrect, for if food be (properly) defined as nutritional intake, it is plain that much more must be included. How long can a man live without ordinary food (including liquids)? It depends upon the person but in the ordinary case he can do so for days if not weeks, and cases have been reported that much exceed the usual. How long can he survive without air? Here the limit is determined with minutes as units. And without sensory impressions? For just 1/10,000 of a second or .0001 second, which is the temporal order of sensory propagation within the human nervous system. In the absence of all impressions man dies almost instantaneously.

Now let us see where he obtains his supplies of these essential materials, for impressions also comprise a physical intake of the organism. There is no need to discuss at length the question of ordinary food and drink; they are taken in at the mouth, pass down through the esophagus and cardiac sphincter to the stomach, thence through the pyloric sphincter into the duodenum, the large and small intestines, and all these preliminary processes of digestion are described in much detail in the physiology of the alimentary tract. This, of course by no means completes the full breakdown of the elements that enter the body in this way, for such substances go through many more transformations during organic metabolism. In regard to man's actual condition they furnish most of the elements upon which his body is operated.

In order to avoid needless misunderstanding and to obviate mystical interpretations of the discussion to follow, it will be well here to describe the few unaccustomed terms to be used. The first is magnetism: magnetic phenomena are not at all supernatural and they do occur in the human body; for centuries following the loss of an accurate knowledge of the phenomenon the term, "animal magnetism," has been used to designate a property of human beings which can often be experienced with great vividness despite its abstract naming. It is the assertion here that such phenomena result from the reactions of substances in the human body of a specific vibration-rate rendering them magnetic in character. Such substances, as substances, are not readily accessible to the measurements of modern chemistry and thus their phenomena are attributed to an abstraction called magnetism rather than to the reactions of magnetic forms of matter. But we do not refer to the phenomena of gases as "gaseosity" and leave it at that; we are able to analyze such phenomena and we attribute them to gases as such. In the same way the phenomena of magnetism are properly attributable to specific matters in the magnetic state and when the term, magnetism, is used here, strictly speaking it means magnetic substances. Similarly with the term, thought: this is a short way of saying thought-stuff, which in turn is a short way of indicating those products of organic metabolism which are required for the nourishment and maintenance of the neural cells of the head-brain in man and for which, in spite of no denial that they exist, there are no names in the modern scientific vocabulary. The term, emotion, stands in the same case; it refers to those metabolic products required for the operation of the organic structures comprising Centre #2 and (potentially) Centre #5. And the term, sex, of course signifies those final products of ordinary food diges-tion which furnish the substances of which the spermatozoa and the ova are composed. All of these terms will have the same meaning, no matter from what food-source the substances may be supplied.

Man's second actual food-source is the air he breathes. It enters through the nostrils and is carried to the lungs where complicated interchanges take place between its substances and those of the blood. This is all that is de-scribed in elementary physiology but of course these substances, too, un-dergo many further metabolic transformations or analyses. Nor is the air we breathe a simple substance, it is not all oxygen, for instance; in a single breath there are included many different gaseous elements and their recep-tion and transformation within the body are matters of the particular organ-ism's capabilities in this respect. Moreover, the proportion of the different elements in the air differs in different localities, so that when a recommenda-tion of a "change of air" is sometimes medically made, we know that this is not always a mere stab in the dark but results from a pragmatic ascertain-ment that in many cases such a change produces noticeable effects.

We are not accustomed to think of man's third food as a genuine food but actually it is. In his present state this takes the form of sensory impres-sions which are continually present organically, whether he be awake or asleep, and which are unconditionally required for his life-processes. These impressions are considered to be more than the mere activation of organs and nervous structures, that is, they are considered as being composed of specific matters of a high vibration-rate which in fact enter the body or, as may be better said in the present state of comprehension, a sort of material energy-intake of a kind too subtle for contemporary scientific measurement and identification. The point to be emphasized is that this food-source, also, is a fully and solely physical one. It completes the actual supplies now available to the ordinary man, and we must remember that the ordinary man is the highest kind of man we are ever likely to encounter.

Now let us follow the various transformations which these different forms of food undergo within the human organism. The first food enters as a solid, passes through the liquid state, and becomes gaseous; if it enters as a liquid then it merely skips the first stage. It is further transformed into magnetism, emotion, thought and sex, where all its possibilities have been used up. The second food enters as numerous gases and thence passes through the further stages of magnetism, emotion, thought. The third food merely enters as impressions, a cerebral phenomenon of the general designation of thought; and there it remains. These various transformations compose a series of interrelated octavic phenomena, as follows:

si	sex					
la	emotion					
		(shock)				
sol	thought		mi	thought	do	thought
fa	magnetism		re	magnetism		
(shock)						
mi	gas		do	gas		
re	liquid					
do	solid					

Ordinary Food	*Air*	*Impressions*

It will be seen that these interrelated octaves account for the entire range of metabolic products demanded for the operation of the organic mechanism in its present condition. As in any octave, that of the ordinary food proceeds, once begun, through its first three notes automatically; but, having reached the shock-point immediately above the note, mi, it halts. At this octavic interval a new force is necessary from outside the given octave in order that it may evolve further and at this point air, made up of gases, is introduced by nature into the body-machine; and, by its introduction, assists the first food octave to continue its evolution while at the same time commencing its own. The first food octave then automatically runs up through its own note, si, where it is completed and its possibilities of nutriment exhausted. Similarly, the second food octave, having begun at its own (gaseous) do, continues to evolve through its own note, mi, at which point it encounters the shock-interval of its own octave and ceases to evolve. The third food octave is present only as an *uncompleted* do and does not naturally serve to provide the external shock to the second food (or air) octave which is required to assist the latter over the interval between its mi and its fa; this circumstance will be further discussed later. But the actual situation, just as it is, furnishes all the substances demanded for the type of automatic lives in which ordinary men spend their existences.

We may place here a preliminary diagram showing the course of food digestion in the human organism. In this early figure there will be no attempt to indicate the relations between the different Centres and the loci of the different stages of the digestive process other than the division of the organism into three general stories, in each of which one actual and one potential Centre are located. The more detailed comparison between the body and a three-storied factory will come later.

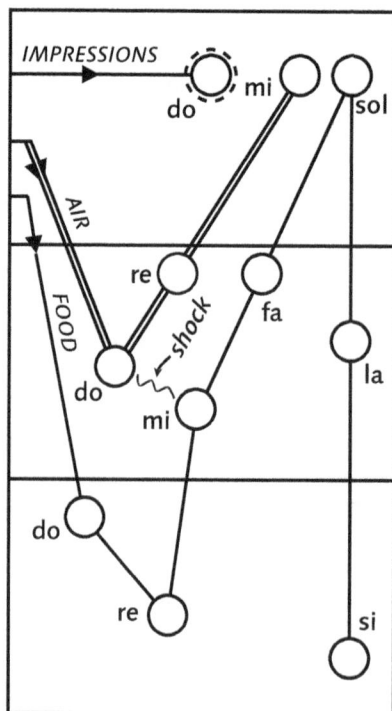

Figure 9. Diagram of Digestion Stages in Ordinary Man.

This very condensed outline has now acquainted us with man as he is, i.e. with his Actuality. He is a semiconscious, mechanically reacting automaton and despite all his grandiose delusions his real predetermined business in the cosmogony of this universe is serving the Moon. It is true that he possesses further potentialities but these are unactualized at the moment and they have their basis in organic regions of the body where he is least likely to suspect their presence since these structures are either now nonfunctional (silent areas) or else at present they mediate only the most minor functions and part-functions of which they are capable.

This situation presents the ordinary man with a total impasse for, no matter how he struggles and strives, all his efforts turn against him in the outcome, all of them eventuate in some attempted or alleged improvement of one of the functions he already exercises. This is the "bigger and better man" fallacy and it is also the fallacy of all reform in general. That error is always the betterment of one or of some functions at the automatic expense of some other function or functions; and if the resultant damage be unseen and thus left out of account by the self-congratulating person, it is all the more dangerous and destructive for that very reason.

A great subtlety is needed here and a very large cleverness. Where shall man look for an escape from his predetermined automatism, from his hazy, semiconscious experience? Anywhere but where in fact he does look; but where is that? He now exercises three main functions, all automatic—reaction, emotion, thought. Where may he find any other function, different in kind from those, which he may be able even to begin to exercise? If he cannot find some such escape, he is lost whether he knows it or not.

That is the Secret, the real and final secret of the Black Sheep who first escapes and then comes back, bringing with him (judiciously) a deeply hidden mystery for such of his companions as may be able to understand. For the Secret can be known. And it can be disclosed.

III. THE BOAT

I.

The Black Sheep's secret—which in this Version is called the Method—is divided naturally into two parts. They may be named respectively the Open Secret and the Hidden Secret, and we shall take them up *seriatim*.

But first let us see why this chapter is called—the Boat. That is just because the secret does consist in a method, that is, in a certain described mode of procedure or in a rigorously defined succession of steps which are to be taken one by one, as strictly directed. With certain exceptions no further step is to be taken until its predecessor has been completed; and here the reader should refer back to the earlier illustration of the chemistry student whose test tube exploded in his hands with disastrous results because he had failed to learn, as instructed, the definitive properties of hydrogen.

Indeed there is much more to be said on this subject, and it must be said, *and heard,* with the utmost seriousness. We do not deal anywhere in mere intellectual speculation, a relatively harmless form of phantasy, but especially we do not deal with it in this chapter. What is to be formulated here is a method of action, it is something *to do*; and if it be done correctly, there shall surely be objective results. It is no more possible to engage actively in this Method and escape those results than it is possible, no matter how incredulously it may be done, to drink a quart of brandy in ten minutes and remain unaffected by the draught. Thus there are bound to be real effects if this work is prosecuted correctly; and if what is done in this discipline be done incorrectly, very *disastrous* effects indeed can be guaranteed.

For that reason such work as is to be described, is only done, and can only be done, safely under the immediate supervision of another person, one moreover who is fully competent and qualified—and has proven it—to hold so responsible a position *vis-à-vis* others who must be for some time confused and helpless in the face of these surely eventuating results.

This is by no means either metaphor or hyperbole; it is a warning as serious as the writer can make it. As to the Open Secret, there is no harm in practicing that part of the Method and much recompense can be gained from it, if the task be engaged in properly. But as to the kind of activity to follow the disclosure of the Hidden Secret, it must not be prosecuted alone or with a group of other uninformed persons, either. Any who may fail to follow this recommendation, do so at their own peril. It is not merely a recommendation; it is a warning and a prohibition.

This again is why the chapter is called the Boat. It involves not only something to do but something which, if done, also will take you somewhere. It

88

is not like the credulities of Christian Science, in the midst of which one will die as quickly of cancer or of a bullet wound as if one had never heard of those credulities. It is not like psychoanalytic phantasies, accepting which one simply substitutes new malfunctions and misunderstandings for old ones. The Method consists in something novel, unsuspected and very different from any of the reactivities of semiconscious men and it will inevitably produce a view, even of one's surroundings, most unaccustomed to all of us. Thus, if we use the analogue of the Map for a formulation of unglimpsed realities, we may likewise describe as the Boat that strict method of procedure which will enable us to approach those realities personally, to view them directly and to make our own confirmation of them for ourselves.

But having had a really personal (not merely an intellectual) view of them, there can be no turning back. Having once in fact constated even a few realities, it will be literally impossible to rejoin the herd of blank-faced sheep and immerse oneself in their dream-life as before. There comes a time when the inquirer is no longer only an inquirer; no matter what terms he uses, he has become an actual postulant; he has abandoned one chair, he has not as yet reached another, he dangles in the void between them. That situation is the worst of all, it is even more hopeless than our semiconscious sleep. And so, even with the possibility of correct instruction and competent supervision, one must be very sure of the seriousness of his interest and purpose before taking so irreversible a step.

2.

In one way this Method resembles that of Science, for its basis is observation, hypothesis, experiment and conclusion. In another way it is dissimilar, for it does not involve the scientific error, the fallacy of affirming the consequent. This will be seen more clearly when the complete chapter has been read.

Now the Open Secret is called open because it can be discovered by perfectly ordinary means and in fact a great many people are acquainted with it, at least verbally. We are told that over the main gate of the Pythagorean Institute at Cretona were carved the words, Gnothe Seauton—Know Thyself. The degree of such knowledge that can be acquired by ordinary, though careful, means constitutes the Open Secret. There are difficulties in this, to be sure, but there are none which may not be overcome by a usual amount of tenacity, of intelligence and of courage.

The first of the difficulties is a purely mental one; it is no more than the delusion that we already do know ourselves. Ask any ordinary man whether he knows Mr. So-and-so (mentioning his own name when perhaps being in ignorance of it) and he will tell you, with a sly or cunning smile, that he knows Mr. So-and-so very well indeed; if you press the point, he will conclude with the triumphant statement: "Why, you see I am So-and-so, naturally I know all about him, I know him better than anyone else possibly could."

No long reflection is required in order to appreciate the absurdity of the assertion. The smallest investigation discloses that his friends and acquaintances hold very different views about Mr. So-and-so than he does himself; and that the opinions of the former are the more likely to be correct. When confronted with a phonograph record of his voice or a moving picture of his actions, he is astonished and bewildered; indeed for some moments he is quite unable to recognize that it is his own voice speaking, his own figure moving across the screen. He possesses a physical, an emotional and an intellectual image of himself, all of which are very far from the facts. It is this image with which he has that real acquaintance underlying his confident assertion but the image is merely subjective and it is false in almost every respect. Of what he is really like, of the picture he presents even to those who are genuinely fond of him, he knows practically nothing at all.

No tremendous sincerity is needed to assure any one of us that his own case is that just mentioned, although here, certainly, a moderate sense of humor will not come in amiss. For there is a high degree of *amour propre* in these images which makes it difficult for us to see them for what they are; always there is much flattery in them and they are a continual product of the confusion between what we would like to be, even what we semiconsciously aspire to be, and what in fact we are. To admit these discrepancies to ourselves is a painful business, indeed just to suspect them sincerely is bad enough. Yet otherwise we are surely the Pauper whose denial of his poverty must with certainty preclude any possibility of future wealth. To destroy a delusion may be very unpleasant, and especially in the case of this one, but to hug it to oneself with a desperate grasp is true abnormality. The first step toward knowing oneself is the realized admission that one does not.

The key to this whole problem is sane objectivity. The possibility of knowing oneself can arise only when a man is prepared to investigate his own attributes and characteristics, and his own behavior, as he would inquire into those of a stranger. Impartiality and objectivity. The subtlety of this undertaking and its difficulty cannot be overstated; at every turn he will, as it were deliberately, misinterpret what he sees and the constant falsity of his ingrained, subjective image of himself will distort what is plainly in front of his eyes. To see what can easily be seen, is not so hard; but the way in which it is seen, *how* it is seen, that is the secret. The very first step in this Method is to look upon oneself as upon a stranger, literally, for a stranger to oneself is what one truly is. A scientist in a laboratory investigating some hitherto unknown creature is not afraid of what he may find, his motive is a controlled curiosity nor has he any axe to grind in favor of or opposed to some subjective judgment regarding that creature's graces. He wants to find out, he looks in order to discover what is. Objectivity, objectivity, objectivity. An objectivity whose demands shall become much greater later.

The second step is to organize the work. Haphazard attempts might turn out fortunately by chance but we shall far more quickly and accurately come to valid conclusions if a definite course is followed and a careful organization of our efforts is adopted to begin with. For this of course is *work*, to be undertaken professionally; simply hearing the instructions that are given, and then dreaming about them, will accomplish nothing. What is to be done, must be done and no one else can do it for you. *No one else can do it for you.* Remember that always. If others take this Boat but you do not, then others can sail somewhere with it but you cannot; also you must propel it. The Boat is given you but only you can take yourself to your destination in it. And although these beginning efforts are slight indeed compared to what shall be required later, yet they are difficult enough at the time one first encounters them. So why should one take the trouble to learn about oneself, anyhow?

But you have to live with yourself, don't you? Divorce of such kind as this is not possible; day after day, month after month, year after year you must live with yourself until you die. Perhaps it would be as well to know something about this stranger you live with; this Mr. Smith (let us say) who places you in such unexpected situations, even occasionally in such unprofitable predicaments. Why do you not accomplish what you secretly wish, what you really seem to strive for? Is it always some outside chance or some outside injustice that hinders you, or may it perhaps be that fellow, Smith, who has something to do with it, too? How can you use Smith to achieve what you want? That is the question. And certainly no answer to it is practicable until you know something definitely and objectively about Smith. Self-knowledge will be painful, your subjective image of yourself will omit no stratagem to deceive you and it will not die meekly; but without self-knowledge you can never be anything at all.

To get the feel of this thing let us have a practice run. Take someone you know well, but certainly not someone you love nor certainly not someone you hate. Just someone of whom you really do know quite a bit. Now come to some considered conclusions about him, impartially objective conclusions; describe him as if you were furnishing a report upon him for an identification to be made by an FBI agent who had never seen him. Write down his physical characteristics from memory, then consider his type, his customary behavior, his personal idiosyncrasies. Check these the next time you see him: Are his eyes really hazel, or would you now call them blue? Is that habit of his of scratching his ear really a habit by which the agent may recognize him or have you given it prominence only because it annoys you? When you have the description to such shape that you honestly believe it would serve as an identification, try it on someone else who knows him;

see if it works and if that second person can put the correct name upon the description you have furnished. If you succeed in this, you have done well.

Now turn upon yourself in the same way. We will suppose your name is Smith; now let us see how recognizably you can describe Smith, as formerly you were describing Jones. Do not get lost in speculations as to who "you" are and what "your" connection with Smith may be. This is perfectly straightforward, perfectly rational, perfectly practical; you are simply that which is considering Smith as anyone else might consider him, who is taking the trouble to come to confirmable conclusions and judgments concerning Smith and who is furnishing a written identification of him. It is important that you write it down, for that will, partially, prevent mere daydreaming.

At once you will comprehend that you have at your disposal a far larger number of data concerning Smith than you had in regard to Jones; but do not permit this fact to sway you toward omitting the obvious. First write down an external physical description of Smith. Check it; you can certainly do that, and don't be too sure you can afford not to. Invent some pretext and persuade a friend to take some moving pictures of you which you can observe at your leisure and for a reasonable time; perhaps he will consider you a vain fellow but you won't feel that way when you regard the picture. Meantime you will be learning what you really do look like. Now continue with all the items you have noticed in the case of Jones, putting down their counterparts for Smith.

Let us organize this attempt more professionally and let us make the inquiry as specific as possible. Here is a list of eight questions; the answers to them should not be couched in terms of generalities, instead the answers should be as exact as it is possible to make them:

1. What do I (Smith) like? What do I dislike?

    a) ordinary food   f) people
    b) clothes   g) amusements
    c) colors   h) company
    d) occupations   i) etc.
    e) situations

2. What do I look forward to? (I.e., what remains in life for me, just within the range of possibility?)

3. What do I fear most from the future?

4. What would I like to be? To know? To do? (To be: what type would I like to incarnate? To know: what field if only one choice but within

that field the possibility of complete knowledge? To do: what primary occupation if I were free to choose seriously?)

5. What have been my happiest and my unhappiest moments?

6. What are my own personality characteristics? Which do I consider weak points? Which do I consider strong points?

7. What things about Smith do I like? What dislike?

   a) physical
   b) emotional
   c) mental

8. Why do I fear to die?

Do not daydream about the answers. Write them down; and take the trouble to do so accurately. Under "food," for example, do not assume that you like caviar unless you really do; under "situations" do not suppose that you either like or dislike military formality unless you have had sufficient experience of it to be able to form a real judgment about it. *Do not guess.*

It will be seen that to consider even so short a list as these eight questions properly and seriously must take some time and involve some effort. However, it is scarcely a beginning. Previously we have discussed the functional human types, practical, emotional, intellectual, and it is now necessary that one determine one's own type among these categories. Each has two aspects, the positive and the negative, as follows:

Practical	positive	active
	negative	inactive or lazy
Emotional	positive	optimistic
	negative	pessimistic
Intellectual	positive	constructive, building up
	negative	deconstructive, tearing down

It makes no difference which aspect of which type refers to you and you must not let your prejudices in favor of one or another influence your judgment; none are "good," none are "bad," it is required only that you discover for yourself which is applicable. And here we must remember that it is not one hour or one day that counts; the criterion is what type you impersonate ordinarily, usually or most of the time, for all of us fall into all six of the above categories some of the time.

This brings us naturally to the Life Review. It also is to be written out and that will take some time. (You are supposed to be doing this seriously.) All of your life is there in your memory; what is required, is to recall it and much of it can be recalled. The greatest difficulty will be with the early years but even there assistance can usually be obtained, from old friends, from an uncle or an aunt, from one's parents. This should be a miniature autobiography, but done without phantasy, done impartially as if it were not an autobiography but a biography of someone else. And do it specifically, dividing the life into the periods into which it naturally falls—infancy, childhood, adolescence, young maturity, middle maturity, and so on. At the end you should have a history of Smith that really tells us and you something about him, what kind of person he is in fact, what sort of thing history has shown that he can do well, what sort of thing ill. A real picture should be beginning to emerge.

All this may be called the first step, the gathering of observable data upon which an hypothesis can be built. The hypothesis or judgment is the second step and then arises the possibility of experimental confirmation or refutation. In the present case this consists in checking the supposed functional type with others and in checking the biographical details insofar as they can possibly be checked; do not assume, for instance, that you did well or poorly at school, get out the old reports if available and, if not, then try to check your supposition in any way you can think of. Of course for serious work of this character a group is assumed with a competent leader; although it will be of little help in respect of the Life Review, in other respects it is not only valuable but necessary.

There are other investigations of the same kind that also should be made at this time. One of them is the Nightly Review, an exercise to be done upon retiring for the night. It poses these questions: What did I do today, i.e., what were my actual activities? What was the emotional history of the day? What was my real thinking today, if any, or was it all daydream from start to finish? No judgments, derogatory or congratulatory, should be allowed to intrude here; we are not trying to make either a better or a worse day of it, we are simply trying to find out how and what it was. Do not despair, do not hope; just look. And for checking these introspective recollections there exists a further interesting exercise called the Motion Picture.

When you have mastered the Motion Picture, you can *see* what has happened. It is done like this. Being in bed for the night and having assumed a comfortable position, the first thing to do is to relax. Complete relaxation is not easy to achieve and it will take much practice; but it *can* be achieved and anyone can do it. The first step is muscular relaxation: begin with the toes and work up through the ankles, the calves, the thighs; as these relaxations are achieved, keep those portions relaxed and begin with fingers, wrists, arms; then the trunk, the face and finally the neck; if tension has become reinstated somewhere during the process, go back and relax that part again, keeping the rest relaxed until finally all the musculature is limp. It cannot be done completely the first time or the tenth time but all of us, as babies, had this ability and it has been proven without question that the ability can be relearned.

Emotional relaxation comes next; and this is accomplished by means of a kind of trick. It is done by reinstating images of a particular kind. Go through your memories and select one or two occasions upon which you really experienced emotional relaxation, the sort of feeling that is expressed by the notion that it would be nice for this to go on forever. Not an active happiness and of course not any discomfort, just a feeling of comfortable drifting. Having selected such a peaceful moment from memory, try to remember as fully as possible the external situation in which this peacefulness occurred; you will try to reinstate not the feeling itself but the sensory impressions that by chance accompanied it. Thus you will call up not only visual imagery (the meadow by the stream, the apple orchard, the quiet library, or whatever) but also olfactory imagery (the outdoor scent, the bookish odor in the library) or other, auditory imagery (the humming of insects, the ripple of the stream) and all other accompanying experiences which are not merely imaginary but really recollected. The instatement in your images of the sensory impressions that accompanied the original emotional relaxation will, if sufficiently accurate and comprehensive, reinstate the condition itself.

It remains now to establish a mental relaxation, a suppression of the constant flux of associations flitting through the brain, a prohibition of the "monkey chatter" continually going on in our minds. This is done by counting a series of numbers, sufficiently intricate to distract attention from the automatic associations but not so difficult as to take up all the attention. One series much used goes as follows: 1-2-3-4, 4-3-2-1, 2-3-4-5, 5-4-3-2, 3-4-5-6, 6-5-4-3, 4-5-6-7, 7-6-5-4, 5-6-7-8, 8-7-6-5, 6-7-8-9, 9-8-7-6, 7-8-9-10, 10-9-8-7, 8-9-10-11, 11-10-9-8, 9-10-11-12, 12-11-10-9, 1-2-3-4, 4-3-2-1, and so on. This may be too intricate to begin with. The trick is to get a series just difficult enough but not too difficult; anything from the simple 1-2-3-4-5-6-7-8, 8-7-6-5-4-3-2-1 to the more complex counting alternately from 1 to 100, thus: 1-100, 2-99, 3-98, and so on. At first it is a matter of personal experiment to find the appropriate series, which thereafter will have gradually to be increased in intricacy as one becomes more accustomed to the attention-distracting effect.*

So far we have three exercises which, when practiced and put together, will establish a state of three-fold relaxation. For this purpose they are valu-

---

* Numerous exercises of this kind are given in *Psychological Exercises*, A. R. Orage, Farrar and Rinehart, New York, 1930.

able in themselves; they also form the preliminary conditions for the Motion Picture exercise.

When the relaxation has been established, the visual component of the emotional relaxation is abandoned while all the rest of the condition is maintained. And instead of the visual imagery hitherto employed, a picture is set up in the mind of the awakening of that morning, preferably in the same bed in which the subject is now relaxing. This visual image should be clear, the body being seen, as it were, from some point outside itself. The image thus established, will commence to move; it will rise from the bed and go through the first motions it performed on the morning in question. Almost at once the film will break and, when it does so, the visual image of the body is reformed deliberately at the point of the break. It will then run automatically for a shorter or longer time, when it will break again and again have to be reformed deliberately. As long as it runs, just let it run and watch it impersonally, while the subvocal counting of mental relaxation continues. When it breaks, discontinue the counting momentarily if necessary, reform the image, let it start moving and resume the subvocal counting. When first undertaking this exercise, of course the breaks in the visual imagery film will be numerous and you will be asleep long before it has run through the day. But with practice the breaks will become continually less frequent, the film will run more automatically and in an amazingly short time the whole day will be covered in this fashion. The chief thing is to let it run *impersonally* and *impartially*; the film will stop at once if you begin to judge of it, as by thinking "this is good" or "that is disgraceful." But if you will let it unroll itself as if it referred to someone else, it will soon show you the day as your body actually went through it.

There are still further investigations which may be made by ordinary means; and in order to outline some of them it will now be necessary to describe the distinction between Personality and Essence which is drawn in this Version. This is a large and complicated subject, whose highlights can only be touched upon here.

When a man is born, he possesses certain qualities and characteristics of Essence; they are undeveloped—indeed they are in an infantile condition—but they are his innately and they are his alone. Moreover these characteristics continue to be truly his, whatever stage of development or undevelopment they may reach, throughout his entire life. At once, however, they commence to be overlaid and hidden and suppressed by the influences of environment external to him, the most potent of these influences being those originating from other human beings and of these last the most potent of course being usually those coming from the parents. Later, teacher, intimate friends and other close associates bring similar forces to bear upon the man's essential and individually inherent qualities.

Thus it soon comes to pass that the man, while yet a child, assumes a kind of twofold aspect; his Essence, viz., what he truly is, begins to alter and mature physiologically but at the same time it is being progressively buried beneath the accumulation of externally dictated behaviors, attitudes and so on which, originating outside of himself, have no necessary relation to his own innate being and which prevent any natural transformation of his infantile essential traits. Moreover, he is only one and, besides that, he is young, feeble and nearly helpless; he relies without recourse upon those very persons whose influences upon him are often contrary to his Essence. As a result of all this his Essence becomes more and more deeply submerged and there is encrusted upon it the outer shell of Personality, originating outside himself and training him in actions and assumed feelings often quite contrary to his own nature and, at the least, incongruous with it. This situation continues without any consciousness of it on the part of the subject and eventually we are confronted with the final product, an exterior Personality hiding an essential core, long unconscious and very different from the presented appearance.

This does not produce the split personalities formerly discussed, for in this case the Personality (including all its split-up sections) is much more developed and predominant than the Essence, which very seldom, if ever, obtains an opportunity to function. It is for the latter reason that the Essence fails to develop and remains infantile, or at best childish, in most people. It is only drastic emergency that brings out Essence usually; and what it usually brings out is panic, terror, a complete disregard for others and their needs. Thus a man's essential qualities acquire a bad name but they are not bad, they are only undeveloped. It can happen that essential fear, normally developed, becomes clairvoyance; and many characteristics of undeveloped Essence are really the suppressed germs of qualities and faculties natural and valuable to the fully developed human being. Meantime these ungrown qualities remain and, in the cases of others, they are never mistaken, even though you may never have encountered them before; there is no mistaking an essential cry of terror or of gladness, though heard for the first time.

At present, as we know, astrology is an activity undertaken by deliberate quacks or by sincerely deluded persons who have at their disposal no knowledge or data adequate to the scope of their profession. But originally the field of astrological investigation included the phenomena of essence when, in very ancient times, astrology was a genuine and exact science.

The facts about Essence itself indicate its relation to this field of knowledge, when the latter was authentic. Modern astrology is an error plain to any biological consideration, for by that time the organism is much grown and developed and no aspects of the planetary system can then have a critical effect upon it. The same is not true, however, for the moment of conception, when the newly procreated cell is totally naked, as it were, and open for a short duration to whatever influences may be present at the temporal and spatial location. That was the commanding instant taken by ancient astrology. At that point—when the male and the female germ-cells coalesce—there are present in the unified cell thus procreated not only the hereditary contributions of its constituent predecessor cells but likewise all the external influences appropriate to and centred at the given temporal and spatial point. Such influences must include solar and starry radiations as well as those originating within our own system from the planets that compose it, but mere proximity will make the latter of the greater determinative value. They do not, of course, change the predetermined contributions of the parent cells but nonetheless they can have an important effect in *patterning* those contributions in the respective strength of their mutual relations. For this reason the position of the planets was considered to be significant at the moment of conception; and this was also where the "fate" of the individual came in, in the sense of the determination of his essential pattern, which could not be without inevitable result in the determination of the future pattern of his life. Such data were worked out with the same care which a modern chemist employs in his calculations and formed the basis of the ancient, and authentic, astrological knowledge. That knowledge is not accessible to us now, however, and even the moment to which it applied has long been mistaken for the birth-date; in certain Schools the genuine science is preserved but it is not included in this Version.

In work of the kind of which we treat here, it is a man's task to discover his own Essence. It is a very difficult task because of the many layers of Personality overlying it. It is also the inner meaning of the gospel saying: "Ye must become as little children." Not in behavior certainly, but in awareness and recognition of what one really is; for one's Essence is what one really is, and that is a very undeveloped being indeed, for the reasons above mentioned. Not that Personality is to be flouted and suppressed in turn; the proper state for a human being is a state in which both Personality and Essence are equally and harmoniously developed. But here the emphasis is upon Essence and the task is the peeling off of one layer after another layer after another of Personality until the Essence is reached, seen and thus permitted to commence its own long delayed maturation. Having missed the chance to develop from its infantile condition by straightforward expression, it now receives a second opportunity to develop by means of impartial recognition.

Orage once made a remark about Essence which ran something like this. Florence Nightingale ought to have been a hostess at a rough wayside inn. That is what she was in Essence. But due to the fact that she was brought up in a Christian family where nursing was considered charitable, unselfish, and so on, she became what she did, though fundamentally she was the wife of Falstaff. An awareness of her Essence might not have induced Florence

Nightingale to have abandoned her career as a nurse; but she would no longer have deceived herself about it.

Closely connected with Essence is a man's Chief Feature. This is sometimes also called his Chief Weakness, for it is usually something of which the man himself is deeply ashamed. It is in fact the basic pattern of his undeveloped Essence; it is deeply buried, deeply hidden, disguised from his recognition by every stratagem of his Personality. But it is the final determiner of our values, something for which, though unacknowledged, we will sacrifice everything else if driven to it. Its effects, direct and indirect, are involved in everything we do; the way we brush our hair, the manner in which and even the steps by which we dress ourselves, our modes of travel, and of course the way in which we meet and deal with other persons. The instance is given of a Russian officer of the Czar's regime who, when told that his Chief Feature was cowardice, laughed heartily. He had been decorated upon the field of battle with almost every available medal for valor, and he had earned the medals. But his Chief Feature was cowardice, nevertheless. His behavior was abasedly craven in the face of his womenfolk, especially of his wife and his mother; and his military feats were fundamentally a desperate compensation for and denial of his real innate, unaltered childhood fears. Another not unusual Chief Feature is self-importance, the expression of which may take nearly any form except pomposity. Chief Feature is never beneficial; except for our chief features we should be the very people that we like to think we are.

"Tell me what you pride yourself upon being," Orage said once, "and I will tell you what you are—not. The very thing we pride ourselves upon *not* being is the very thing that we are. 'I'm not a jealous person.' 'I'm not afraid of being told the truth.' When once you have yourself said the real truth about yourself, there is nothing that anyone can ever say to you again that can hurt you."

Chief Feature is a predominant feature, an outstanding characteristic. It is not, however, the element that is apparently most pronounced; instead, it is an *arrangement* of qualities. Until you have arrived at your own or another's Chief Feature, the definition does not come clearly into view. How shall one find one's Chief Feature? And, when found, what shall one do about it?

One may sometimes surprise the Chief Feature of another in a chance description or an off-hand, happy remark. Someone happened to speak of G. B. Shaw as a man whose wits had gone to his head; and it was an almost perfect delineation of his Chief Feature. One may possibly turn on oneself in this sudden and unexpected way and make an equally striking discovery. But the sure way is to watch one's general and detailed behavior over a considerable period impersonally and to let their picture gradually and impartially form in one's mind. An outline will emerge, suspicions will thrust themselves forward; disregard them for a long time, until you are relatively sure. Then go to someone competent to confirm or to deny your own judgment; you can never be sure of this aspect of yourself by yourself, you will always need an outside confirmation. Naturally it must be a competent one and your equally uninstructed friends will not be of avail here; but it is one of a group leader's functions to supply assurances like this at the proper time.

Then comes a serious moment for, although to others who do not possess this particular Chief Feature it will seem a matter of little importance and nothing to occasion much of a fuss, to the man himself it usually appears as an almost unfaceable shame. It is, indeed, something which he has only brought himself to mention to his teacher after a real inner combat. And his immediate impulse is to do away with it by any available means.

This pitfall must be avoided at all costs. Struggling and striving, as our Mr. Shaw has said, are the worst possible ways in which to accomplish anything; and a direct struggle against one's Chief Feature will not only accomplish nothing valuable but is also only a naïve way of increasing one's service to the Moon. The salvationist attitude has no place in an undertaking so serious as this one; it is always the mark of the religious or emotional fanatic, no matter how much he may seek to deny his role.

What, then, is to be done, if a direct suppression of Chief Feature is prohibited? The answer is a simple one but it is also a hard one. The subject must watch his own Chief Feature, once he has identified and confirmed it, in operation in his own behavior. As he watches it—and the more he watches it—*it will change of its own notion and by itself*, a little by a little. It will do so, moreover, without the substitution of something more harmful in its place. This is not at all so astonishing as it might seem at first glance; there are a number of chemical reactions that can take place only in the absence of light, and on the level of psychology this is a similar phenomenon, in that an awareness of the action of Chief Feature will automatically alter the action, at first only imperceptibly but after a long enough period very noticeably. Chief Feature, like any other aspect of Essence, will commence to mature. When it has matured, it may well turn out to be one of the man's most valuable human qualities. But it is obvious that its ill-advised suppression, being already the real cause of its presently undeveloped, objectionable condition cannot change it normally but can only cause further harm. Never permit anyone, under any guise or pretence, to persuade you to struggle directly against your Chief Feature; that is no more than the naïveté of reform and, in this case a more than usually disastrous naïveté.

A man's Essence is likewise responsible for his Animal Type, which of course must be altogether distinguished from his Functional Type. There are such realities as animal types among human beings; a decay in the accurate knowledge about them has led to totemism among so-called primitive but actually decadent peoples all over our planet. But it is most likely that the animal-headed gods of the Great Egyptian School represent totemism only to those modern archeologists who present a suspicious appearance of being totemists themselves.

Have we not all met human beings whose presences suggest that of a rabbit? Think for a moment of Caspar Milquetoast, the cartoon prototype of numerous real people. Dog-types and bird-types are represented among nearly everyone's acquaintances and are sometimes exemplified in their nicknames; these are real types whose characteristics are, and will continue to be, mirrored in their possessors' behaviors. To know oneself at all fully must therefore be to be aware of one's own animal type. But unfortunately these are not always so obvious as they may be in certain cases and sometimes the animal, though real enough and even contemporaneously existing, may be unknown to its human counterpart. Here the assistance and the knowledge of others may again come in handily, for this inquiry is not nearly so subjectively embarrassing as the search for Chief Feature.

It must not be thought, however, that mere appearance will be much of a guide, although occasionally it may be so most amusingly. But for the most part animal type is not evidenced by external similarity; its correspondences lie rather in the realm of behavior patterns. It is there that the investigation must be made, by an extended observation of the behavior without a priori assumptions, until a typical pattern begins to appear of its own accord. And the knowledge thus gained is valuable knowledge; our types are natural to us and their ascertainment can tell us much as to what we may continue to expect of ourselves, for it is a foolish person who expects the leopard to change is spots or the cat suddenly to behave like a whale.

Self-knowledge of this kind tells us what we are and, in view of our real automatism, what we shall continue to be under ordinary circumstances. In the Life Review, if it be at all properly and carefully done, we shall find many repetitions or typical patterns of happenings and behavior which seem to recur time and again and which often have as their basis the habitual ways in which we confront external circumstances; thus at any given moment what is happening to us, greatly resembles what has happened to us before in other periods of our lives and the same shall also continue to happen to us in the future unless we much alter. The attempt here is not to alter ourselves but to know ourselves and the value of our estimating of any given circumstances or plans in relation to ourselves. For we can be sure that our functional types and our animal types will go on operating, and that Chief Feature will continue to be the secret mainspring of our behavior in everything.

Another important question arises just in this respect. Why are we interested in this kind of work? Why are we interested in the Hidden Learning itself? Those questions can be answered, if a man will interrogate himself sincerely and fearlessly, and by the same techniques previously suggested. No doubt he has more than one motive for his interest, supposing it to be a genuine one. And if it is not, nothing could be more valuable than the discovery of that fact before he has gone too far and can no longer turn back. So let him seriously consider what his intellectual interest may be, what his emotional and what his practical interest may be in this activity to which he is now on the verge of committing himself. It is not yet too late; he has so far learned only the Open Secret and he may yet turn back before an irretrievable commission has been made.

In group association much more work of the kind we have indicated and many more investigations may be made; and indeed it is only in group work that those already described can be carried forward successfully. Otherwise there cannot be a sufficient checking of results or the necessary control by a qualified teacher who himself has before passed through the same kind of self-investigation and is aware of its difficulties and pitfalls for that reason. The purpose of the work involved in the Open Secret is to come to some truly correct and accurate conclusions about oneself, conclusions that can validly be checked by others and which receive their final confirmation by their impartial recognition on the part of other than oneself. As in scientific work guesses or assumptions will not do and self-deception, though undeliberate, must be guarded against continually. The facts discovered must be confirmed, sometimes by instrumentation (where this is possible), always in the end by competent outside judgment.

But plainly the results have the greater importance to the subject himself of the investigation and the discoveries, later to be externally confirmed, must be made in the first instance by the man on his own account. Indeed his own discovery and his own recognitions are the prime purpose and fruit of the work. In this endeavor he must learn to take an impartial, scientific attitude toward himself, without hopes or fears, just looking in order to see and to learn. And, after all, he is not responsible for what he may find. He is not responsible because he cannot be; as he begins this work, he is the inevitable product of an heredity and of an environment over which he has had no decisive control, in fact no real control at all. Why, then, should he clutch at a sense of sin and be afraid to see what is? Surely he shall be surprised; and surely he shall be far from pleased, as his phantastic, subjective image of himself begins to be replaced by the reality-picture of himself as he actually is and lives.

There is a danger here, especially for those who comprehend best what is said and possess a natural aptitude for understanding and realizing the attitude recommended. Such pupils naturally progress faster than others and they may commence to see certain aspects of themselves before they are ready, that is, before their impartiality is sufficiently established by accustomed effort. No one can see himself fully without being horrified by what he sees; horror can lead to terror and panic, and to serious emotional disturbance. It is here that a teacher's presence and ability are strictly required, to re-establish relative values, to remind the pupil thus disturbed of his real ultimate purposes and to render to him the external reassurance that, although what he sees is bad, indeed terrible, he is not alone and that others have passed through a worse case. He can never, he feels, forgive himself; how, then, shall others forgive him? Right here he must be *shown* that they do. For these feelings, no matter to what degree they may mount, are of no genuine importance aside from the unconscious effects which they produce within; what is of real importance, is that the man should commence to come out of his daydreams about himself and start to see at least this intimate aspect of reality with some relative clarity.

The greatest value, as well as the inescapable requirement, of this work of the Open Secret is the impartiality that must be manifested by the subject toward himself. He must learn here to look at himself without prejudice of any kind, either positive or negative, just as in fact he can look at a complete stranger. Otherwise all his attempts will automatically come to naught in any case. But if he learns the "feel" and the "taste" of this *experienced* attitude, he will have taken a primary step toward waking up and will also have acquired the beginning of an ability that must soon be developed further.

Impartiality towards oneself is the inner crux of the Open Secret activity. It is the indispensable demand of the work disclosed by the Hidden Secret, if calamity is to be avoided.

3.

We now approach the heart of this whole matter, which is subtle and not nearly as simple as it may first appear; and we shall need a careful introduction to it. Such an introduction may be furnished by a hidden item of A-type knowledge possessed by the Schools. This knowledge is not of a forbidden kind; it has simply been lost for so long that ordinary men no longer know anything about it and, when it is told to them, they either miss its significance altogether or else, partially comprehending it, manifest the Pauper's Fallacy and Phantasy that they indeed already possess what in fact they are so far from possessing as to miscomprehend.

Modern psychology, we have said, recognizes two chief states or levels of consciousness, the sleeping and the waking states. The experience of mankind recognizes another in addition, a state which in our usual vocabulary is often called cosmic consciousness. This may or may not be recognized by a given scientist (some of them do recognize it) as a genuine type or condition of consciousness but only incredulity can doubt that it occurs, and has occurred, to many thousands of men. The usual difficulty in respect of it is a double one; first, that the subject experiencing a shorter or longer period of cosmic consciousness cannot recall clearly, if at all, what he has understood while in that state after he has resumed his usual condition and secondly, that he is quite unable to communicate later whatever recollection he may have retained. Besides this, there is the fact that he has no control over either entering or leaving the state. Any one of these circumstances is enough to show that the experience is pathological in character and together they establish that conclusion. Naturally, this is not to say that the state itself is pathological but only that the experience of it by an ordinary man is pathological.

In any case these three states of consciousness—Sleep, Waking and Cosmic Consciousness—are the only fully differentiated levels known to ordinary men, even verbally. It has been entirely forgotten that there is another, equally differentiable state of consciousness natural and proper to human beings, the name for which in this Version is Self-Consciousness. That name is one of our technical terms and the first thing to do, is to define it.

Self-Consciousness is that state of consciousness in which the subject is currently and accurately aware of all the operations of his organic body.

The result of Self-Observation and Self-Consciousness; the latter is an impartial, non-identified awareness *of one's body* as distinguished also from the "I" which is making the observation.

The four different states or levels of consciousness form an experiential hierarchy, as follows:

#4. Cosmic Consciousness: characterized by an awareness of cosmological phenomena

#3. Self-Consciousness: characterized by a direct awareness of the subject's physiological organism

#2. Waking: a subjective state, hypnotic in kind, characterized objectively by daydream and delusion

#1. Sleep: normally characterized by unconsciousness, usually characterized by experience lacking in "logical" connection and consistency due to the general exclusion of sensory input to the head-brain

Of these states #1, #3 and #4 are normal, #2 is abnormal. One may pass from #1 to #2, from #2 to #3 and from #3 to #4 directly and normally; but it is impossible to pass directly from #2 to #4 normally and this can occur only in pathological cases. In other words, supposing the attainment of Cosmic Consciousness to be a man's goal, the ordinary man omits a required step when he assumes that it is possible to enter the condition of Cosmic

Consciousness directly from the Waking state, for this is possible only after the state of Self-Consciousness has been established.

As to the state called Self-Consciousness, reference to the above definition will show that it is clearly distinguished from what is usually termed "self-consciousness." The latter condition is one characterized mainly by illusions, in which one's hands appear amazingly awkward if not completely unmanageable; one is aware indeed, precisely *not* of one's actual body and its true proportions, but instead all one's attention is devoted to the assumed impression which is made upon someone else by that body. At the least, this obvious distinction must be understood right away and it will be well to commit to memory the technical definition of Self-Consciousness, which has been made as short and direct as possible for that purpose.

No doubt it will be objected that we have not done justice to the Waking state, in which "masterpieces of art" are written and painted, atom bombs are invented, civilizations are born, grow and die away and a great many other astonishing absurdities are committed. But all of that is quite literally dreamwork and we have already had occasion to remark that the alleged purposes for which all this activity takes place, are almost never accomplished. The last fact should suggest to us very clearly how dreamlike, unstable and really unconscious the Waking state is. Neither for ourselves personally nor in cooperation with others do we reach the hazy and wavering goals which we are accustomed to flatter ourselves that we so clearly entertain.

A person in the Waking state is thus not truly awake. For a normal person the Waking state is not a really proper level of consciousness at all; it is, instead, only a transitional state of normal infancy and childhood, between the relatively unconscious Sleep of the neonate and the Self-Consciousness that ought normally to be established fully at some point during the adolescent period. But this has not happened to us; we have been brought up and trained to the Waking state by those who themselves had never been taught how to pass through it to a more normal condition, and thus we also have remained in the transitional state between really sleeping and really being awake. To wake up in a genuine sense is to enter the state called Self-Consciousness but, though adults now to whom such a state is proper and natural, we ourselves have no experience of it.

Well, almost no experience of it. For brief flashes of Self-Consciousness do occur to many people very infrequently during their lives. Sometimes in a moment of great emergency, the sort of moment that calls out essential qualities, one becomes acutely aware of one's body in much detail, sometimes this happens pathologically at the point when fever breaks suddenly in the course of a severe illness; other occasions, too, such as very unusual or unexpected surroundings, may provide a brief flash of the experience. It is gone as quickly as it came; we have no control over it, we cannot reinstate it and it is of small use to us. The real state of Self-Consciousness, when genuinely established, is a stable and enduring state.

Now let us go a little fully into the different states of consciousness and their characteristics, from the viewpoint of the threefold nature of the human being. His positive factor, we recall, is experiential content, the negative factor is the end-products of neural functioning in his body, the neutralizing factor is consciousness itself, transforming the objectivity of neural functioning into the subjectivity of experience. These three factors constitute his being and behind them all stands "I," the fourth point of the triangle, its centre which, when projected, forms a pyramid. (In a sense, the Great Pyramid may be a tomb after all, although not exactly in the archeological sense.)

As regards Sleep, it is normally a deep and dreamless state; babies experience it but for us only an extreme threefold exhaustion can bring it on and it is necessary for us to speak of the kind of abnormal Sleep with which we are acquainted. The main feature of this sort of Sleep is the absence of the tremendous sensory input to the head-brain from the sense receptors, which is so prominent a feature of the Waking state. This is brought about reflexly by a certain degree of bodily relaxation and it leaves the end-products of neural function in the head-brain now represented chiefly by the activities of Centre #2 and of Centre #3. The instinctive subdivision of Centre #1 continues to operate as usual, taking care of metabolic phenomena and deep homeostasis, but these activities, except when something goes drastically wrong, are ordinarily connected with consciousness in our cases in any event; the moving subdivision of Centre #1 is mostly inhibited from intrusion into the head-brain in Sleep and thus that entire centre is excluded from the negative factor in the Sleep state.

Thus consciousness is related only to the neural end-products of Centres #2 and #3, transforming them into the subjective experience of dreams. The so-called illogicality of dreams is therefore explained, for of course the logic which is absent is not an intellectual logic at all but simply the usual cause-and-effect successions imposed by the sequences of the phenomena of the external world as reported in the Waking state by the sensory equipment of the organism. The logic which is absent in dreams is not mental logic but sensory logic, and both emotional and mental logic remain, to relate the items of Centre #2 and Centre #3 activity in unaccustomed but consistent ways. (It is by a tentative probing of these relations that psychoanalysis and other systems of dream interpretation construct their partially stable, though incorrect, edifices.) Thus in Sleep the presence of the three fundamental factors is accounted for as follows: negative factor, neural end-products of Centre #2 and #3; neutralizing factor, consciousness of Sleep level; positive factor, experiential dream content; subjective transformation of negative factor by neutralizing factor.

The reason that a normal man sleeps normally, i.e., dreamlessly, whereas we do not, is that, awake, he functions harmoniously in a threefold way, i.e., practically, emotionally and mentally, whereas we do not. As we have seen from the food scales, all three types of energies are produced in the body, but, if they are not used during the day, then they remain unexhausted and still functional throughout the night. In our ordinary Waking condition we are not functionally balanced, due to the absence in us of any controlling, really any properly neutralizing factor; we seldom manifest any real thought and our emotional experiences are haphazard and inharmonious with our other functions, since they are not deliberate upon our parts but instead are dictated automatically by external events. Thus, even if we happen to have had sufficient physical exercise during the day to obviate insomnia, we still go to bed with excesses of unused emotional and mental energies and those furnish the negative factor of neural end-product which, in relation to the neutralizing factor of consciousness, provides the experiential Sleep content of dream.

When a man enters the Waking state, the situation remains substantially the same as in Sleep. The chief difference is the entrance of Centre #1 into the picture as an active component of the negative factor of neural end-product. Sensory input, always present during Sleep in the peripheral regions of the organism (for otherwise the man would have died at once) now pours into the central head-brain region, overwhelming many emotional and purely mental elements; consciousness fulfills its role relating to the mental elements; consciousness fulfills its role relating to the now predominantly sensory neural phenomena and, transforming them into subjective experience, the usual sensory logic of cause-and-effect is reinstated experientially. Moreover, the moving subdivision of Centre#1 contains many motor constituents and the experience of their activity leads to an illusion of being awake, when one in fact is not fully awake at all. The whole thing is automatic and mechanical, including the resuming delusions that we are actively thinking when really we are only being hazily aware, not at all of the neural end-products of a mental kind which are present but merely of their indirect effects which we call thoughts. In the same way, when we passively experience emotions, the violence of some of them convinces us that we are being emotionally active; but the activity is not in us, it is in the neural end-products of emotional character of which we, indeed, are actually the passive victims. This passivity of consciousness in the Waking state is what mainly characterizes that level of consciousness and renders the state an abnormal one for an adult man. It must not be thought that consciousness is absent because it is passive; it is very much present but, instead of the normal activity which would, if functioning, instate the condition of Self-Consciousness, there is a lethargy which results in a merely registrative functioning of the

conscious factor and which further precludes anything like a complete reg-
istration of the full negative factor present. This extreme passivity is what
renders the condition hypnotic, also; the trance-state of hypnotism, which is
only a variation of the Waking state, is characterized by great subjective pas-
sivity and it is worth mention that the electroencephalic recordings from the
head-brain, the so-called brain waves, are indistinguishable in type in both
Waking and hypnosis but change their character drastically in Sleep, even of
our disturbed kind.

The state of Self-Consciousness is defined by a complete contrast in this
respect. The conscious factor then registers the neural end-products of the
body actively instead of passively and the positive factor of experience al-
ters to a clear awareness of the details of bodily operations and functions.
The relationship is then in accordance with the realities of the situation, for
we must remember that all the world external to the body is actually rep-
resented to the subject of experience exactly and only at the points where
the end-products of neural function occur. These phenomena of the outside
world are there represented, not as they actually are, but only through their
effects upon the mechanisms of the body which already have themselves
conditioned the final product through their own nature. The phenomena of
the body itself are likewise represented at the same locations and in this case
there is far less distortion (at the exact points there is none at all), for what is
here reported, is represented in its own terms. Thus a direct awareness of the
body is a direct awareness of reality and the comparable experience is a real
one in a sense beyond that which can be attributed to any indirect experi-
ences. Moreover, in the state of Self-Consciousness the external world must,
and does, assume a very different appearance than is present in the waking
state and the novelty of such a view, encountered unexpectedly, is sometimes
a serious shock to one unprepared for it. The keynote of Self-Consciousness
is the activity of the conscious or neutralizing factor; it is further character-
ized by the immediate objects to which consciousness is related, viz., the
phenomena of the man's own organism. Another distinguishing feature of
Self-Consciousness is that it is a state which, in general, can be entered only
deliberately and purposefully by the subject.

Cosmic Consciousness is a state in which the subject may be aware of
cosmic phenomena in the same manner in which he is aware of the local
phenomena outside his own body. The same three factors characterize his
being but now the end-products of neural function represent much more
than they did previously. For one thing, the functioning itself has been al-
tered by the condition of Self-Consciousness from which the state of Cosmic
Consciousness is entered and, for another, there are subject to the transform-
ing effect of the conscious factor in this state more subtle and delicate end-
products than are reachable at lower levels of consciousness. Sometimes it is
objected theoretically that the human body possesses no sensory organs of

a kind suitable to place it in contact with cosmological phenomena of large scale. But it does. Some of these mechanisms in our cases are undeveloped and immature, some are fully maturated but non-functional in any state lower than that of Cosmic Consciousness; and some are present and incorrectly functional even now, as in the pathological instances of clairvoyance, precognition and like, so-called parapsychological phenomena. But Cosmic Consciousness, being a state which at present is far beyond our abilities to experience normally, can now be described only in the general and inadequate terms employed above.

These states, from #1 to #4, are characterized successively by a respectively expanded consciousness or a respectively higher level of consciousness. In Sleep a man is not normally conscious of anything; in the Waking state he is distortedly conscious of external phenomena; in Self-Consciousness he is aware clearly and accurately of internal phenomena; and in Cosmic Consciousness he is aware accurately, though indirectly, of external phenomena and their reality-relations.

It is our nature that consciousness must be one of our basic and fundamental values; a subjective denial of this fact in no wise alters it. At bottom we all realize that it is better to be awake than asleep; and even our present abnormal Waking state permits a scope of behavior and experience much more desirable to us than even a normal Sleep. But between Waking and Self-Consciousness there is a greater difference and a greater increase in human value than between Sleep and Waking. And with Cosmic Consciousness these increases are still more greatly augmented. The highest value in this respect is the highest level of consciousness attainable by human beings.

Confronted with such possibilities, they sometimes occasion timidity and fright to the subject. He instinctively fears to undergo experiences so novel, so entirely unaccustomed to him. What will he see in such states? Of what perhaps dreadful objects and relations will he become aware? And above all, would not such experiences change him out of all recognition to himself, might he not be lost and vanish altogether in so strange an interior milieu?

To the one hand such fears are groundless and need not be entertained. One is the same individual or person when asleep and when awake; although the experience and cognition of reality greatly change as between the two states, the experience remains the same unique entity in one as in the other. The same is true as to Self-Consciousness and Cosmic Consciousness and it is always the very same subjectivity or "I" which experiences any or all of the possible states of consciousness open to a human being. One does not become lost because, when removed from Sleep, he then can attribute the warmth he feels to a steam radiator instead of to the subjective phantasies of dream; nor will he be lost when he is able to experience reality more clearly and accurately at the higher levels of consciousness.

To the other hand there is a kernel of truth in his first hesitancies, to which he will do well to accord his attention. To pass directly from his present state into a full degree of Self-Consciousness, not to mention Cosmic Consciousness, would certainly bring him face to face with a view of reality so strange and unexpected as to cause him very great shock and perhaps to injure him disastrously. He has no "atmosphere" as yet to buffer such shocks and their impact upon his raw being is assuredly to be avoided. He must thus be introduced to the next higher level of consciousness slowly and gradually, so that he may become accustomed to it little by a little, just as a man who has been blind for many years must treat his eyes with the greatest caution when his sight is in the process of being restored.

For this reason the Hidden Secret, which is the Method next to be formulated, is devised with foresight in strictly successive steps and with rigorously predetermined stages. Of course it must be fully understood also that work of the kind we are about to describe, cannot be done alone, and that a suitable group of people under the immediate instruction of a competent teacher is a *sine qua non* of any such attempted activity. If these requirements are not met, calamity and ruin are sure to result. Yet the very core of the Oragean Version cannot be omitted on that account. It is only necessary—but it is very necessary—to emphasize that what is formulated, is *not* recommended *to be done* except under the above conditions. And it must be remembered likewise that the steps of the Method are not haphazard steps, that their results have been foreseen and confirmed and that their sequence is as important as their successive activities themselves, which are designed for that gradual introduction of which we have spoken. So, we now proceed to the Method.

4.

The Method is the very heart of this whole matter. But the reader must be warned that it is far more difficult and subtle than it appears to be on the surface. To formulate it is hard enough but, even in the presence of a perfect formulation, to understand it in a correct sense is still more ticklish.

It is not unusual to hear those who have received this information and are supposedly familiar with it, discussing it in a quite incorrect way; the terms they use are the right ones, but there is a subtle misdirection in the way they are understood, and misunderstanding of this sort is very dangerous misunderstanding. Just as one who starts out due north in the midst of a wilderness but who has the misfortune to involve a tiny deflecting in his original direction, will return in a constant circle to his starting-point, just so do those who underestimate the subtlety of the present information circle the further from their goal the farther they proceed, and in such a case they merely dream delusions about their supposed progress. Let the reader, therefore, not assume that he has properly understood what is to be said until he has examined it carefully from all angles and seriously considered just what it is that is meant. And especially let him not import any meanings or expansions of his own into the formulation; what is said will be *literally* the case and, unless a qualification be presented directly, none is to be assumed.

To assist us in understanding the nature of the present Method it will be well to remember what it is not. In general there exist three Ways or Paths for the development and perfection of human beings, which correspond to their basic functional types. There is the Way of the Fakir, of Centre #1, of asceticism and mastery of the physical body, of generally ascetic religions; this develops the Will. There is the Way of the Saint, of emotional religions, of faith and feeling; here the Higher Emotions are the goal. And there is the Way of the Yogi, of the mind and understanding; it leads finally to a high degree of Reason. All of them, however, possess an objection in common, that one faculty or ability is developed at the expense of the others. Thus when Will is attained, the Emotions are weak and the intellect feeble; when the Emotions are great, the Will is undeveloped and the mind nil; and when Reason has been established, both Will and Emotion are lacking to the subject. Accordingly the attainment of the almost impossible primary goal in all these cases leaves the man with more work yet to accomplish than he has already mastered, in order to bring himself to the complete development which is the final goal.

But there is also the Fourth Way, which is the Way of the Gurdjieff formulations and of this Version. It is quicker than the others, and correspondingly harder. On this Way all the chief functions are developed simultaneously, not to any final degree at once, to be sure, but harmoniously and in balance with each other. Thus it constitutes a different Path, on which Will does not precede Reason nor Reason precede Emotion and the ultimate goal is the concomitant attainment of Individuality, Consciousness and Will. This Way is seldom taught or propagated among men; the reader must be prepared for a viewpoint unaccustomed among the usual developmental creeds. From the beginning he must not confuse it with the better known Paths.

The first step of the Method is the technique of Self-Observation. Its purpose is to establish the previously discussed state of Self-Consciousness in a gradual and normal manner; and its difficulty, if the technique be correctly understood, is so great that no sudden success, and resulting shock, need be apprehended.

Self-Observation is a psychological activity of a genuinely novel kind. Its distinction from any other sort of psychological reaction whatever can be seen when the following question is considered: what can a human being do which is neither thinking nor feeling (in the sense of emotional experience) or moving? These last three are his chief and typical functions and everything he has hitherto done is to be found among them, either as a main or as a part-function comprised within the totality of his activities. It is quite impossible to think or to feel or to sense any legitimate answer to the above question if its full meaning be properly accepted; and the answer has to come from outside, as a disclosure from someone else to whom it has already been disclosed from another external source. That is why the answer is here called the Hidden Secret.

For there is an answer. There is a fourth type of activity in which a human being can engage and which is not thinking or feeling or doing in the usual meaning of the terms. To realize this distinction clearly is the first necessity of the first step of the Method. For instance, it will at once be supposed that the activity of the work of the Open Secret has been Self-Observation, but that is not true at all. There has been a sort of observation involved, in that the personality and the behaviors of the subject have been viewed and examined by him as impartially as possible; but the means used in doing so have been thought-processes, introspection, memory-processes and the like, all of which without exception are included among the intellectual functions of man and, far from being distinct from them, are thus identical with them. These processes lead to judgments which may be more or less correct objectively but judgment, too, is a mental function and specifically it is not the fourth type of activity which is Self-Observation. Many persons find this very difficult to accept in the beginning—and many easily lose the once-understood distinction later—but it is absolutely essential that the reader comprehend for himself convincingly that the distinction is valid and final and that there is at least as great a difference between the self-observatory activity and the other three functions as there is between thinking and moving or between practical and emotional activity. When Self-Observation has been more fully described, it will be possible to come to this demanded realization.

Self-Consciousness is that state in which a man is fully and currently aware of the operations of his organic mechanism, i.e., of his body. Self-Observation is the means whereby the state of Self-Consciousness begins to be established and it is evident at once that the activity of Self-Observation implies and presumes a definite dichotomy within the man's general presence; that is, Self-Observation presumes a real and valid distinction between the observer and the observed, between the being himself and his observed organism. In the Oragean Version this distinction is formulated in the phrase, "I" and "It." "I" is a so far empty word, referring at present to the passive experiencer of whatever automatically proceeding content the organism furnishes, such as thought processes, emotional processes and sensori-motor processes; the consciousness of "I" manifests that abnormal and lethargic passivity in its registrative functions which has already been discussed. But "I" manifest conscious activity and the only way in which "I" now can do so, is by the active instead of the passive registration of those very processes which up to now have formed the background of a passive consciousness. When the formerly passive registration becomes active, it becomes awareness. As to "It," the matter is perfectly clear; it is the body, the organic mechanism to be observed, the automatically performing organism which basically furnishes the content of experience.

These two distinguishable elements, "I" and "It," must be clearly present in the pupil whenever he performs an act of Self-Observation. In order to accomplish this he must be clearly aware not only of what he observes but also that it is he, or "I," who is making the observation. Such a realization on the part of the observer is called Self-Awareness. Self-Awareness is not synonymous with Self-Observation; it is, instead, a fundamental requirement of Self-Observation.

To establish this particular constatation and to assist the man in realizing that the distinction between "I" and "It" is a valid one which must be present to him at the moment of the self-observatory process, there is a mantram that can be of use. A mantram is not a prayer, although in the original versions of all genuine religious prayers were mantra. A mantram is a series of words, pronounced slowly aloud or subvocally, to each of which a clear and specific meaning is attached in the consciousness of the subject as he pronounces them. In Orage's own expression: "A mantram is not a mere series of words; it is a series of experiencings so joined that their sum becomes a force." The mantram now mentioned goes as follows: "I"—have—a—body; have—a—body—"I"; a—body—"I"—have; body—"I"—have—a; "I"—have—a—body.

As each of these words is pronounced in their different transpositions, the man strives to have before him its specific and particular significance. Thus with "I": he strives to realize just what he means by this term, that it is an empty word to which much delusion has become attached and that its only genuine reality is now furnished by the self-observatory activity in which he proposes to engage. With 'have': he strives to realize the full meaning of 'possession,' to which this term refers. With 'a': he attempts to have clearly before him the ideas of specificity and uniqueness that are signified. And with 'body': he brings to mind all that he knows about bodies in general and this one in particular, their mechanisms, their automatisms, the functional relations between their main and subordinate subdivisions, and so on, and so on. This carefully instated relationship between the words and their meanings assists him to a more authentic realization that in fact he, or "I," has a body which may be the object of the self-observatory activity upon his part. This pronouncing of the mantram, of course, is preponderantly a mental process and is not itself at all the Self-Observation.

The psychological activity of Self-Observation is defined by seven limiting characteristics, of such a kind that, in the absence of any one of them, it cannot correctly be said that Self-Observation takes place. Here they are, exactly as stated by Orage:

1. Self-Observation includes no element of criticism. This means that the impartial attitude of the scientist must still be adopted. No genuine inquirer investigates anything with the notion that he is to be prepared either to condone or to approve; he looks to see and only to see. In the same way in this particular activity, when one is aware of some aspect of one's body, that of which one is aware can only in fact be so; it cannot be either good or bad. But in our cases, due to our abnormal condition, impulses will often arise to approve of what is seen or to criticize some functioning of which one becomes aware. These impulses can, and must, be excluded. The reason is not that they are bad, either; the reason is that, if they are present, the authentic activity of Self-Observation is not present.

2. Self-Observation includes no element of tutorialness. If criticism is out of place, a tutorial attempt to alter and to improve is more so. There must certainly be no attempt to change what one is observing in any way for, if it be changed, the opportunity to observe or to experience it, vanishes instantly. In scientific work great care is taken to obviate all effects upon the specimen under observation which might be due to the investigation itself, lest the findings be such as to refer not to the object of the inquiry but instead to back-effects of instrumentation or other techniques employed; in the latter case the work is of course fruitless. Similarly it must be plain immediately that, if one is self-observing some phenomenon of his organism's activity, he cannot continue to do so when, *for any reason* that activity alters.

3. Self-Observation includes no element of analysis. This analysis is a typical mental action and its prohibition includes that of other intellectual activities as well, such as comparisons or even descriptive formulations of the object or objects of awareness. Consciousness is not a thought-process and neither is awareness; but Self-Observation is a particular kind of awareness and therefore it is present only when thinking is excluded.

4. Self-Observation is possible only with non-identification. This is the essential and definitory crux of the entire activity. Only when one deliberately separates oneself from the organism under scrutiny, only when one establishes firmly the position that "I" have a body and that "I" am not It, can one self-observe. Without this realization there is no possibility of correct Self-Observation; and it is subtle, difficult and hard to maintain. Nevertheless, it is demanded without equivocation, for in its absence whatever occurs cannot be the self-observatory activity.

5. Self-Observation must take place within the prescribed area. That is to say that not anything or everything can be the object of Self-Observation. The objects of this activity are definite, not vague; they are the phenomena of the organic body which one has. These phenomena are many but they are not infinite in number and they can be classified into specific and numerable categories, The reason that the admonition, Know Thyself, has been familiar for so long and yet has produced no actual results even in the cases of those who are prepared to accept it seriously, is that that precept is almost always directed toward an incorrect object. For example, in the work of the Open Secret it is incorrectly directed; and consequently, although the results of that work can be valuable, especially in a practical sense, they cannot be of a final and objective value to the subject. Know Thyself = Know Thine Organism; that is its correct meaning and, moreover, in this sense it can be valid just because in this sense it outlaws introspections and guesses and judgments whose inevitable delusions prevent objective results.

Let us therefore begin defining the prescribed area of Self-Observation by a series of exclusions, by stating categorically what it is not. To begin with, it is of course not concerned with the observation of anything outside the subject's own body. No external phenomena whatever are the objects of this kind of observation.

But there are internal phenomena also which are not, for a long period, the proper objects of Self-Observation, either. Self-Observation is not observation in the usual sense or in the usual meaning of the term; it is a specific kind of awareness. By the same token, and as a rational corollary, unless it is a pure awareness without intermixture of thought-processes and/ or emotional processes, it is not Self-Observation. For this reason thoughts themselves are excluded as objects of Self-Observation. To be aware of one's thoughts impartially and objectively is a very difficult and advanced exercise; if one tries it, he finds as a matter of course that he is thinking about his thoughts. Thinking about thought or about thoughts is introspection, it is not Self-Observation. The same is equally true of emotions; and neither are these the proper objects of Self-Observation. To self-observe either thoughts or emotions objectively is to be accurately aware of the neurological phenomena which are their physical bases and which give rise to them; and to do this within one's own body is so obviously beyond the abilities of the pupil, on his introduction to the self-observatory technique, as to be worth no further discussion. There is, however, an indirect way in which a beginning can be made in the Self-Observation of thoughts and emotions and this will be indicated a little later.

We have therefore excluded all outside phenomena and all thought and all emotion from the self-observatory activity. What is left? There is a very great deal left that it is possible to self-observe, and the easier categories of this residue are precisely the gross behaviors of the bodily mechanism. They must not, however, be considered in a vague and general way; let us first of all categorize them:

a) Posture. There are many bodily postures typical of or habitual with a given person; there are also many postures dictated by passing external conditions which are not habitually repeated by the subject. All of these are to be observed, not in the sense of listing them but in the sense simply of *being aware* of them when and as they occur. They are not to be reasoned about nor analyzed, nor is there to be any effort to alter or to improve them; what is required, is simply to be aware of them as they take place. It is quite possible, for instance, to be aware that one of one's hands is warmer than the other (when this occurs) without in any way seeking to account for the fact or even thinking about it at all; in other words it is possible simply to be aware of it, period. In the same way, this is all that is required concerning the gross fact of bodily posture, solely that one should be aware of the current position of one's body when it occurs.

b) Gesture. In a like fashion one may observe the gestures that one's body makes from time to time. Like our postures, these are almost entirely unconsciously performed and what is meant here, is that one must be aware of them in detail and accurately as they occur. Do not consider whether this or that one is often repeated or whether or not it constitutes a habit. If the attention is put only upon an awareness of these gestures, all the other questions about them will answer themselves in due course without any artificial attempts on the part of the subject to solve the problems for himself. As one becomes increasingly conscious of the gestures that one's body makes, he will soon come to recognize which of them repeat again and again and thus are his gestural habits; this is the way to find out about them, not by any direct cogitation but indirectly and only by becoming more and more aware of them. Besides, the purpose of Self-Observation is not primarily information but instead it is an intimate alteration of conscious experience.

c) Movement. In addition to its postures and gestures the body manifests bulk or general movements, in walking down the street, in seating itself in a chair and thereafter in rising from it, and so on. Gestures, too, are movements but they are local movements of parts only of the body; and the present category comprises the movements of the body as a whole. These latter are to be observed in the same way as are the previous categories, that is, in the sole and vivid sense of being aware of them as they take place.

d) Facial Expression. Expressions are constantly flitting across our faces and usually we are totally unconscious of them. But our thoughts can be read more accurately by others from such expressions than from the words which we may be saying at the same moment. It is interesting to note how other people do this; they do not become acquainted with our real meanings by analyzing our expressions and theorizing about them, instead they recognize the expression and its meaning just by noticing it. The same can easily be a by-product of our own observation of our own facial expressions but the main thing, once more, is simply to be aware of when and how and in what detail they occur.

e) Tone of Voice. Here again we seldom realize in what manner we are speaking and are often surprised that our companions disregard the literal meaning of our words but take instead what our tones of voice contrarily indicate. Thus we often suppose that we are making an undeniable point in argument when in fact the point itself is denied by the very tone of voice in which we put it forward. More than our words, our tones of voice signify what we really mean and it will astonish the beginner to discover how much of this he always misses and how hard it is to be aware of these intonations as others hear them. A wire-recording of his own voice will quickly convince the subject that this is so. Of course he is not to try to change his tones in any way, for in that case he will lose what he wishes to observe. He is once again simply to be aware of them as they occur.

We now have the five categories of gross behavior which are to be the first objects of Self-Observation. They are:

> Posture
> Gesture
> Movement
> Facial Expression
> Tone of Voice

The way to accomplish this is not to attempt them all at once but to take them one at a time in succession. Take Posture first. It will be found to be very difficult merely to remember to be aware of postures when they occur; and of course to remember about them afterwards is not Self-Observation but instead is a thought-process called memory. Then, when one remembers about it currently, one must do it, for a cue is only a cue and Self-Observation is the activity itself. It is further necessary to stick with this one category of Posture until one has been able to make some progress with it, until one is assured for himself that he can really be aware of this aspect of his body at least reasonably often. It may take a week, two weeks, a month in any particular case. Only then should the subject drop this first category and go on to the next.

After they have all been gone through and some proficiency attained in each one, the next step will be to put them together, at first in pairs, and to be aware, for instance, of Facial Expression and Gesture at the same time. The final step is to put them all together and to have a simultaneous awareness of all five categories; but this is a long way off.

6. Self-Observation is to be conducted by means of all available percep-

tions. This means that one is not to use only one mode of sensory perception in the exercise of Self-Observation, but all available modes. For example, one can see the position of one's crossed legs well enough, if one looks at them, but this is not the only means available. The muscular tensions and the pressures arising from the position will inform one immediately of this part of the posture, as well as of other integral parts of it, and a Self-Observation of the posture consists in an accurate awareness of those sensory aspects which together create a picture of the posture in consciousness. Muscular tensions likewise chiefly inform us of our facial expressions, while our auditory sensation will tell us about our tones of voice. In the latter case it is necessary not only to hear them but to hear them as others hear them, i.e., impartially, i.e., with non-identification; and this same element must be present in all other observations, too. The point of the present feature of Self-Observation is that all appropriate senses are to be employed in the awareness directed toward any category and that as complete a picture as possible is to be constructed.

Furthermore, in respect of the sensations by means of which the Self-Observation of specific categories of bodily behavior is made, there arises another possibility of awareness. This is not the possibility of observing the sensation itself; to do that would imply the ability to observe directly the neurological phenomena which comprise the sensation. Nevertheless, it is possible to be far more aware of the sensation than we ever are and to bring it more vividly into the field of our consciousness. For instance, we are mostly unconscious of the many impulses affecting our eyes and making up our changing fields of vision; only the focus of sight is partially clear to us and we miss most of the periphery entirely. But it is possible, by an active effort of consciousness, to be aware of the whole field of vision, of the outer elements above and below and to right and left of the central portion. This is what is meant by the Self-Observation of sight or of any other sensation, and it is necessary to be unconfused about it; it does not mean an observation of the sensation itself but instead it means an increase in the vividness and completeness of the sensation, brought about by an active effort of consciousness in relation to it.

Here again the number of our sensations is not infinite and it is required to make a definite list of them in order to deal with them in order and professionally. Such a supplementary list for Self-Observation may be stated as follows:

Vision	Temperature: a) heat
Audition	b) cold
Olfaction	Pain
Pressure: a) deep	Equilibrium
b) light	Gustation
c) tickle	(Heart Beat)
	(Pulse Beat)

The last two, heart beat and pulse beat, are put in parentheses because they are not sensations but internal behaviors reported to us by sensations, chiefly of pressure; but they are also items of which it is possible occasionally to be aware.

The present list is supplementary to the main list of gross bodily behaviors given previously but awareness is also to be exercised in regard to this supplementary, sensory list. Its items are also to be taken first separately and then in combination; and efforts of this kind, correctly directed, will inevitably increase the Self-Consciousness of the subject.

7. Self-Observation is to be confined to no particular time or place. The activity is not to be exercised only for some given half-hour in the morning or only for ten minutes before retiring for the night or only in the privacy of one's study. To the contrary the purpose is to be aware of these specific bodily behaviors and of the above sensings every time it proves possible to do so and the final goal is to be able to do so all the time, straight through the day first and eventually even during the time the body becomes quiescent at night. Of course this is entirely out of the question immediately and the acquirement of such an ability is a long way off. Indeed, if it were possible to be currently aware of the items listed and in the sense described for only a very short time, one would have established the state of Self-Consciousness in a final way, repeatable at will. If this happened too quickly, it would, as has been said, produce a severe and undesirable shock but the effort involved in the present technique is far too difficult for that and it will be found that even a slight progress will be so slow as to dismiss any fear of premature success. The whole significance of this last feature of Self-Observation is that the effort is to be continuous, or at least as continuous as the subject can make it. Self-Observation is to be practiced under all the conditions of ordinary life, not just at special times or in particular places.

To sum it up, the present technique is defined by the specific features below and, if any of them be omitted, then it is not the technique described. Self-Observation is to be practiced:

1. Without criticism
2. Without tutorialness

3. Without analysis
4. With non-identification
5. Within the prescribed area
6. With all available sensory perceptions
7. With confinement to no time or place

Of these seven criteria the first four are all concerned with non-personal impartiality of the subject; but by far the most important of them is non-identification, indeed this is the very touchstone of the whole matter. It is this separation of the subject from what he observes which is the inner definition of the activity and which sets it off distinctly from any other activity superficially resembling it. Non-identification is even more than impartiality; it is the foundation beneath true impartiality and the only foundation upon which the latter can genuinely be built. Also it is the most difficult to fulfill of all the criteria concerned. We are in the habit of identifying ourselves with all sorts of things, external moral crusades and internal moral and emotional attitudes, business propositions and purposes, and even mentalistic philosophies and creeds; but of all of these the ultimate and basic identification with our own bodies is the strongest, and the core of all of it is our identification with our own Chief Features. Unconsciously one assumes that one *is* one's own Chief Feature. It is this false identification (for essentially Chief Feature is no different from any other automatically acquired feature) which must be broken, before so apparently an unconnected activity as Self-Observation can be carried out. It is not easy to do so but it must be done. One must repudiate his identification with *all* aspects of his body and make the real separation implicit in the assertion, "I" have a body; only so can "I" exist at all or be other than the empty word which hitherto is all that "I" has been. Only "I" can self-observe and to do so, "I" must first gain the actuality of non-identification.

There are a number of further remarks to be made about Self-Observation. Of course it must be done concurrently with the behaviors and sensations that are its first objects, that is, the Self-Observation must occur at the same time and *with* the occurrences of the behaviors and the sensations. We have already said that a later "awareness" of them is really a memory and not an awareness; the type of awareness or consciousness that is involved in Self-Observation must always be an awareness of what is happening just *when* that happening takes places. When it is understood that Self-Observation is not primarily concerned with the accumulation of any type of information but instead is basically related to an alteration in the very level of consciousness itself, it will be seen that its concurrence with the phenomena toward which it is directed, is an essential part of the process.

As a by-product, however, a great deal of information will be accumulated of necessity. Moreover, this information about one's body and one's behavior will be far more valuable and accurate than what can be gained through the work of the Open Secret, just because it consists of realizations rather than of deductions.

Deductions are fallible not only because of the possibilities of error in the process by which they are reached but, even if the deductive procedure be correct in every respect, they also suffer from the lack of assurance that the premises from which they derive, are actually correct premises. The case is very different with the personal realizations resulting from Self-Observation; what has been intimately experienced in clear consciousness has an indubitable validity far greater than anything affected by theorizing or mental manipulations. In this regard Self-Observation throws a forceful illumination upon the tasks of descriptive analysis previously undertaken.

It is also a source of information quite different from text book knowledge of one's organism to be gained from a course in physiology. One's own body never corresponds exactly to the sort of generalization diagrammed in a text and often the discrepancy is notable in more than one sense. If you really want to know about your body, you must learn how to be aware of it in detail. But it must always be remembered that all this is a by-product; it is never the chief goal or the purpose of Self-Observation itself.

The categories taken as the first objects of Self-Observation are selected in accordance with a certain principle, and the principle is that in their cases the observations are open to outside confirmation. They are checkable. This novel activity is so subtle and mistakes are so easy to make regarding it that the subject's own affirmations and impressions about what he has done and is doing, cannot safely be taken at face value; indeed more than anyone else the man himself stands in need of confirmations. As concerns gross bodily behavior, proofs of accurate Self-Observations can usually be obtained from other persons and, if necessary, instrumental checking is possible by means of motion pictures, sound-recordings and similar devices. This is necessary, for above all it is demanded that the subject must develop, and become accustomed to, the self-observatory technique in a real and proper sense; an assurance must be had that he is not phantasying or dreaming about it but has begun to experience what it genuinely is. Later he must enter fields of Self-Observation where confirmation is not so easily to be obtained and, unless both he and others can rely on previous accomplishments established beyond doubt, he may be lost indeed.

Haste here is inexcusable because its results are so serious. Many persons have been known who supposed themselves competent in this first step of Self-Observation long before they in fact were and who prematurely essayed the far more difficult tasks of observing Centre #2 and Centre #3 phenomena; they have emerged from this with almost unbelievable phantasies regarding their results and, if nothing more serious has happened to them, they have lost all possibility of continuing this kind of work on themselves. No small time is required to complete adequately this first step in which gross bodily behavior and its associated sensations are the sole objects of Self-Observation; the writer has never known anyone who has accomplished it adequately in less than a number of years.

But paradoxically, although it may take so long, it consumes no time. This must be plain from the fact that the observations are made concurrently with the happening of what is observed. That is, there is no special time for making them set apart from the times of all the other activities in which one's life consists and it is not necessary to allot some period, subtracted from other occupations, in which to prosecute Self-Observation. Just the contrary, these observations must be made exactly *when* other events are taking place and thus they cannot diminish the time available for such different activities.

It is also sometimes objected that to engage one's attention upon the self-observatory activity must distract one interminably from other matters in hand at the moment and that, if one becomes involved in this, he will never get anything else done the whole day long. But again the opposite is true. Far from rendering one inept or clumsy in the usual conduct of ordinary life this activity actually increases both the accuracy and the speed of one's reactions to the conditions one confronts and to the various stimuli that make up those conditions. This assertion does not stand in need of reinforcement by argument or theory; all one has to do is try it, to be convinced at once that the statement is a correct one. For, although Self-Observation can only be directed solely toward the phenomena of one's organism, the increased activity relating to internally originating stimuli will spread to and will affect externally originating stimuli also, rendering them clearer and more vivid; and thus, as a by-product, one becomes more accurately aware of his external surroundings. But it must be emphasized that this is a by-product only; if one permits his attention to wander incorrectly and directly to outside events, then the genuine process ceases and even the by-product will be lost.

There are certain pseudo-methods somewhat resembling the Method, and there are other traps and ambushes into which one may fall, that merit some mention here. Especially in certain Eastern so-called schools there exist numerous exercises, often supposed to be of an esoteric nature, whose fallacy consists generally in this: that having received some traditional information regarding higher levels of consciousness and even regarding some of the objective physical symptoms accompanying such normally established states, such exercises are designed artificially to instate the corresponding physical symptoms in the hope thereby of establishing the conscious state by indirection. It is as if a sufferer from smallpox should entertain the hope that by painting the exterior of his body in hues of normal health he might thereby have recovered from the disease of which his skin eruptions are only a symptom. It is true that, by an artificial reinstatement of sensory images, an emotional experience can be re-established (cf. the exercise directed toward emotional relaxation); but it is not true that by an artificial reinstatement of physical symptoms a higher level of consciousness can be established. The difference between such a technique and Self-Observation ought to be perfectly clear: the activity of Self-Observation, as defined, is a directly self-conscious activity and, instead of seeking to produce some or other symptom of the state of Self-Consciousness, it is a direct attempt to establish partially that higher level of consciousness itself. From its very first step Self-Observation is directly concerned with that type of active awareness which defines and *is* the state of Self-Consciousness.

Among the exercises of the mentioned Eastern schools there is a series which holds a prominent place and which is concerned with various deliberately controlled modes of breathing, such as alternating breaths through one nostril at a time, and the like. Now it is true that the reflex modes of breathing are different in the states of Self-Consciousness and of Cosmic-Consciousness, just as they are mutually different in the sleep and waking states. But by setting up artificially that mode of breathing which may be natural to the state of Self-Consciousness, for instance, what is obtained is not that level of consciousness itself but instead it is a counterfeit and abnormal state resembling the genuine condition only in respect to the breathing symptom.

Such exercises are here definitely stated to be harmful. And indeed even the Self-Observation of those modes of breathing natural to the Waking state are prohibited by our technique at the present stage of the work. No doubt it will have been noticed that breathing, although it is as easily observable as posture and more easily observable than heartbeat, has been omitted from the categories of behavior toward which the first steps of Self-Observation are to be directed. That omission is by no means an oversight. The fact is that breathing is a very delicate and a very complicated reflex action and that the pupil's meddling in it at his present stage of incompetence may upset its intricate balances injuriously, even to the extent of so disarranging it that it might conceivably fail during the Sleep state and by such failure cause his death. For such reasons it is too dangerous a category to be admitted during the early work of this kind and its omission is obligatory.

But more likely to be embraced at the beginning of any of the above, are the fallacies concerning the observation of thoughts and emotions by the subject. Logically it would be seen that, if the technique be directed toward Centre #1, it might also be directed toward Centres #2 and #3. But actually it is not directed toward the histology of Centre #1 but only toward the gross behavior of the body as a whole; and the Centre #2 and Centre #3 phenomena are not gross but minute phenomena.

If one seeks, at the present stage, to observe a thought, he cannot do so because there is nothing there to observe; his consciousness will not at all reach to the objective neurological phenomena that in fact constitutes a thought. At the same time, to formulate that a thought is clear or confused, complex or simple, is not Self-Observation but instead it is introspection; just as to notice one's walking is slow or fast or that a muscular tension is strong or weak, is formulation or description but it is never the primary awareness that is Self-Observation. The delusion that one is self-observing when in fact one is either introspecting or just formulating, is very easy to entertain and the difference between the latter and genuine observation constitutes one of the real subtleties that must be distinguished clearly by the subject at this first stage.

The case is the same with emotions, only more so, due to the fact that they are more rapid and unstable than thoughts. To observe an emotion directly now is quite impossible; and, just as with thoughts, merely to describe them currently in general terms or to categorize them as being positive, negative, strong, weak, and so on, all this is introspection and it is not Self-Observation.

The case with the observation of gross bodily behavior is authentically different. In the observation of the category of movement, one does not think that he is walking; he thinks of something else altogether and is just simply aware that the walking activity is taking place. When from this there is excluded all emotional reference and when to it there is added a detailed awareness of all the various physical aspects of the walking, that is Self-Observation. When in actual practice this kind of pure and unmixed awareness is experienced personally, it is then possible to come to that realization of the difference of awareness from thought and from emotion and from sensing which was spoken of on page 112, above.

But as to both thoughts and emotions there is a preliminary and indirect way in which they may become the objects of Self-Observation even at the present period of the work. Since the various subdivisions of the body are closely connected intra-organically, i.e., since close interconnections exist between Centres #1, #2 and #3, various thought-processes are accompanied by symptomatic muscular tensions in one or another part of the body and different kinds of thought-processes are also associated with typical bodily postures, even sometimes with an habitual series of gestures or local movements of hands and feet. The same is true of emotions; indeed the latter are so closely conjoined with corresponding postures and facial expressions, for example, that they may be artificially instated by a deliberate assumption of these bodily phenomena. Thus the Self-Observation of different categories of physical behavior is already a kind of indirect observation both of mental and of emotional states and provided, as always, that analysis, formulatory processes and judgments be resolutely excluded from the technique, just as a by-product of such observations the true nature of his thoughts and emotions will gradually become clearer in the subject's consciousness without his own specific efforts to that end. For the present that is enough. No direct approach to thoughts and emotions as such is yet feasible and Self-Observation is to be confined strictly to the definite categories previously listed.

There is another way, too, in which mental and emotional attributes must be excluded from the work of Self-Observation in accordance with its own limiting definition. The exclusion of criticism and analysis refers directly to the absence of thought-processes in the technique and the exclusion of criticism and tutorialness refers to the comparable absence of emotional interference. But since the work of the Open Secret proceeds hand in hand with the work of the Hidden Secret, and in fact the former is much strengthened and illuminated by the latter, it is necessary continually to keep the pupil reminded of the real distinction between the two and to be on guard against the temptation to confuse them.

Often as a result of discussions among the pupils themselves at this stage and sometimes as a consequence of information they may have gathered correctly or incorrectly concerning another Version of the Gurdjieffian ideas, there may arise a desire to mitigate, so far as possible, the more arduous tasks of Self-Observation itself and to expend the greater efforts upon the more interesting and introspective investigation of their personalities. There will therefore be those who would have the rest of us believe that these introspective judgments, provided only that they be made regarding legitimate matters, constitute legitimate work. But this is the case only in respect of the Open Secret and the latter work is itself only preliminary to the genuine work of establishing the state of Self-Consciousness through the technique of Self-Observation; it continues during the self-observatory activity, not because it is a more advanced type of work but because it is a so-far-unfinished kind of work. To imagine that one can lightly and hastily skim over the work of Self-Observation and then return to introspective judgments relating to personal habits and behaviors, Chief Feature, Types, and so on, is to indulge in a fallacy destructive to the entire project. Furthermore, this latter wishful aspect evidences a certain mechanical emotional fanaticism and serves to estrange newer, but serious inquirers who, themselves being rationally level-headed, will not accept such an attitude as corresponding with their own gravity of inquiry, and in this fashion many men of genuinely objective purpose may be lost. The truth is that the proponents of faith and introspection, of struggling and striving, are out of place in the Fourth Way; their place is the second Way, the Path of religion, and when they present themselves as proponents of the Fourth Way, they present counterfeits. It has been the experience of the writer, in the conduct of his own groups, that when people of this type are discovered to be members of the group, they should be dismissed from the group work upon one pretext or another as soon as possible, for the objective benefit of the remainder of the group. This is not because such people are of the emotional functional type, for persons of that type can adopt the Fourth Way and become valuable group members in association with other types; it is because in these cases emotionality has become so indulged and so exaggerated at the expense of the other prime functions that the possibility of developing the necessary balance has been lost for good. For such persons there is now open only the Way of Religion and that is the Way they should seek.

Up to this point we have been discussing only the first step of the first stage of the Method. This first step consists of the Self-Observation of the defined categories of physical behavior. To prosecute this particular work there is demanded the expenditure of a special kind of energy which specifically is not mental, emotional or muscular energy. What, then, is this special energy, whence does it come and how may its supply be increased? In the first place, it is Centre #4 energy. But Centre #4 is at present nonfunctional and so cannot furnish a supply of its own proper energy. In some cases, however—and these are the cases of the only persons who can inaugurate this work, for not everyone can do so—there is a tiny, chance-accumulated supply of the requisite energy at hand. It derives from those few genuine self-observations or close near-misses which they have already happened to make once or twice during their lives up to the moment when they encountered this work; and this very small supply of so-far-unused energy of a comparable kind suffices for the first beginning of the self-observatory activity. Thereafter every genuine self-observation which is made produces an excess of the same Centre #4 energy which in turn may be utilized for further self-observatory work. Thus the very beginning is the most precarious stage of all from the view point of the energy required, which thereafter will increase as the work progresses.

But the apparent corollary to the above situation is not true. As anyone can testify who has taken part in the work, a very active effort is necessary in order to make the observations required by the technique. This active effort is necessary upon *each* occasion when a single observation is made. But, although the energy available for the purpose does in fact increase as further observations are made, the active effort demanded upon every manifestation of the activity does not decrease. In other words, Self-Observation can never become a habit, as can any activity of the body, including not only muscular reactions but also certain ways of thinking as well as particular emotional attitudes. That is because all those latter functions really are organic functions, no matter how much we may falsely identify ourselves with them, whereas Self-Observation is not an organic function but instead is a genuine function (and the *only* currently possible function) of "I." Any bodily activity whatever can be, and often is, habitized; but no activity of the ultimately subjective, the "I," can become a habit, and there is a real distinction between the two. In the experienced fact that Self-Observation does not become easier, i.e. does not become habitized but continues to require a similarly active effort no matter how often the activity has been manifested, lies a further confirmation of the reality of the distinction between "I" and It and a further evidence that the mantram, "I" have a body, is not either an analogy or an as-if proposition. Instead it is a statement referring to genuine Reality.

It is often asked how long it will take the subject to master the self-observatory technique, to be able, that is, voluntarily and whenever he wishes, to be aware of the indicated categories of his bodily behavior in the defined sense. On the face of it this question is impossible to answer. How long will it take one to master the subject of mathematics or become acquainted with that body of knowledge which comprises modern chemistry? The time required is a function of the energy expended and also of the degree of correctness with which it is expended. The conditions surrounding the pupil have a bearing here—the kind of group in which he is making his effort and of course the relative competence and degree of sympathetic mutuality between himself and the leader or teacher of the group. But the main factor will be how much energy he himself is able to expend. For this reason no two members of any group progress exactly equally. Theoretically the self-observatory ability can be mastered in a day or less; actually it cannot and, as we have seen, this is really a beneficent circumstance. Months will certainly be required, more likely years, and for some a million Recurrences may be demanded before the ability has fully been obtained—the term, Recurrence, may be considered here as referring simply to a single life-period; it will be more fully discussed in the subsequent chapter.

But fortunately the first step of the first stage of the Method does not have to be fully mastered before one may proceed further. The Method consists of two stages as will shortly be explained, and the first stage comprises three successive steps. The first step is Self-Observation directed toward the categories of behavior previously defined and this has now been discussed at some length. In the second step exactly the same categories of behavior are dealt with but the activity employed is greater than just observation. This new activity is called in this Version, Participation.

There is a subtle psychological difference between impersonally and impartially watching or observing the movements, say, of one's legs in walking and actively participating in those movements. Here again it is very easy to deceive oneself and to confuse real Participation with mere deliberation; and only after one has acquired the authentic experimental "taste" of non-identification by long and successfully confirmed Self-Observation, should this next step be attempted.

For there are two kinds of deliberation, one mechanical and the other conscious. To the outside observer it is next to impossible to distinguish this difference and there should have been established within the subject himself a criterion by which he is able to guarantee which kind is operating. When one walks deliberately, perhaps when one is trying to imitate the gait of another, his natural movements are both altered and slowed; and even if he is trying to imitate past supposed movements of his own, both of these effects will be present. That is mechanical deliberation. In conscious deliberation the movements are also slowed but otherwise they remain unaltered. This is why only a person who has achieved the ability to self-observe his movements without altering them, can now participate in them without likewise altering them; and this fact, although difficult of external confirmation, holds out the possibility of confirmation by opposite instructional techniques of a precision kind. That may be necessary, but by this time there should also have been developed and be present in the subject himself at least the beginning of trustworthy, objective criterion by which he may have some interior assurance of a genuine kind in such matters.

The basic problem in Participation derives from the ease with which one can identify himself with the object of Participation, for instance with the walking activity which his body is manifesting, and this difficulty only becomes greater when it is attempted to participate in activities other than moving ones. To participate in the olfactory sense or in any sensory activity of the organism is a very subtle business and the separation of "I" from It while at the same time "I" is participating in Its activities, is a matter with which the novice will experience considerable trouble. The solution of this problem depends upon a firmly established non-identification, so well grounded by the correct practice of Self-Observation that the more subtle and difficult participation will not unseat it.

The situation has been likened to learning to drive an automobile. First you simply sit in the front seat and observe how the car is driven; this is comparable to Self-Observation and teaches you how the car is run. Then, but without taking the driver's position, you place your hand upon the wheel and upon the gearshift lever and your feet next to the pedals and participate in the driving of the car. You are not yet controlling it yourself, you are simply participating in its operation by someone else. This for the moment is enough.

Participation is more active than Self-Observation and will give the subject a new and different "feel" of his organism. But it cannot be too greatly emphasized that the chief effort must be placed upon making the Participation of a genuine kind and avoiding a dreamlike, delusional pseudo-participation, in the practice of which the pupil may conclude by deceiving himself grossly. A genuine Participation is characterized by the same general features that serve to define a correct Self-Observation.

  1. Participation excludes criticism. To participate in a series of bodily movements will bring them into consciousness even more vividly than in the case of the self-observatory activity and thus any automatic criticism which may be suggested to the subject, will occur to him more clearly than previously. The reason for the exclusion of such a critical faculty from the process ought by now to be evident: it is that, just so soon as the attention becomes involved in the process of criticism and to the exact degree that it does so, it is progressively withdrawn from the Participation itself, which thereupon fades and soon vanishes.

  2. Participation excludes all tutorialness. Tutorialness is the impulse to alter and to improve. Let us suppose that one inevitably notices some real or fancied awkwardness in his habitual gait or some incompetence, e.g., lack of smoothness, in a gestural habit. The immediate impulse will be to improve upon these physical activities by the substitution of more appropriate movements. Similarly with facial expressions and with the speaking activity which produces the tones of the voice. But how can one participate in the activities of the machine as it runs itself, if for any reason those activities suddenly be changed? Actually the machine knows how to run itself much better than you do; and, as always, an alteration, phantasied to be for the better, can be guaranteed to instate some harmful substitute activity entirely unsuspected by the subject. The mechanical organism must always, and will always, be in some kind of integrated balance or imbalance and there can be no change in its habitual activities without at the same time the inauguration of a corresponding, but unnoticed, alteration somewhere else in it. And in any case the purpose is not improvement, it is Participation; and Participation, moreover, in the activities of that particular machine just as it does in fact habitually operate.

  3. Participation excludes analysis. Analysis, as the chief sort of mental activity likely to occur, is meant here again to include judgment and all other kinds of intellectual interference. The reason for the exclusion in this instance is primarily the same as that for the debarment of criticism from the process, namely that to the degree that such an interference is present, the Participation itself is absent.

  4. Participation involves non-identification. As just remarked, this is more difficult in Participation than in Self-Observation. The former is the more active process of the two and in it one does purposely become involved in the given bodily activity. To do this and simultaneously to maintain one's separateness from that in which one voluntarily and deliberately involves oneself, demands a very subtle combination of restrained activity and voluntary passivity which can only be learned and understood through intense concentration and considerable practice. It demands a degree of interior, psychological discrimination that is not soon to be attained but which must be attained. Despite the difficulty each pupil in turn must achieve this for; once again, non-identification is the inner core and final criterion of correct Participation.

5. Participation is to be conducted within the prescribed area. Not anything-one-wishes can be the field of Participation at this point and throughout the entire first stage of the Method the same categories of physical or bodily phenomena remain the targets of the activity of "I," whatever form the latter activity may take. One may, and should now, participate in the same activities of his body which have already comprised the objects of Self-Observation and he must also refrain from the activity of Participation in anything else.

The categories of such activities are specifically:

> *Posture*
> *Gesture*
> *Movement*
> *Facial Expression*
> *Tone of Voice*

6. Participation is to include all the phenomena of the body's sensations. This is more difficult than in the cases of the above listed gross behaviors. How is one to participate in Audition or in Gustation, for example? The answer is that one can learn how to do so through Participation in the categories of gross physical behavior that constitute the fifth defining feature of the technique and which are listed in the paragraph above. These latter participations can be confirmed by outside sources, as has already been remarked and, if the technique be properly and professionally pursued, provision must be made for such external confirmation of the pupil's abilities. No means at present exist, however, for that kind of confirmation in respect of the subject's Participation in his bodily sensations and here it is necessary that an interior criterion has been firmly established by which the subject may have a correctly confident judgment regarding his own objective success or failure. It is therefore required that a high degree of real impartiality and of genuine psychological discrimination, confirmed externally in previous work of this sort, be possessed by the pupil before he can be allowed to undertake the sensory participations included within this sixth defining feature of Participation.

*The fields within which Participation of this kind is to be exercised are the
same as those previously considered under Self-Observation, to wit:*

Vision		*Temperature:*	*a) heat*
Audition			*b) cold*
Olfaction		*Pain*	
Pressure:	*a) deep*	*Equilibrium*	
	b) light	*Gustation*	
	c) tickle	*(Heart Beat)*	
		(Pulse Beat)	

*The last two are again put in parenthesis for the same reason as before.
As to how one participates in these sensory categories of behavior, only a
short verbal description can be given; in the case of a pupil who has correctly reached this part of the technique an understanding has already been
obtained concerning the implications and character of this kind of activity,
which no longer stands in need of long verbal formulations. If the Self-
Observation of sensations has been properly understood and achieved (and
this should previously have been confirmed), then the difference between
that activity and Participation is that the latter is still more active. To notice
and self-observe the gross sensation (not the underlying neurological phenomena) of Audition is different from participating in it, in the sense that the
former procedure, although certainly active, is more passive than the latter;
in the latter one projects oneself, as it were, into the hearing process and
becomes more intimately associated with it while at the same time always
maintaining the inner distinction between the "I" which participates and
that in which it participates. One is farther away from the object of Self-
Observation than from the field of Participation but in both instances one
must keep oneself equally distinct. That is why Participation is a more difficult procedure and constitutes a later step in this first stage of the Method.*

*7. Participation is to be conducted at no particular time or place. That
is, it is to be conducted at all possible times and in all possible places. As
with Self-Observation, Participation is not something specially distinguished
from the ordinary course of life but is to be made a part of the entire life-
process. There is no item of the defined categories either of gross behavior
or of the listed sensations which does not offer itself as a field of Participation whenever and wherever it occurs. And the purpose, here too, is to make
Participation as continuous and complete as possible.*

*It is perhaps worth adding that the same supplementary remarks apply
to Participation as to Self-Observation. By the very meaning of the term it
must be an activity concurrent or simultaneous with the behaviors toward
which it is directed. For the same reason it cannot take away any of the time*

which would otherwise be used in the manifestation of those behaviors, for they themselves consume an equal amount of time whether or not one is participating in them. Nor, if properly exercised, can Participation prove a distraction from the day's ordinary pursuits. Breathing, of course, is strictly to be excluded as a field of the participatory activity, on the ground above discussed. Any attempted direct Participation in either thoughts or emotions is likewise excluded as before; at the same time the experience of these cannot avoid becoming more vivid as and when Participation takes place in their bodily symptoms. (It is to be noted that, as a by-product of the Self-Observation of the bodily symptoms of negative emotions, those emotions themselves tend rapidly to disappear. And they vanish even more quickly when there is Participation in their physical symptoms.) We may, then, sum up the technique of Participation as comprising the following defining characteristics, in the absence of any one of which it is no more the correct activity than is Self-Observation in the same case. Participation is to be practiced:

1. *Without criticism*
2. *Without tutorialness*
3. *Without analysis*
4. *With non-identification*
5. *Within the prescribed area*
6. *With regard to all available sensations*
7. *With confinement to no time or place*

At about the time when the pupil or student has reached and undertaken the exercises just described as Participation—but sometimes earlier and sometimes a little later—there will arise in him an experience temporarily, but nonetheless painfully, distressing. The occurrence of this experience is in fact objective evidence that real progress is being made but that will at first prove of small mitigation to the subject. The phenomenon has been aptly described as an experience of the draining of all color out of night. It is as if the hues of his interests were rapidly fading; and suddenly those things and activities that formerly concerned him and formed real attractions in his life-experience, seem of little or no importance to him. Actually the process has been proceeding gradually in him from the moment he took his first serious step in this work; but now it has crossed a threshold (the threshold of the 'fa' of this particular process) and the man is both astonished and dismayed to discover that he has lost a number of his relations to life which he quite properly suspects it is now too late to ever regain. When, as may easily happen, this loss of interest may refer directly to his main practical occupation, a feeling of real emptiness invades his whole being and he may begin to look about desperately in the hope of finding out how fully lost he is. This can be another point of crisis at which the counsel and assistance of a fully competent teacher is of great necessity.

For the kind of interests which are dying in the pupil and cannot now be reinstated, are precisely those subhuman interests which have formerly attracted him in the most literal and mechanical sense. Nevertheless, such attractive-interests with which he has in greater or lesser degree been accustomed to identify himself up to now, may well have formed the energizing basis of his life. Such may be the practice of some contemporary pseudo-art in which he has aspired to gain an outstanding reputation and perhaps has already done so to some extent, as in painting, writing, music, and the like; or it may be the performance of practical work in engineering or farming or more probably a commercial business, to which he has been seriously devoting his time and in which he has been striving for an ultimate success; or it may be a professional interest in philosophy or theoretical science, in which the man already holds a position providing his livelihood. Whatever his occupation, he has long since taken it up, usually just because it did attract him, i.e., because it interested him naturally on account of his own type and his own mechanical abilities. What is he to do now? How can he continue when all the warmth and fire and interest which he formerly felt in this task of his, have either vanished or are on the verge of doing so?

Sometimes it is practicable to abandon the previous occupation; those of the emotional functional type are always anxious to do so on the spot—but this is seldom, if ever, advisable. It is a man's duty to earn his own and his family's livelihood and, even if the pupil be a woman whose career happens not to be necessary for her own particular support, this experienced happening of increasing disinterest furnishes an opportunity for further self-development which should not be lost. Here, above all, it is necessary to employ Common Sense.

In the Oragean Version Common Sense is not assumed to be a minor or unimportant attribute of human beings. Just as there is always, even in an undeveloped Essence, a small point of imperturbable calm where, if one can find it, one can take one's stand under the most panicky and terror-stricken conditions, similarly there is an attribute, even if a weak one, of unshakeable Common Sense. It is a more important attribute than is often credited. If the organism, including all its behaviors, thought-processes and emotional processes, be likened to a ship, Common Sense is the captain. On a real ship, when danger is present, the captain is on the bridge and he is there, moreover, with full and final authority. In the analogical case, when a real crisis arises, appeal must be made to the captain-of-the-ship and his decision must be accepted as final in the emergency. At such a time Common Sense must be put in command. You are lucky that there is such an often-disregarded assistant in your employ; you are a fool if, in these conditions, you do not avail yourself of his services.

The pupil has now come to be confronted by an inevitable revaluation of values. In other words, what was formerly of automatic value to him has lost its value; and for the time being there is nothing of equal substance to take its place. This is not only a new but a disconcerting dislocation. It can occasion no surprise that he feels lost; the pupil asks urgently: how can a man live without any interests at all? The answer is that he cannot; and here we find evidence of the serious importance of the much earlier inquiry into what interests the candidate may have had in work of this kind and in the whole topic of the Hidden Learning. It is only values connected with these ideas and with this work which may now remain to him. And of course at first he overestimated their intensity; but if they were at least genuine in their real degree, they will now stand him in good stead, for they alone can now provide him with something to live for and fill, at least partly, the horrible void he correctly perceives to be developing within himself.

However, these remaining values have not as yet been transubstantiated within him to any tangible or embodied result and the reduction of his living to this meagre pitch must not be allowed to endure. There is no easier way to inculcate a growing fanaticism then to confine everything to a premature immersion in his work without any external counterbalance at all. It is necessary in these cases, therefore, that the pupil be encouraged and very definitely instructed to continue at least his primary practical occupation *as if* he were still drawn to it by the former attraction of his interest. This will be much harder for him than was his previous automatic and mechanical involvement in whatever his main life-work may have been, but it will also provide him with a valuable opportunity for his own self-development. For the automatic goal of success for which he was before striving, he must now substitute the goal of carrying out an exercise both exceedingly difficult in itself and almost certainly beyond the present development of his abilities. In attempting in all his behavior in respect to his occupation to present those appearances and to accomplish those actual results which would correspond to his former interest in it, he will learn some very valuable lessons and will likewise obtain more for himself then he can realize at the time. He will, in fact, be playing a conscious role in life for the first time and, although he will not fully succeed—for the playing of roles is a more advanced exercise than we have yet reached—he will prepare himself for this later work and, above all, he will begin to discover how he can utilize the very emptiness which poses the problem, in order to fill it with something new and valid.

Such opportunities are not, of course, open to those who prosecute work of this kind in special surroundings, such as schools established for the purpose of excluding the distractions of ordinary life, where the pupils may live and work together only with each other and their instructors. On that account even at the Institute at Fontainebleau, when it was in operational existence, it was not permitted that any student remain indefinitely and, when Gurdjieff had decided that such a one had been there long enough, he was sent away, although naturally this provision could seldom apply to the instructional staff itself. The fallacy of such "retreats" or "monasteries" is called in this Version the fallacy of Going-to-Tibet. Orage did indeed send some of the students under him to Fontainebleau for periods of from a few weeks to several months, he might have done more of this if the Institute had been in full operation while he was conducting his groups in New York City; but he very definitely discouraged the attitude that this was necessary and in some cases declared it to be inadvisable. No Institute lasts forever, nor does the man who conducts it, and if the candidate has not been accustomed to prosecute this work in life, without the artificial help of a specially prepared environment, he will be at a complete loss when at length he must sink or swim by himself. Sooner or later, and whether or not the Institute had continued, he must do that and be thrown entirely upon his own resources if he is to fulfill the self-development he has begun; and the periodic meeting of groups, while their members remain for the rest of the time in the usual conditions of their ordinary lives, is the better preparation. It is also much less calculated to induce in them an always lurking fanaticism. This requirement that the pupils continue to be surrounded by the customary circumstances of their lives while they prosecute the work of the Method, is an outstanding feature of the Oragean Version.

The third and final step in the first stage of the Method is an activity here called Experiment. It can correctly be practiced only after the discipline of Self-Observation and Participation have been undergone and mastered to a considerable degree of competence. One of the most important aims of the Method's first stage, including all of its successive and increasingly difficult divisions, is to show the pupil how to work with the concrete and physically tangible aspects of his organism, to deal only with phenomena whose characteristics are open to the observing and consequently to the confirmations of others besides the subject himself, and thus to bring the whole matter down to earth from the fancy realms of reforming self-improvement and daydreaming mysticism. Above all, this Method purposes to be matter-of-fact, practical, common sense and down-to-earth. Just because in the Oragean Version we wish to, and we must, deal with items of information and of A-type knowledge which has long been lost by ordinary men and are now preserved only by genuine schools, there will always exist the temptation to lose oneself in the fascinating vistas opened up by information of this (to us) remarkable and interesting kind. There is certainly no reason to apologize for our profound interest in questions of universal scope and in the ultimate problems of man's real relation to the Universe and to God and of the correspondingly proper aim of his existence; all these are matters natural to the concern of serious men who aspire to become normal, to fulfill their proper obligations and to reach a true understanding of Reality. Nevertheless, because of our deep ignorance of Reality and of the unacquaintance with its details which has always surrounded us, it is very easy for us ourselves to become more unreal just in the contemplation of genuinely illuminating but to us most remarkable truths. Thus it is more than ever necessary that the work itself should be undeniably real and practical, that it should be such as to exclude by its own nature our abnormal propensity for Phantastic Imagination, that it should relate us more, not less, closely to hard, objective fact. Accordingly, the experimental work, now to be proposed, will not be of any extraordinary, esoteric kind and it may well seem to the reader to be too simple and elementary. That, of course, is because he has never tried it from the serious and impartial viewpoint of the Method.

Here it must be carefully explained once again that the idea is neither reform nor self-improvement; nor is this the same as the work of the Open Secret, although here there will be gained a good deal more directly personal information than with the preceding Self-Observation and Participation. The practice at this stage will deal chiefly, although not altogether, with habits but it will not begin, nor will it ever be primarily concerned, with so-called "bad" habits. In a proper sense all habits, in no matter what particular manifestations they consist, are bad because they are mechanical and unconscious. And we have lots of them.

Let us start with one that lacks any emotional reference. Almost everyone puts on the same shoe first every morning; it may be the right or the left one but it always the same one. See, then, having observed what your habit is in this respect, if you can change it and put on the unaccustomed shoe first, for here for the first time we are concerned with an alteration of behavior. The alteration, however, has no ulterior motive behind it nor does it relate to any real or fancied betterment regarding the habit; the alteration is to take place not for any other purpose than just for its own sake. And if it should happen that as a result of the exercise it soon becomes customary to have reversed the past order in which the shoes were put on, then see if you can alter the situation again and on alternate mornings don first the right, then the left one, and so on. The real purpose of this type of Experiment is to live less mechanically, more consciously; *and it is not anything else.*

For a considerable time the pupil should be restricted to experimenting with such neutral habits in order that he may get the "feel" of non-emotional alteration for its own sake and come to understand in his own experience the conscious value of Experiment unrelated to so-called moral goals. For instance, from his practice of Self-Observation he should now be aware how long during the average evening he sits with his legs crossed and how often he is likely to change their positions automatically. Let him decide to spend one selected full evening without once crossing his legs. Just as he has previously discovered with the shoes, he will find how almost impossible it is to remember his decision in time and suddenly he will "wake up" to the fact that his legs are already crossed and that his unconsciousness has betrayed him again. If there is at this point any lingering doubt still in him as to how strong are the automatisms of his body and of how little control he has over it, the experimental work with simple habits will kill it for good. Also, of course, he can scarcely help learning how numerous these mechanical habits of his are and in what they consist.

With a healthy respect already instilled in him regarding their power he may now proceed to deal experimentally with even stronger habits. For the habitual smoker there is one readily to hand which is not only a sensori-motor character but also most probably involves aspects of his subjective image of himself as well as other elements affecting his general behavior. Let him give up his smoking until it no longer exists as a habit, that is, until he no longer experiences any desire or need to smoke. With nicotine, as with alcohol, the minimum period, no matter what the subject may suppose his condition to be, is thirteen weeks. This is the time it takes for the residues of the substance to be eliminated fully from the organism, although the desire for their ingestion may have disappeared considerably earlier in certain cases. During this time the pupil is to devote his Self-Observation especially to the physical changes of gross bodily behavior brought about by his deliberate alteration of the habit. He will find that there is a great deal to notice and he will be tempted to attend mainly to such items as the symptoms of intense emotional irritability at once set up in him when he begins the experiment; but judgments on such scores are the least valuable of his opportunities and he should concentrate on the same Self-Observation in the same specific categories as he earlier practiced.

At the end of the period he will doubtless find that he has no further interest in smoking or any of its aspects, including the "companionship" feature which he supposed to be associated with it. He will discover that his sense of smell or Olfaction is much keener and perhaps that he feels better or more "toned up" then he did before he undertook the experiment. He will therefore automatically, or as he will say naturally, conclude that it was a good idea to break this habit and that he will now have done with smoking for good. But this is absolutely forbidden *and he must be required to reinstate the habit.* Failure to do so, constitutes good and proper ground for dismissing him permanently from the group with which he is working.

If the reader has at all understood the aim and purpose of this step of the work, he will appreciate the grounds for the above requirement. In the first place, during this particular experimental procedure the subject has quite drastically thrown his organism out of balance, for nicotine has a profound effect upon the nervous systems of the body. When the habit has been broken, the organism has already readjusted to the new situation and has adopted compensatory arrangements to bring it into integration under the new conditions. But the subject has no idea whatever concerning the new adjustments and compensations, which in this case will be at a deep level and, whatever their nature, are probably more harmful than any previous effect of the nicotine. Before these new arrangements have had time to crystallize thoroughly, he must reverse the procedure and bring himself back to the former situation. This is one reason for reinstating the habit.

Another, and much more important one, is that he is now learning the experimental attitude toward life. The experimental attitude toward life consists in Experiment for the sake of consciousness, not for the sake of reform. It likewise involves a full and realistic non-identification, which is completely denied and repudiated by a concern for the usually imaginary organic benefits of non-smoking, for instance. All the previous work of the Hidden Secret has been directed toward the installation of impartiality toward himself and first of all toward his organism; and impartiality most assuredly does not signify a yearning toward the "good" or an enmity toward the "bad." There is no more moralism connected with the third step of the first stage of the Method than there is with any scientific experiment.

In fact in modern life our acquaintance with experimental techniques and with the experimental attitude is largely derived from science. In scientific experimentation there is no personal axe to grind and no *a priori* assumption as to how the result may turn out. The position of the Version is basically the same and the differences result only from the difference in the object of experimentation, which in this case is the man's own organism. It is not necessary to take that object into a specially provided laboratory in order to experiment with it; life itself is the laboratory in which the work is done. And while certainly a great deal of information will be acquired by the subject as the outcome of his experimental work, the primary and direct purpose of this step, as of the other steps of the Method, is the increased activity and expansion of the conscious factor in the subject's totality. This work of Experiment is, too, the small and early forerunner of his eventual control of his organism and all its mechanism. But he is by no means able to exercise any genuine control as yet and the delusional pseudo-control of reform is to be avoided sedulously.

There are a great many experiments that can be made in this way. A given pupil, for example, may be accustomed to seven hours sleep per night. Let him take a series of some weeks and for a week at a time sleep, or in any case stay in bed, for periods of nine hours, eight hours, six hours and five hours respectively. It will be his purpose also to notice what general effects these different daily sleeping periods have upon his waking actions, which period generally makes him feel better and more energetic during the day, and so on. Through this it may happen that he will discover that five hours' nightly sleep produces a "better" effect upon him than his previous seven hours; but when he has concluded this experiment, he must return to the seven-hour schedule for at least another month.

For of course he may find out by such procedures that a different resting period or an abstention from smoking actually does suit him better than his previous practices in these regards. After the experiment is over and after the original situation has been *re-established*, naturally he can do as he pleases, by abandoning smoking or sleeping as much or as little as he wishes. But the point is that such alterations have nothing whatsoever to do with the work of Experiment or with any other aspect of the work of the Method; they are the subject's own personal concern and it cannot fail to be plain that such mechanical changes in behavior are unrelated to the conscious good which is the fundamental aim of the Method and its work.

Drinking habits, of course, present a profitable field for Experiment, assuming that the subject is neither an alcoholic nor a teetotaler. "Going on the wagon" for a thirteen-week period sometimes produces unexpected results and in any case will furnish the pupil with a considerable amount of information about the actual effect which alcohol has upon his organism. If this experiment is repeated fairly regularly, say at one-year or two-year intervals, he will also learn about the way in which these effects themselves change at different periods of his life.

Another exercise relating to alcohol and which is of long, indeed ancient, standing, is the experimental intoxication of the whole group of pupils at some meeting which has been purposely arranged ahead of time in appropriate surroundings. At such a meeting not only will behaviors appear which are not available for observation at other times but the length of time during which Self-Observation can continue as the drinking proceeds, will furnish a good estimate regarding the abilities of different pupils and their progress in the Method's work. No doubt this exercise will shock conventional moralists but the point of view of the Oragean Version is not concerned with mechanical morals.

In a treatise it is not possible to do more than indicate such procedures as the technique of Experiment; the richness of its benefits can only be appreciated in the experience with a group which is engaging in the work under competent instruction. The competent instruction is more than ever necessary here because in its absence there will function the inevitable mechanical fallacy of confusing the moralistic itch for reform and improvement with genuine and correct Experiment, as in Self-Observation and Participation, the inner and definitory core of the practice is non-identification; and there is no more indisputable proof of one's identification with one's organism than the rabid desire to improve it, even a small tendency in this direction being sufficient to focus the suspicion of the teacher upon the pupil who manifests such a trend. When this happens, the pupil must be required to return to the simpler exercises of Self-Observation and for the time being abandon Experiment, which is shown to have proven too difficult for his abilities of non-identification.

Assuming, however, that the group is now able to conduct correct Experiment, the work proceeds. It has commenced with the simplest and most mechanical habits and gone on to deal with more important habits, important in the sense that the latter involve larger areas of the subject's behavior patterns.

The automatic roles which one plays in life automatically and unconsciously are dictated by one's falsely subjective image of oneself, which in turn derives from the hidden Chief Feature. To alter such roles consciously and to attempt to play other roles, not on a stage but in life itself, is an extremely advanced exercise in its final development but a beginning can be made at this stage. Of course there is nothing "better" about the artificial role which the subject selects to attempt than about the automatic one he has always been playing; the whole value of the exercise depends upon the practice of a *different*, not a better impersonation. Here also we have a field in which outside confirmation is both possible and required; the criterion of success is not the opinion of the experimenter himself but is based upon his demonstrated ability to impress others who are not involved in the experiment, with the validity of his impersonation.

Consider the picture as the King of England steps forth in full ceremonial regalia to address the Opening of Parliament. Ah, sigh the spectators, genuinely impressed—the King of England! "But we know," as Orage remarked, "that it's only old George." The point here is that the impersonation must be correct and authentic, as in this mentioned role it is, for here the part is deliberately (even if unconsciously) played.

The student-experimenter will not accomplish the result unless his behavior is consistently that of the type whose role he is playing. The mere imitation of certain movements, gestures and gross physical behaviors will leave many inconsistencies present that will at once disclose to the onlooker the falsity of the attempted role. It is necessary not only to move and act but also to feel and think as the impersonated type. George must be not only George but also he must *be* the King of England, circumstance by which habit soon makes it extraordinarily difficult for famous people ever to be anything else—such, for instance, as normal men. But the same sort of temporary and deliberate identification is required in conscious roles; a genuinely conscious role is one that one fully lives and this involves simultaneously all the main functions in the consistent pattern that actually constitutes the role.

The general public can be made the unconscious participants in Experiment of this kind and especially can be made to provide confirmation of an objective character; either they are fooled or they are not. Can they, for example, be made to believe that the subject is really in an indignant frenzy when in fact he is experiencing no emotion at all but is solely concerned with producing an intended effect? In this sort of work one can, and should, place oneself in exceedingly difficult situations but care must be taken not to overestimate one's abilities beforehand and the exercises must be conducted in close consultation with the teacher. As an instance of the kind of work now discussed, there was an exercise recommended in the Orage groups, but of course only for those qualified to undertake it. In this exercise the subject arrays himself in his most formal attire, proceeds to the most currently fashionable restaurant in town and orders a sumptuous dinner accompanied by expensive wines and liquers. At the conclusion of the meal he informs the *maître*, and eventually the management, that he has no money with which to meet the bill; and in fact he has not, for he has carefully left all his cash, as well as his checkbook, at home. Furthermore, he is not to settle the account except in a last extremity, which will be proof of his failure in the experiment. By this means the subject creates both an embarrassing and a most difficult practical situation for himself, in the meeting of which he will need all his ingenuity in the playing of roles as the circumstance develops, in order to escape from the predicament and bring the experiment to a successful conclusion.

Not all full experiments need be as embarrassing as the above (which is an excellent test of non-identification) but they can be even more difficult. The public is off-guard and unsuspicious but one's fellow-pupils are quite the opposite and to manipulate them without their realizing it, is a considerable feat. To deceive the teacher himself in such an exercise is still more difficult and may even annoy him slightly; the writer recalls with much satisfaction his own single success in such an enterprise, which may be worth recounting simply as an illustration.

Orage at that time was conducting a number of different groups in New York City and among them one for beginners without previous acquaintance with the Gurdjieff ideas, a group all the older members were forbidden to attend. I doubt whether anyone except myself wished to attend it but I wanted to see how he handled these beginners and, instead of seeking his permission (which doubtless I could have obtained), I decided to make an exercise of the circumstance and to attend without his knowledge. It was not difficult to ascertain the meeting-place in a roundabout way and, to my advantage, it turned out to be a large and poorly lit room in downtown New York. Other advantages which made the undertaking relatively easy were the facts that none of the audience would ever have seen me before and that of those present who knew me there would be only Orage himself and Miss Jessie Dwight, both of whom were properly confident that in the ordinary way none of Orage's pupils would disobey his explicit instructions regarding attendance and would thus not be on the alert.

The great disadvantage, however, was that both of them knew me well and that I should thus have to disguise my appearance at least against recognition by a casual glance. To this end I liberally powdered my dark hair until it appeared grayish, shaved off the mustache I had worn for years, donned an old business suit and an unaccustomed derby hat, adjusted on my nose a pair of glasses which automatically impaired my sight and made my movements hesitant, and finally stuck a large cigar in my mouth, which at the proper time I lit and smoked with some discomfiture.

But all this was only the exterior and the beginning. I had decided to play the role of a businessman of some, but not very much, practical ability who possessed no intellectual curiosity at all. For this purpose I selected a man of the mentioned type with whom I had only a slight acquaintance, persuading him to have dinner with me and then to accompany me to the meeting on the pretext that I had just heard of these discussions and had been told that they offered advice of a practical nature that might prove useful to both of us, in fact that they disclosed some kind of new and advanced Pelmanism. During the dinner I endeavored in every way to draw out my companion and to enter into and identify myself with the actual interests he on his part entertained. In other words, both in my feelings and in my thoughts I tried to realize his own attitudes and to be as much like him as I could.

We then went on to the meeting and at the door, where Miss Dwight sat at a desk and collected the entrance fees, we passed by among others with no especial attention being accorded us. We took seats toward the rear of the room and from there listened to the formulations and later discussion, in which my friend took no part. I, however, felt that I must ask at least one question in order to make the test a fair one and I finally propounded the most meaningless query I could think of, in a gruff voice as of one suffering from a cold. My companion looked at me, a little surprised by my suddenly rasping tones, but Orage considered my question with his usual patience and succeeded in making his reply far more intelligent than my question had invited. Soon afterwards the meeting broke up and we went out into the street where we parted amicably, my friend having no further interest in the matter, as I had predicted to myself that he would not.

Some days later, being alone at luncheon with Orage, I repeated my stupid question which, in connection with my lack of a moustache, told him all. He was, to my surprise, at first annoyed. But when he had realized that my behavior indicated a lack neither of respect nor consideration for him but was in fact an experiment which, though simple enough, had been difficult for me to carry through, his attitude at once altered.

Connected with the playing of roles is the attempt on the part of the pupil to live a fully balanced day, that is, the attempt so to expend all three kinds of energies, mental, emotional and physical or practical, that at the end of the day the expenditure will have been at least somewhat comparable in all three categories. It is connected with the playing of roles because it will often be found that conscious roles are required in order to obtain the result. If this exercise is done impartially and with non-identification, it can produce valuable by-products and it will certainly increase the conscious activity of the subject.

Another exercise of a similar kind makes the weather one's accomplice. We are inclined to underestimate the effect of the weather upon us; a dull and rainy day brings the lack-lustre eye, a lethargy of movement and a generally let-down and unambitious feeling, whereas we are all acquainted with the bounciness induced by a bright and cheerful spring day. The idea here is deliberately to reverse these effects, to instate a vigorous activity on the rainy day and an experience of dull monotony on the bright day, the latter no less than the former. The pupil should now have at his command a repertoire of means to effect the desired result, among them a series of postures, gestures, movements, facial expressions and tones of voice which, if deliberately performed, will establish the intended mood. If on the rainy day these bring grumbling remonstrances from one's associates or expressions of surprise on the bright day, one may feel assured of some degree of success in the exercise. Also one is by so much a little less the mechanical slave of passing planetary conditions.

A much more serious exercise is the taking of experimental vows. The Vow is not by any means an act of genuine Will but it is the beginning of a practice directed toward the eventual establishment and acquirement of Will. In a real sense this is a dangerous exercise of which the teacher must be in full control. Failures and repeated attempts are to be expected in other kinds of Experiment from the simplest to the complex but in the accomplishment of vows there must never by any failure. This is because one of the most important results of this exercise is the formation in the subject of an unshakeable conviction that he can never fail in a really serious undertaking, i.e., the formation in him of a genuine self-confidence which has no relation at all to the false conceits he may previously have entertained. Such a conviction of success is founded upon the experience of repeated successes and one failure can destroy the effect of twenty successes already attained and bring the subject back to the point where he must start all over again, if it does not, as it may, forever defeat him.

A vow is a promise to oneself that may not be broken. The first two requirements of such work are 1) that the pupil must be absolutely certain of his ability to fulfill the vow without any possibility of failure and 2) that the object of the vow, the action or the purpose to be accomplished, must be gratuitous. The beginning of Will is the ability to make gratuitous efforts, viz., efforts which produce no result of any benefit to him who makes them and which are made solely for the sake and purpose of making them. This is what Gurdjieff refers to, when he says: "Only super-efforts count." Such an effort is the act of digging a hole and then filling it in again or of writing a letter and then tearing it up; and it is precisely the unreasonableness of such an act that renders it a pure effort. Another example is that of a man who makes his way home through the storm with much exertion and then upon his arrival at his door, decides to walk down the road a quarter of a mile and return again. It is because this action accomplishes nothing which has not already been attained, that it constitutes pure effort, without the admixture of foreign elements. At the commencement of undertaking vows, then, there are two characteristics of the second, or gratuitous, requirement: a) that the vow itself must refer to something of no importance to the subject; b) that by the same token it must certainly not refer to anything either disagreeable to him or which he considers it either advantageous or disadvantageous to perform.

This means that the first vows must be very simple ones indeed. For a commuter to get off his train at the station before or after his regular stop and proceed home from there, is much too difficult to begin with, for it may easily happen that he simply forgets to do so on the very day when he has taken a vow to that effect, and neither forgetfulness nor any other circumstance must prevent his accomplishment; it makes no difference what the cause of failure, failure itself is disastrous. Thus likewise he must not undertake any vows that may be rendered impossible of fulfillment due to circumstances beyond his control; excuses, no matter how proper and reasonable, cannot alter the interior effect of failure, which under no circumstances must be allowed to occur.

Thus so simple a vow as not to wear any gloves tomorrow is a good one to start with. But the subject never does wear any gloves? All the better, for this will render it more unlikely that he will fail. Nevertheless, he will do well to put a note—"No gloves today"—in front of his shaving mirror before retiring, lest for some unexplained reason an occasion to don them might arise and he have forgotten his vow at that very moment.

Opportunities to increase the difficulty of such vows, but by a very little at a time, are innumerable and they should be embraced with much caution and in full consultation with his teacher. Among other duties the latter has taken it upon himself to guard the pupil against an overestimation of his abilities of this kind, which it is very easy but really injurious to make. After a long practice under careful supervision the pupil may be permitted to undertake a more serious and paradoxical vow: he will be told to select something he has always wanted to do or some purpose he has always wished to accomplish, and to vow to perform it. This may appear easy on the surface but the very fact that he has never done it despite his wish, shows that it is not easy; and on no account must he be allowed to fail. This is about as difficult an exercise as can be undertaken with safety as an experimental vow at the present stage.

The matter of vows may be summed up thus. The purpose is to build a foundation for Will. The greatest care must be taken, in undertaking vows, to insure that they are easy enough. This is because one failure can wipe out all previous successes; the very great necessity is that *all* vows shall be carried out successfully. They should commence with things so simple that the subject can *guarantee* his ability to fulfill them; this will establish his familiarity with the feeling of certainty that, when he has made a vow, there can exist no possibility of his failing to fulfill it. They may then be increased in difficulty gradually. The goal of this self-discipline is the attainment of a certain kind of ability; the highest form of that ability is genuine Will.

Upon consideration it will be seen that all of the exercises included under the third step, the step of Experiment, are interrelated and mutually supporting, that they reinforce one another and that the earlier phases continue to be included in the later. Nevertheless, one must begin somewhere and the following list may be presented as that of the successive practices under Experiment:

1. With habits:
    a) simple, physical habits
    b) complex habits involving the whole organism

2. With roles:
    a) simple, type roles
    b) more complex roles

3. With external situations:
    a) involving strangers
    b) involving co-pupils

4. With vows:
    a) regarding the simplest actions
    b) regarding more complicated actions
    c) regarding something one has always really wished to do

We have now completed the outline of the first stage of the Method, which consists of the successive steps of:

1. Self-Observation
2. Participation
3. Experiment

The same feature characterizes the entire first stage that we have found operating within its last step, namely, the mutual reinforcement and bearing of all its parts. These steps are not completed and then abandoned in order to take up the next in turn; to the contrary, they continue and are added to step by step, as the activity of Self-Observation and Participation continue to be practiced during the conduct of Experiment. One never gives up Self-

Observation, for this activity is itself a defining characteristic of the state of Self-Consciousness which is the goal of the Method and is as yet beyond the experience of the pupil. And the same is true of Participation and of Experiment, which are to be made a part of life itself and are active constituents of the living of a normal man.

During these steps of the Method's first stage the difficulties have increased progressively until they are now incomparably heavier than during the work of the Open Secret. Especially the demands upon the ability to non-identify have grown as the work has proceeded. But we have no more than made a beginning and it may as well be said now that in this work difficulties shall always increase. The pupil should be reminded, and must continually remind himself, of the altitude of the goal to which he aspires—to become a normal human being. Greater responsibilities will always accompany greater being. To take a simple example, in the army the sergeant has more responsibilities and encounters greater difficulties than the private, the lieutenant than the sergeant, the captain than the lieutenant, the major than the captain, the colonel than the major, the general than the colonel, and the General of the Armies has the greatest responsibilities and the greatest difficulties of all concerned. But it is an analogue of this last position to which you aspire. Certainly the difficulties shall increase, and continue to do so. That is what you want, isn't it? One of the basic definitions of the normal human being is this: Man is the creature whose nature it is to encounter, to create and to overcome difficulty.

Since, if one wishes to learn how to live normally, the undertaking must be conducted at least as professionally as the task of mastering chemistry or the supposed "facts" of history, the question of keeping records arises. Their primary value for the subject himself does not lie in the records—although they may be of use to the teacher—but in other advantages, as will appear.

In the beginning of the work of Self-Observation, for example, it is possible to procure a counter, to be worn on the wrist, of such a kind that it will register two series of numbers independently by means of little levers which may be pushed in by hand to alter each series by a unit at a time. The subject, endeavoring to remember to observe himself, will push in one of these levers every time he succeeds in such recollection and will push in the other one every time when, following immediately upon such recollection, he actually does make an observation. In this way at the end of the day he will have a record both of the activity of his memory and of the times also when he has conducted Self-Observation. They will not necessarily coincide, for he may momentarily recall the task he has set himself but, before he has accomplished it, again forget about it; this will happen frequently in the beginning. Then at the day's conclusion, upon a simple chart which divides the day into periods, as morning, noonday, afternoon, dinner, evening, etc., he may note down the approximate distribution of the sparse moments during which he engages in Self-Observation. This will be easier than foreseen, for such moments, being those of active consciousness, impress themselves much more strongly upon the memory than others and their later recall is relatively easy. In this way he will both have a record of his progress, or its opposite, in the technique and will also find that the mere presence on his wrist of the counter will serve as a valuable reminder to him to prosecute his efforts more often.

The same strategem, of course, is equally applicable to Participation. And in this connection the pupil should be encouraged to invent all sorts of further artificial reminders for his own and his companion's use, for the effort necessary in order merely to remember to engage in the self-observatory activity is unusual and most difficult at first.

In the more advanced work of Experiment the accompanying records may be made as complete and formal as desired. Such records are only auxiliary and have no importance in themselves—it is the experiment as such that is important—but for some persons, especially those who are attracted to scientific procedures and research, they may add to the interest and actually serve as an incentive for more work than would otherwise be done. A full-dress experiment can be treated just as it would be in a university research laboratory or as the basis for a formal thesis prepared by a doctoral candidate.

Thus first the matter of experimental design can be considered. What form shall the experiment take and how shall its different portions be related progressively? Is it desired to submit the results to statistical treatment? If so, then the procedures must be planned out ahead of time in order to provide results to which such techniques may be applicable. And so on. Next comes the deductions consequent upon them which are to be tested experimentally. Then the experiment itself and the immediate recording of its results. After that it will be necessary to analyze the results in the manner foreseen in the experimental design; and finally to compare the actually obtained results with the deductive predictions and to draw up a schedule of those conclusions which may be established by the outcome of the experiment.

All this, of course, is by no means necessary and is not to be recommended in cases where it will prove a hindrance rather than an incentive. No records at all are required in the prosecution of this work but they can be of value, especially as continuing reminders. And as the employment of records to some degree or other will usually be encountered in group work, a mention of them is made here.

Since we are speaking of reminders, it will be well at this point to remark upon a technical term of the work which is of much significance. This term is Self-Remembering. Orage himself used it sparingly but it holds a prominent place in other Versions, particularly in the Ouspenskian Version where it is the cause of some confusion, and it will prove worthwhile to make its meaning perfectly clear.

The term has a reference both to Self-Observation and to Non-Identification but it is synonymous with neither. The conscious act of Self-Observation is performed as follows: 1) a deliberately conscious distinction is set up between "I" and the organic body; 2) one consciously identifies oneself with the "I"-portion of this established dichotomy; 3) from the latter standpoint one observes, in the sense of being aware of, the defined phenomena proceeding simultaneously in the organism. There is thus a division of attention accompanying the observatory act; to the one hand one withdraws from the usual identification with his organism and is aware that he is the now separated "I" and, to the other, one is aware of the specific organic phenomena taking place, as it were, outside of "I." Self-Remembering refers precisely to the *first* of the latter awarenesses, viz., it refers to that part of the attention which at the moment is focused upon the "I" and not upon the "It" or organism.

This process of division of which we speak, is called Non-Identification and in it "I" is placed apart from the body; the act of Self-Remembering is that included part of the act of Self-Observation which is directed upon "I" and not upon the phenomena that are the objects of Self-Observation. In fact, Self-Remembering is identical with Self-Awareness. For anyone who is capable of performing the act of correct Self-Observation there is therefore no excuse for supposing that Self-Remembering is identical with Self-Observation or that in itself the act of Self-Remembering is sufficient to constitute Self-Observation. Self-Remembering no more constitutes the complete act of Self-Observation than does the cue or reminder which causes the subject to recall his intention to self-observe. And if the process stops merely at the point where Self-Remembering takes place, then no Self-Observation has been performed. Every one of the above distinctions is required in order properly to understand and also to realize (i.e., to make real for oneself) what Self-Observation is.

Much earlier, when discussing the different states of consciousness, we have mentioned that Reality, including naturally the external environment, appears differently to the subject when in these various states. And by this time the pupil who has correctly practiced Self-Observation and Participation has experienced inevitably some unexpected glimpses of the appearance of the outside world at the level of Self-Consciousness. As stated, it is one of the purposes of the Method to bring on this kind of experience gradually and without premature shock to the pupil. Because he cannot perform the acts of Self-Observation and of Participation consciously enough and for sufficiently long periods at a time, no matter how hard he tries, he will not have had many of these glimpses of another kind of real world and, instead of producing any sort of shock in most cases, such experiences serve as further incentives to work and, more importantly, as definite confirmations that the results of the Method are not imaginary but that something very real and non-subjective is being accomplished.

It is, of course, no more possible to describe to a man in the Waking state what the world looks like from the level of Self-Consciousness than it is to describe exterior reality as perceived by a man awake, to one who has never experienced anything except Sleep. In neither case does the transition to a higher level of consciousness involve contact with anything especially horrible or terrifying but the outside world does begin to be seen in clearer aspects and as involving much more movement and activity. To one whose perceptions have never proceeded beyond those of the Waking state this new view at the least is very unaccustomed and exceedingly strange; and both to assure him that he is not suddenly "losing his mind" and also to permit him the opportunity of confirming something previously predicted, the pupil is informed beforehand, so far as can be possible, as to what he will encounter with his first self-conscious perceptions.

As remarked, very little can be said about it. But at least two aspects can be indicated. One is the extraordinary and astonishing *aliveness* presented by the appearance of so-called inanimate objects; for instance, an ordinary brick wall may look no longer dead and inanimate but instead may give one the most surprising impression of a peculiarly living thing and the view of so much more active an object as a tree may occasion a considerable amazement. Another, rather opposite effect is the unusual appearance of *deadness* presented by the human beings who may come into view at such moments. Of course it is not that they are really dead but that they suddenly seem to be somewhat less than half-alive; and for the first time one registers in personal experience that they are really sleeping, really submerged in unreal daydreams, really scarcely conscious at all. All this is not a matter of reasoning, deduction or even intuition; it is a directly sensory experience and, as such, creates a deep impression. One can never afterwards forget how the outside world looked to him at a moment approximating to Self-Consciousness. And if he has been prepared so that it does not come upon him too startlingly (for it will certainly come abruptly) or in exceptionally unfortunate conditions, there will be no reason for him to be shocked by it. If, nevertheless, he is, another occasion has arisen for the teacher's services.

It is now time to transfer our discussion to some theoretical aspects of this first full stage of the Method. But there is a final word regarding the above practices, that is, regarding these instructions for doing. What has been described sounds like hard work and it is; it is very hard work indeed, for what is utilized in these non-identified efforts is a kind of energy we have never heretofore used and of which we have no tremendous supply.

But there is nothing lugubrious about this Version and too often those who engage in serious activities of this kind, begin by drawing a long face whose dimensions are never afterwards lessened, so that for an outsider to observe them is to become convinced on pretty good evidence that their discipline must be a tolerably depressing one. There is, and there should be, no such implication in, or result from, this work.

It is certainly necessary to struggle and to strive but it is not necessary to embrace the usual fallacy on this score. The struggle here is a direct internal struggle conducted within one's ultimate subjectivity; it is not turned toward what is outside ourselves in any respect. Our organisms are in reality outside ourselves and thus we are never struggling against their manifestations, habitual or not; we are not striving to reform them or to make them "better" or to convince ourselves that we are sinfully responsible for what is actually automatic and long since determined without our slightest consciousness of the determination. What we do with such manifestations, of every kind whatsoever, is first to self-observe them, then to participate in them, and finally to experiment with them. Moreover, we do so always with non-identification. This whole procedure is very different indeed from the writhings involved in the Way of Religion or the Path of the emotionalist, and enough has previously been said to distinguish the Fourth Way ultimately and finally from any of the first three usual Ways. It is not a question of disparaging any of the Paths by which men may become normal, it is a question of distinguishing clearly between them. It must be obvious that our Way is not that of the religionist or of the emotionalist.

As to the Oragean Version, it does not propose that men are bad but that they are abnormally subhuman. Nor does it believe that their situation is irremediable but to the contrary it is engaged exactly in defining a remedy. The purpose of the Method is to bring each candidate more energy, more activity, more consciousness, more life—not less in any of these cases. Nothing is really harmful that does not injure "I"; and our chief and final criterion is consciousness itself. We hold nothing at all against cheerfulness or the full experience of all emotions, both positive and negative; indeed it is our assertion that such experience is far too meager and our program is to make it fuller and more conscious. Nor do we consider this in any way a hindrance to our ultimate goal of normality.

There is no proposal here to immerse the candidate for humanity in self-reproaches or despair, but quite the opposite. And we are not concerned with those who are bowed down by an automatic sense of sin and the desire to struggle and strive against it, whether or not upon the pretext of struggling and striving against something else.

If you are not capable of more actively enjoyable, more conscious and greater life than you have ever hitherto experienced, it will be well for you to keep away from this Version.

5.

Let us now consider the effect produced upon the physical organism by Self-Observation, in general by the first stage of the Method. We may discuss this from two related viewpoints, first with regard to the digestion of the substances taken into the body as foods, and second in regard to the activation of the different organic Centres.

We recall the situation of the ordinary man before the Secret has been disclosed to him and before he takes part in the present kind of work, as concerns the octaves of food digestion within his body. It was as follows:

si	sex					
la	emotion					
		(shock)				
sol	thought	mi	thought	do	thought	
fa	magnetism	re	magnetism			
(shock)						
mi	gas	do	gas			
re	liquid					
do	solid					

Ordinary Food	*Air*	*Impressions*

Here we have the completed digestion of the first food octave; the second, or air, octave half-digested; and the third food octave represented only by an incomplete 'do' which cannot further evolve, even automatically. Let us investigate the last point more fully.

The basic feature of digestion is that it is an *active process*. Following babyhood, food is not pushed into anyone's mouth automatically; he has to convey it there himself. After it is in the mouth it has to be masticated and swallowed and then the alimentary canal has to deal with it, also actively. It is the same with air; hundreds of muscles cooperate to draw it into the lungs, which in turn are so constructed that in them an active interchange takes place between the gaseous substances of the air and the chemical substances of the blood. All this has been arranged by nature to proceed automatically and mechanically, with little or no consciousness upon the part of the subject. Moreover, at the place where the first food octave becomes stalled in its evolution at the note, 'mi,' of its development, the evolutionary air octave joins it, providing the necessary shock for the continuation of the first food octave through its 'fa' and further notes. The point about all this is that, although it is automatic and largely unconscious, there is a great deal of activity involved.

But when the developing octave of air digestion in turn reaches its own 'mi' and encounters the inevitable barrier to its further progress, there is now no active shock present outside its own octave and its evolution ceases, depriving the organism of the further products which might be, and ought to be, derived from its substances. Nature makes no mechanical provision for this second necessary shock from outside which, if it is to occur, must be furnished consciously by the subject himself. Yet the possibility is present, for there is still a third food constantly furnished to the organism in the form of sensory impressions and, since these are of the same character as that of the derived substances at the point where the air octave has become stalled, they hold out the possibility of providing the required shock for the continuation of the evolution of the air octave.

They fail to do so for the simple reason that, although continually present, they are not "eaten." No more than ordinary food will give any nourishment if it is just held passively in the mouth and then gradually drooled out again, will the food of the third kind either begin its own evolution or provide a shock for the second food octave, if it just enters and lies there, as it does. The whole bearing of this matter is precisely that nothing whatever is done about the entering impressions; they are always pouring in but their result is an entirely *passive* registration on the part of the subject, who displays no activity at all toward them but merely accepts them and at once forgets them if indeed he was ever even partially aware of them in some semiconscious way. This is the typical characteristic of the dreamy, less than half-conscious Waking state.

The activity of Self-Observation is exactly the eating and digestion of the third food, sensory impressions, viz., the bringing into an active, detailed awareness of the sensory input continually arriving both from without and from within the body itself. This active effort of consciousness must, and does, have two complimentary effects: first, it actually "eats" the incoming impressions and thus initiates their own digestion within the organism; second, this initiation of digestion of the third food thus provides the necessary shock to the second food evolution to assist it across its "mi-fa" interval and to continue its own digestion. The situation then alters from that of the table above to that of the table below:

				(shock)	
si	sex	sol	sex	mi	sex
la	emotion	fa	emotion	re	emotion
		(shock)			
sol	thought	mi	thought	do	thought
fa	magnetism	re	magnetism		
(shock)					
mi	gas	do	gas		
re	liquid				
do	solid				

Ordinary Food   Air   *Impressions*

It will be seen that there are now much greater supplies of energy available within the organism. With the conscious taking of impressions into active awareness the mental-type energy has been increased by fifty per cent; and the further result is a tripling of the emotion-type energy and a tripling of the sex energy. Sex energy is the highest form of substance produced by the transformations of digestion in the so-called physical body and its normal uses in general are of two kinds. In combination with a member of the opposite sex this energy can procreate another organism of a kind similar to that of the parents; by the subject alone, and under the proper conditions, this energy can be used to procreate within his own body another organism of a kind different from that of the original body, although still a fully physical organism. But these are matters to be discussed below, as is also the fact, which no doubt has been noticed, that the air octave under the above conditions will proceed automatically through two further notes which have not been included in the above table. At present it is sufficient to show the much greater energies available for human living as a result of the Method's first stage work.

We may also now continue Figure 9 (page 86) which showed the stages of the digestive process in the ordinary man before undertaking this work. There are two of these figures, which refer to exactly the same processes, diagrammed differently simply to exhibit different relationships of the same food transformations; since they will be needed later, we shall give them both now, up to and including the stages represented in the table just presented.

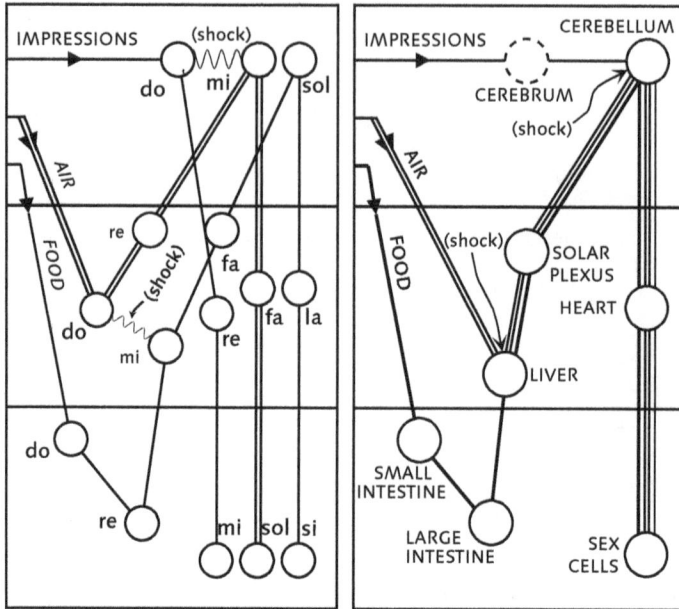

Figure 10. Diagrams of Digestion Stages after first conscious shock.

In order to elucidate further details of the second (the first conscious) shock, two inserts are appended, corresponding to parts of the preceding diagram:

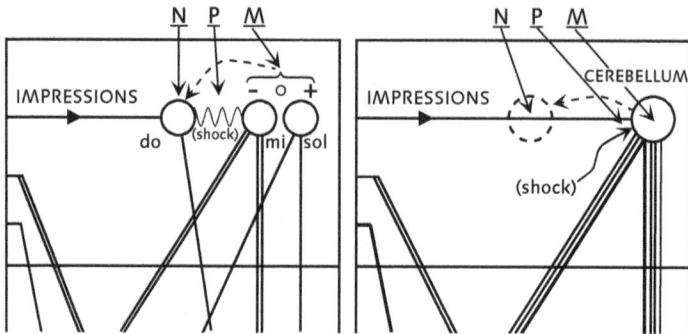

LEGEND: + positive factor   M: designates derivation of energy
         - negative factor   N: designates application of energy
         o neutralizing factor P: designates effective result

Figure 11. Detail of second (conscious) shock.

The energy for N derives from M. There is a distinction between the application of energy and its effective result. This diagram is proposed by the writer upon his own responsibility, since it was not originally presented in the Oragean Version.

Occasionally incredulity is expressed regarding the location of the air-food shock in the liver, although the anatomical facts are plain enough. From the lungs the air-substances absorbed by the blood are transported through the heart and thence from the left auricle into the aorta; but all this is simple transportation, not transformation. Thence the blood-borne air-substances are taken directly to the liver; and at the same time there enter the liver via the portal vein the transformed food substances carried by the venous blood from the intestinal walls. There in the liver the first confrontation takes place between the arterially carried air-substances and the venously carried food substances; and that is why, diagrammatically, mere transportation stages are omitted. Similarly, any competent student of neuroanatomy ought to suspect why and how the second (conscious) shock takes place, and can only take place, in the cerebellum. A detailed exposition of all the involved factors is more appropriately to be found in a neurological text book.

Figures 10 and 11 which have just been presented, as well as the accompanying explanation, set forth the present matter in the terms of the Oragean Version. But since it is the purpose of this treatise neither to proselyte nor to seek believing converts to these views, it will be well here to state that at the present point we encounter very grave theoretical difficulties, the responsibility for which lies nowhere but at the door of Gurdjieff personally. The fact is that the sources of information regarding the above question derive from three sources only: from the formulations of Gurdjieff himself, from the Oragean Version and from the Ouspenskian Version. Not a single one of these sources agrees with any of the others in all details.

Since it is agreed that the information for all versions came originally from Gurdjieff, the obvious solution would appear to be to rely upon the Gurdjieff formulation and to attribute any discrepancies in the other versions to errors upon the part either of Orage or of Ouspensky. Unfortunately this cannot be done, the reason being that the Gurdjieff formulation is not only fragmentary and incomplete but also customarily vague.

The attitude of Gurdjieff's of refusing intellectually theoretical information makes it impossible to determine just what his own careful formulation would have been; but from the only detailed statement* of his known to the writer Figure 10-A has been prepared, which will be found on the following page. This should be compared with Figure 10 (on page 154, second half of diagram) in order to disclose the discrepancies. It should be noted

---

* Gurdjieff, G.: *All and Everything, First Series, Beelzebub's Tales to his Grandson*, Harcourt Brace & Co., NY, 1950; pp. 788 ff.

that in Figure 10-A only the food octave and part of the air octave are represented—the impressions octave being omitted entirely—and these should be compared with the relevant portions of Figure 10.

The Ouspenskian Version* does not specify the organic locations of the digestion stages within the body but is concerned solely with the parachemical aspects of the matter; it should be compared with Figure 10, first half. The question of the Gurdjieffian parachemistry will be further discussed in the next chapter of this treatise.

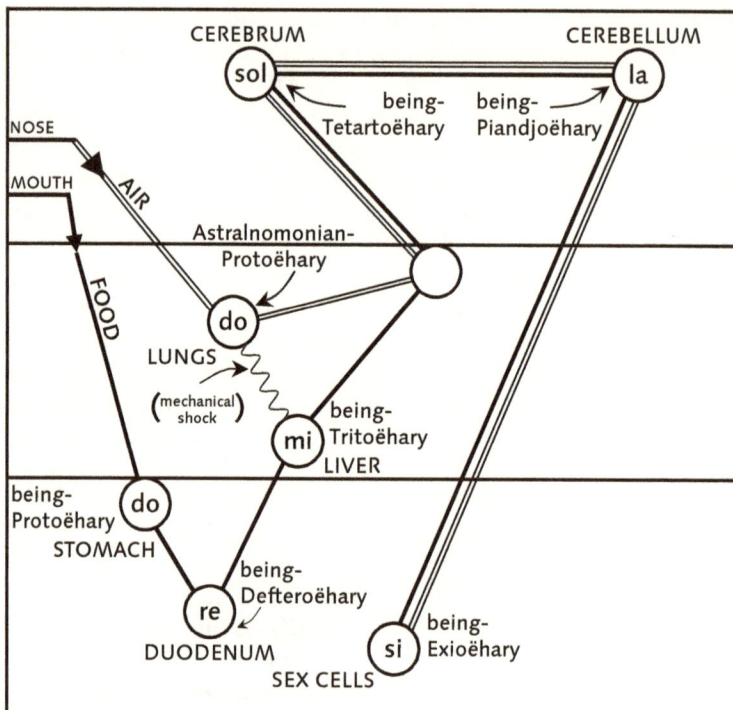

Figure 10-A

To show discrepancies between the Gurdjieff formulation
and both the Oragean and the Ouspenskian Versions.

This includes the first (mechanical) shock but does not include either the second (conscious) shock or the impressions octave. This formulation bears no exact correspondences either with the Oragean or with the Ouspenskian Versions.

---

* Ouspensky, P. D.: *In Search of the Miraculous*, Harcourt Brace & Co., NY, 1949; pp. 181 ff., especially p 100.

The foregoing discussion has been included both for the sake of clarity and to obviate the possible criticism that the discrepancies in the Oragean Version are due either to carelessness or to oversight. The chief discrepancies consist in the Gurdjieffian attribution of the air octave 'do' to the lungs and the Oragean attribution of this same 'do' to the liver, and also the location of the food 'sol'—air 'mi' in the cerebrum instead of in the cerebellum as in the Oragean Version. The writer cannot claim to be able to resolve these questions in a final sense and he offers it merely as his personal opinion that the Oragean formulation is simply a careful and more detailed working out of the information rather vaguely formulated by Gurdjieff; incidentally it is more in accord with ordinary physiological knowledge but this of course does not alter the fact that it may contain one or more minor errors. For these several reasons and also because this treatise is definitely a formulation of the Oragean Version, we will continue to adhere to the latter.

A result of the presence of these new transformations of the available food substances in the organism, and thus of the availability of new energy-sources, is the activation of the higher centres, #4, #5 and #6. The first effort of Self-Observation is actually made through the utilization of some small amount of Centre #4 energy which may previously have been accumulated by chance, for it is only in Centre #4 that impressions may become active in the present sense. But the phenomenon itself, being an active one, affects neighboring cells, stimulating them to become active in turn and thus increasing the total amount of Centre #4 energy every time a successful self-observation occurs.

It may also be said that every impression, made active through Self-Observation, furnishes content to the hitherto empty Centre #4 structures which now for the first time commence to function properly. And once the 'fa'-interval between Centre #3 and Centre #4 has been crossed by the consciously activated impulses, the process continues to its octavic conclusion. Centre #4 activity furnishes content for Centre #5, which in turn performs the same service for Centre #6, while the growing normal channel of interconnection between #5 and #6 gradually begins to weaken the previous abnormal connections established between #6 and Centres #1, #2 and #3. Thus the subject, by concentrating his attention at the point of obstruction between Centres #3 and #4, i.e., by expending his conscious effort solely upon the work of Self-Observation, will automatically commence bringing all three higher centres into normal function. The activation is due physiologically to the now normally established discharge of impulses from the cerebrum to the cerebellum through the cortico-pontine-cerebellar tract. The nature of these changes is diagrammed below.

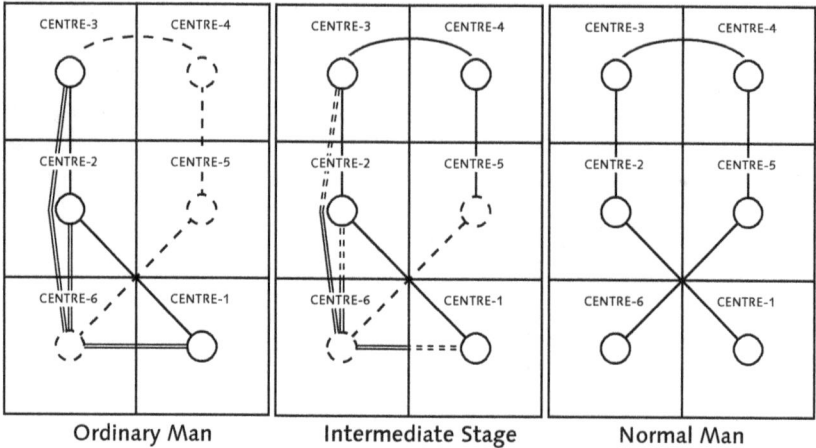

Figure 12. Activation of Centres.

By a schematic adaptation of Figures 5, 9, 10 and 11 a diagrammatic representation may be had of the relationship between the octaves of food digestion and the functioning of the centres in the normal case. The following diagram was not presented in the Oragean Version nor, to the best of the writer's knowledge, in the Ouspenskian Version, either; and he therefore takes full responsibility for any error or misrepresentation that may be included in it.

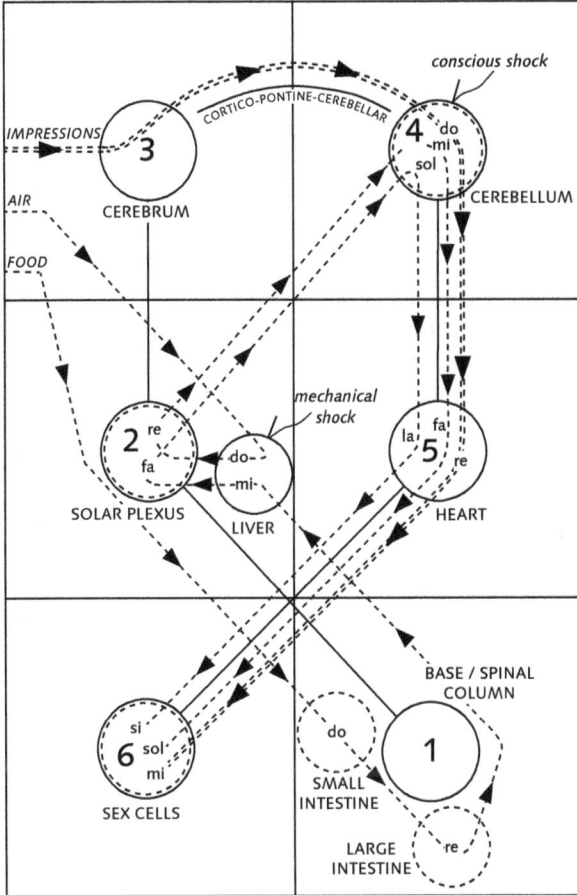

Figure 13. Relationship between Food Octaves and Centre functioning.
(Not presented in Oragean Version.)

The human organism has been likened to a three-storey factory which receives supplies at each of its levels. The ground floor supplies are actually used, as also one-half of the materials entering the second storey; the other half of the latter, as well as the top storey supplies, are received but are allowed just to lie where they are delivered and there to rot. This not only clutters up the factory but the inevitable necessity of getting rid of them interferes with the work already going forward. Under these conditions the operations of the establishment suffice merely for maintenance and required repairs and no further output is achieved. Thus the factory produces nothing at all; and any factory whose operations result in nothing more than its own mere maintenance, is obviously an unsuccessful enterprise.

But with the proper utilization of its delivered materials all this is changed. There is now a conversion of supplies into finished product, which product consists in higher mental activities, higher emotions and, above all, in those energies that permit the exercise of genuine Will and the consequent ability to Do. Doing, or consciously directed action, is precisely the final output which the factory is designed to produce and it in no way resembles the automatically determined movements and actions of the "factory" during its mere maintenance. Real doing is always deliberate and consciously directed both in its intended effects and their actualized achievements; it is thus very different from the mechanically produced reactions of the ordinary man in his Waking state. And the entire reorganization of the factory commences with the conscious effort of Self-Observation and the resultant effects upon the factory's transformation of its received supplies (food digestion) and upon the functions of its different departments (the activation of the higher centres), which were previously unused rooms gathering dust and debris. Plainly enough, this simile can be worked out in much greater detail; that can serve as a later exercise.

We now come to a formulation of the further Potential for Man. And a word of warning is required here. What we are to formulate is not now the case, it is not the Actual for us or for any ordinary men; it is perfectly real but it is *potentially* real and the temptation is always large to accept such formulations as already accomplished facts when actually they are facts yet to be accomplished. This fallacy has invariably followed the original formulations of concepts such as the Gurdjieff ideas and it will certainly happen in respect of them also, for such is the inevitably functioning law of the octavic involution when correct information is put at the disposal of the ordinary man. One of the most striking illustrations of this involutionary process is the assumption by modern Christians that they possess souls (and thus gratuitous tickets to heaven, if they behave themselves). But in no genuine religion of any sort—and this includes Christianity—has it ever been stated that ordinary men possess souls. To the contrary it has been stated explicitly that they do not, that they must acquire souls the hard way, i.e., by working correctly to produce them, and that if they do not follow the given instructions correctly, their last chance of any part of a soul is gone forever. Good intentions count for nothing in such an enterprise; nor is following instructions correctly, at all the same thing as listening to them, dreaming piously about them or even repeating them verbally with unctuous self-satisfaction. Christians are among the foremost examples of the Pauper's Parable: phantasying that they already possess souls, they assuredly shall never acquire them.

This sort of thing derives from the common practice of skipping the first step, which is hard and practical, and beginning with the second step which, if the first be skipped, is daydreamy and impractical. It is daydreamy and impractical because without the preliminary accomplishment of the first step, it is *totally impossible*; nothing then can be done about the second step *except* to daydream of it. There can be no skipping the first stage of this Method, nor the first step of the first stage, and it is no more than phantasy to imagine that what follows can possibly apply to a man that has not achieved, and proved that he has achieved, the results of correct Self-Observation, Participation and Experiment. The fallacy of skipping is a customary part of the Self-calming disease. What will now be formulated relates to the normal man, and it applies to the normal man but not to us or to the reader; for us it is a real potential but our actual reality is very different.

The first thing to be noted is that our formulation of the physical potentiality of the human being up to now has been far from complete; we have pronounced only the "one hundred" portion of the expression, "one hundred and twenty-four." We now take the case of the man who has reached the position of Figure 12 and within whose body all six centres are functioning. The effect of such a functioning is to amalgamate the centres in pairs, Centre #3 combining with Centre #4, #2 with #5, and #1 with #6. Very naturally the base of the spinal column, the solar plexus and the cerebrum do not disappear. It is that the functional centre of gravity gradually passes from the lower Centres to the higher; and instead of the jangling of mutual mechanical interferences in the body (as must be the case when the first three centres control functional operation) there is a smoothly harmonious functioning of the organism as a whole, because the very premise of the activation of Centres #4, #5 and #6 is the operating presence of the organic regulator which is the subject's active consciousness. When this functional shift has taken place, he is left with only three operating centres as before, but now they are the three harmoniously related higher centres instead of the three mutually contending lower centres. This is the three-storeyed factory.

The concept of sub-centres must now be introduced. And the reader must be told that, although it may seem simple at first, it will not be simple by the time we have finished with it; indeed this concept is so very complicated that its full exposition will not be possible until we have considered larger cosmic features of the Greater Map in the next chapter.

We will begin with the statement that the organic machine which we know as the physical body is itself the human being's First Centre. What we have just been calling its three Centres or the three storeys of the factory, are in fact its three Sub-centres. These three Sub-centres always bear to each other the relationship of the three primary universal forces (positive, negative and neutralizing) but they cannot be so drawn in a figure because, since the relationship is always altering as between them, a *moving* diagram would be required. The type-relationship, however, is this: intellectual Sub-centre—positive; emotional Sub-centre—neutralizing and instinctive Sub-centre—negative.

The second and third Centres of a human being consist also of bodies, just as material and just as physical as is the First Centre or physical body. For an ordinary man they are potential; for a normal, or fully developed, man they are actual. Each of these further organic bodies has three physical Sub-centres within it and they correspond exactly with the three sub-centres of the First Centre or physical body.

These surprising statements need some greater amplification. According to the Gurdjieff information *everything* in the universe is material; this body of ideas is more materialistic than Materialism, for it means what it says, viz., that thoughts are material, that emotions are material, that the sun's radiations are material, that everything is material. For instance, when it calls itself a body of ideas, it means that an organized relationship of ideas is material, too. Material substances in the last analysis consist of differently vibrating primordial matter which is far too tenuous for measurement by modern scientific instrumentation, and some of them are not even available upon the surface of this planet; their definitory difference in all cases is the difference of their respective vibration-rates. The lower the vibration-rate, the coarser the matter; the higher the vibration-rate, the finer the matter.

A function of the physical body, or First Centre, is to ingest matters of given vibration-rates (food, air, impressions) and to transform such substances by raising their vibration-rates to permit of the construction within itself of the Second Centre and of the initiation of the Third Centre.

There is nothing either supernatural or miraculous about this. Let us remember the ontogenetic development of the First Centre; begun with the union of two procreative cells which fuse into one and then commence mitotic subdivision within another First Centre, i.e., within the mother's womb. This newly conceived and presently embryonic First Centre is soon nourished by food substances ingested and transformed by the mother's body and its growth is rigorously controlled and directed by the steady-state DC organic field already present in the original cell from which it began. This neutralizing factor (the organic field) is what determines the various stages of development and the final adult form of the new organism or the First Centre, and the same organic field remains inherent in the organism until its death. There is therefore nothing very remarkable in the fact that the same biological field forces (the neutralizing factor of the First Centre) can, and do, serve as a neutralizing factor for the replica organism which is the Second Centre, whenever the necessary substances of the required vibration-rates are present within the First Centre for the corresponding organization. These substances are not, of course, available within the First Centre except as a result of actively conscious effort, correctly directed, on the part of the subject himself. They are the result of the completed evolution of the second food octave.

These three large Centres, which in reality are three organic bodies composed of increasingly finer material substances, have gone by various names throughout the history of Schools and of genuine Religions. It will avoid confusion to list some of these terms here, including the ones which are used in the Oragean Version:

	First Centre	Second Centre	Third Centre
Gurdjieff	Planetary Body or Earth Body	Body Kesdjan	Soul Body
Oragean Version	Physical Body	Astral Body or Psychic Body	Mental Body or Psychological Body
Christianity	Body	Soul	Spirit

N.B. The Etheric Body, which can be, and has been, photographed with the ordinary camera by means of dicyanin screens, is not one of the above but serves the purpose of a sort of umbilical cord connecting the First Centre with the higher Centres. It is the least permanent of all the bodies.*

(In the writer's opinion few of the above terms are particularly well chosen. Every one of these bodies is physical and to apply the term, physical, to only one of them, is confusing, to say the least. Furthermore, the derivation of the Second Centre being from substances common to the Planetary System as a whole and of the Third Centre being from substances common to the Suns of the Universe, the logical terminology should be Earth Body, Planetary Body and Astral Body. However, this latter terminology is nowhere to be found and we shall adhere to the terms employed in the Oragean Version.)

We must now remember that the ontogenetic development of the physical body within the mother's womb passes through all the chief phylogenetic stages of the Organic Kingdom during its embryonic phases. According to the present Version these phylogenetic stages are shown in Figure 7, page 79.

They represent the action of the biological field in relation to the cellular constituents of the organism during its growth, although whether the cells

---

* Kilner, W. J., *The Human Atmosphere (The Aura)*, E. P. Dutton & Co., NY 1920, 1926.

are arranged in these successive ways due to their respective numbers at different periods or due to a changing pattern of the field itself (from back-effects of the organism's growth) or to some other reason, is not known. That is, no cause can as yet be assigned for the fact that during the organism's development the cells arrange themselves within the field pattern in just these and no other successively more complicated patterns. Nevertheless they do; and again we are confronted with a fundamental octavic phenomenon.

Since the three Centres or the three organic bodies pass through these given octavic stages during the course of their development, it is to be seen in the case of the ordinary man that the result of his partial digestion of the available food substances gives him a completely evolved physical body, an astral body developed only up to the invertebrate stage and a mental body whose growth cannot be said to have even begun:

	Physical Body			Astral Body			Mental Body	
	(MAN) si			()				
	(MONK.) la			()				
MAN si sex o	(VERT.) sol sex	()		mi sex	() (VEG.)			
MONK. la emotion o	(INVERT.) fa emotion	()		re emotion ()	(MIN.)			
VERT. sol thought o	VEG. mi thought o			(potential) shock do thought ()	(MET.)			
INVERT. fa magnetism o	MIN. re magnetism o							
VEG. mi gas o ← shock ←	do gas o							
	(actual) ... MET.							
MIN. re liquid o								
MET. do solid o								

Ordinary Food	Air	Impressions

By subjecting the specified sensory impressions to active digestion by the conscious activity of Self-Observation the potential shock from the impressions-'do' to the air-'mi' is altered to an actual shock; the air octave then completes its evolution and provides the transformed matters required for the full development of the astral body and for the beginning of the development of the mental body, in relation to the biological field forces (neutralizing factor) present in the developed physical body. The situation, when the astral body has been developed, is diagrammed below, in relation to the food octaves and to the three Centres or bodies of Man:

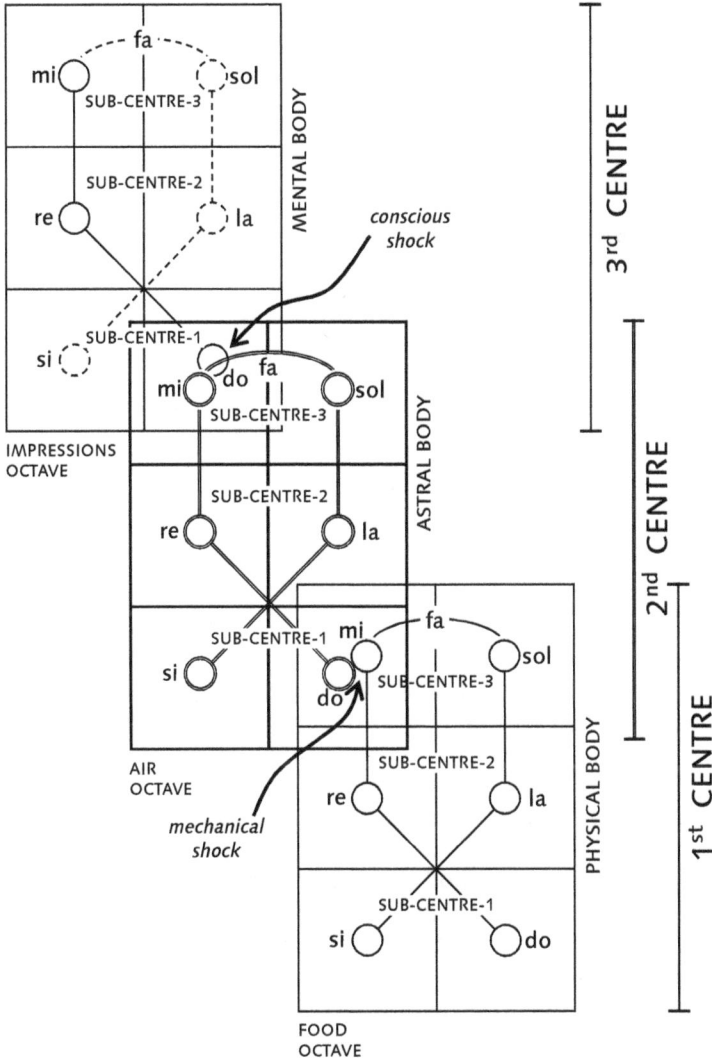

Figure 14. Food Octaves and the three Centres.
(This diagram was not presented in the Oragean Version;
the writer takes responsibility.)

The table corresponding to the degree of evolution of the three bodies represented in Figure 14, preceding, will then stand as follows:

				Physical Body				Astral Body				Mental Body
							MAN	si	"nectar"	o		
							MONK.	la	"ambrosia"	o		
									(conscious shock)			
MAN	si	sex	o	VERT.	sol	sex	o	VEG.	mi	sex	o
MONK.	la	emotion	o	INVERT.	fa	emotion	o	MIN.	re	emotion	o
				(conscious shock)							
VERT.	sol	thought	o	VEG.	mi	thought	o	MET.	do	thought	o
INVERT.	fa	magnetism	o	MIN.	re	magnetism	o				
(mechanical shock)											
VEG.	mi	gas	o	MET.	do	gas	o				
MIN.	re	liquid	o								
MET.	do	solid	o								
Ordinary Food				Air				Impressions			

In this table the air octave completes itself through its full development, providing all the substances needed for the procreation of the astral body; and it will now be seen why the notes, 'la' and 'si' of the air digestion octave cannot be represented in a table (page 153) which relates to the transformation of food substances in the physical body (or First Centre) alone. Although all the substances transformed in the air digestion octave go to the formation of the astral body, they correspond up to and including the note, 'sol,' to substances also utilized by the physical body; but the air octave notes, 'la' and 'si,' are substances actualized only in the formation of the astral body and are not represented in the physical body at all. They are the "ambrosia" and "nectar" of the Greek tradition, both of which are completely material even if they are the "food of the gods." Similarly, the eventual 'fa,' 'sol,' 'la,' and 'si' substances of the impressions octave are not assimilable by the physical body or First Centre except for utilization beyond its own functions, for utilization, that is, in the procreation of the mental body.

One further general proposition regarding all the stages of food digestion and all the substances derived from their transformations is to be noted here. It must not be supposed that the ingested substances simply evolve and do nothing else, for of course at all their evolving stages they are necessary for the maintenance and operation of the organic machine itself. But the organism, the First Centre, is so designed that it can ingest more than is required for its own operation and the surplus is used for the evolution of the increasingly finer substances that also are demanded for further organic operations; this is also true of the Second and Third Centres when the required substances are available for their construction and they too commence to function organically. Thus from the very first 'do' of the ordinary food octave, a part of the ingested material in solid form goes to the nourishment and operation of the relevant portions of the organism and the rest becomes available for the transformation into substances of the 're' or liquid stage of the food octave. This transformation is aided by the prior presence in the organism of substances already at the 're' stage and currently functioning as such in the body. Similarly, part of the ordinary food substances at the 'mi' stage of the first food octave is utilized in this form in the operation of the organism and the other part (aided by the entrance of gaseous substances of the air octave at its own stage of 'do') is transmuted to the 'fa' or magnetic stage of its evolution; while at the same time the entering air substances at their 'do' are divided, part of them being used in the functioning of the organic machine and the rest evolving to the next, or 'mi,' stage of the air octave evolution. This same process will hold with regard to all digestive stages in all of the three bodies or Centres, some of the substances being used in their current state for organic functions and the surplus evolving further into finer substances of higher vibration-rates for the further organic utilization.

We come now to the final question concerning the evolutionary digestion octaves, the question as the second conscious shock necessary in order that the impressions octave should proceed past its own note, 'mi,' and complete its evolution, thus forming the Third Centre or mental body in its final configuration. Nature makes no more provision for this required shock than for the first conscious shock which is necessary in order to complete the evolution of the air octave and which is supplied by the technique of actively conscious Self-Observation. The subject himself must therefore supply this kind of shock by his own conscious activity, just as in the case of the second kind of shock, viz., the first conscious one. The full table of the digestion octaves, below, will identify the physical location where this last shock must take place; the practical means whereby it is produced, will be considered in the next section in which the formulation of the complete Method will be concluded.

Physical Body				Astral Body				Mental Body			
								(MAN)	si		()
								(MONK.)	la		()
				MAN	si	"nectar"	o	(VERT.)	sol	"nectar"	
				MONK.	la	"ambrosia"	o	(INVERT.)	fa	"ambrosia" () (conscious shock)	
MAN	si	sex	o	VERT.	sol	sex	o	VEG.	mi	sex	o
MONK.	la	emotion	o	INVERT.	fa	emotion (conscious shock)	o	MIN.	re	emotion	o
VERT.	sol	thought	o	VEG.	mi	thought	o	MET.	do	thought	o
INVERT.	fa	magnetism (mechanical shock)	o	MIN.	re	magnetism	o				
VEG.	mi	gas	o	MET.	do	gas	o				
MIN.	re	liquid	o								
MET.	do	solid	o								
Ordinary Food				Air				Impressions			

The location of the second conscious shock is underlined; it will be seen that, when this shock is actualized the impressions octave will then complete its evolution and provide the necessary materials for the procreation of the Third Centre or mental body. The material source when this physical shock derives is not formulated directly, to the best of the writer's knowledge, anywhere in the body of the Gurdjieffian ideas, or in the Oragean Version, or in the Ouspenskian Version; it cannot therefore be diagrammed here, although suggestive implications will appear from figures included in the next chapter. We shall now proceed to further practical applications of the above information.

6.

The first stage of the Method, which has been described in Section 4 above, consists of the three successive steps of Self-Observation, Participation and Experiment. It is the actively conscious efforts of the subject during this stage of the Method which provide the first conscious shock enabling the digestion octave of the air substances to complete its evolution and transmute the ingested foods into the correspondingly finer matters furnished at the top of the air octave. Since these transformations must continue to take place, the Method's first stage is not one that can be passed through, simply learned as it were and practiced for a short time, and then dropped. Just as one must continue to eat every day, these consciously active efforts, once initiated, must always thereafter continue to be prosecuted; they are literally digestive activities which of course must go on as long as there is any organism in which they may take place. Their real significance is simply that in this respect one continues to live actively and consciously instead of passively and unconsciously.

The three steps of the first stage are further subdivided and their parts may be classified as follows:

Stage 1.

Step 1. Observation: a) First Centre, Sub-centre #1
                      b)   Sub-centre #2
                      c)   Sub-centre #3
                      d)   Sub-centres #1, #2, #3 together
Step 2. Participation: a) First Centre, Sub-centre #1
                      b)   Sub-centre #2
                      c)   Sub-centre #3
                      d)   Sub-centres #1, #2, #3 together
Step 3. Experiment: a) First Centre, Sub-centre #1
                      b)   Sub-centre #2
                      c)   Sub-centre #3
                      d)   Sub-centres #1, #2, #3 together

Furthermore it will be seen that these subdivisions may be yet further subdivided, as for example Step 1. Observation:

a) First Centre, Sub-centre #1—
   1. Posture
   2. Gesture
   3. Movement
   4. Facial Expression
   5. Tone of voice
   6. Posture, gesture
   7. Posture, movement
   8. Posture, facial expression
   9. Posture, tone of voice

10. Gesture, movement
11. Gesture, facial expression
12. Gesture, tone of voice
13. Movement, facial expression
14. Movement, tone of voice
15. Facial expression, tone of voice
16. Posture, gesture, movement
17. Posture, gesture, facial expression
18. Posture, gesture, tone of voice
19. Gesture, movement, facial expression
20. Gesture, movement, tone of voice
21. Movement, facial expression, tone of voice
22. Posture, gesture, movement, facial expression
23. Posture, movement, facial expression, tone of voice
24. Gesture, movement, facial expression, tone of voice
25. Gesture, posture, facial expression, tone of voice
26. Posture, gesture, movement, facial expression, tone of voice

These classifications are not set out because of a delight in complicated listings but because this work must be specifically and accurately detailed in order to insure its practical application to actually real phenomena and in order to avoid any possibility of supposing that speculating and daydreaming about it is the same thing as in fact doing it.

If the work is done correctly, a great amount of real knowledge will result, information regarding physiology, personality characteristics, behavior patterns, and the like. We may compare this process with what is known as the scientific method, which is also a proceeding directed toward the accumulation of knowledge. Scientific procedure involves four steps:

1. The gathering of data appropriate to the given problem.
2. The construction of an hypothesis subsuming large numbers of the data.
3. The setting up of an experimental technique to test the hypothesis.
4. The resulting disproof or alleged proof.

In the present Method the step of Observation corresponds to the first step of the scientific procedure and the step of Participation adds to the data already accumulated. The direct construction of hypothetical explanations of what is observed, is prohibited (because this involves judgments, analysis and other mental activities obstructive of the work itself); but, provided they are not directly sought, such hypotheses will gradually construct *themselves* in the subject's experience. The step of Experiment will serve in fact either to confirm or to refute them.

Knowledge gained in the latter way, even though merely as a by-product of an increase in consciousness and of a normally active transformation-process, must plainly be superior to scientifically gained knowledge in two specific ways. First, it is direct knowledge; no instrumentation intervenes between the observer and his data, and instrumentation distorts the data of science both in ways which are recognized and in sometimes unsuspected ways. Thus the data resulting from the direct awareness of Self-Observation are pure and undistorted data, reflecting the actual characteristics of the reality under scrutiny, for it is a very different thing to deal with the actual units of physiology in this way than it is to be concerned merely intellectually with such mental concepts-by-postulation as cells, hormones, molecules, and so on.

And in the second place the verification of conclusions, although compared with others and in part justified by their agreement, no longer suffers from the intrusion of the fallacy of affirming the consequent, as is the case with the alleged verifications of science. This is because it is not an hypothesis, but instead it is direct experience, which is being confirmed. The verification of a datum of only mental experience, viz., of an hypothesis, must suffer from the presence of the above logical fallacy, for the reason that it must be the deduced consequences *only* of the given hypothesis. But in the case of direct experience this difficulty does not arise, since what is being confirmed, is neither a deduction nor an hypothesis; when one legitimately confirms a datum of direct experience, such confirmation is final and complete. Naturally the verification must be legitimate and the proper safeguards must be taken against both phantasy and self-deception, either of a deliberate or of an unconscious kind; but these precautions are inherent in any correct investigation, scientific or other, and of course they apply equally here.

Now is it necessary to continue the formulation of the Method and to go on to a discussion of its second stage. Such activities are possible before one has fully mastered the first stage but they should never be undertaken (because they cannot be undertaken correctly) until sufficient ability has been gained in Self-Observation, Participation and Experiment to guarantee the pupil's verified objectivity in regard to himself, his organism and especially his emotional moods and fancies. This means that a genuine non-identification must have been established without doubt or question before the Method's second stage can be entered upon.

7.

The second stage of the Method consists in two difficult and easily distinguishable activities. The technical terms denoting these activities are Voluntary Suffering and Conscious Labor.

The first thing to be said about them is that, if they be engaged in prematurely, they will almost certainly become freakish facsimiles of the genuine activities denoted; instead of Voluntary Suffering there may arise a sort of twisted emotional asceticism even merging into the disease of altruism, and instead of the authentic results of Conscious Labor phantastic daydreams may be experienced which are the more dangerous since the subject, by an unnoticed error, may become convinced that his delusions constitute a direct insight into reality.

The defense against the first of these misfortunes is a true impartiality founded unshakeably upon a correct non-identification not only with the personalities of others but with the subject's own organic mechanism and his own personality. In the second case the safeguard is an impartial objectivity which cannot be satisfied in the absence of a proper confirmation by competent outside sources, viz., by other members of the group and especially by the group's leader. For these reasons it is plain that much prior work must have been done and its results can be carried out safely and successfully only in association with a correctly conducted group.

The beginning of Voluntary Suffering is the deliberate suppression of the symptoms of negative emotions in the presence of others. Examples of such emotions are anger, fear, jealousy, hatred, annoyance, exasperation and so on. An acquaintance with the organic symptoms of such emotions has already been obtained through Self-Observation; and some ability in their manipulation must have been acquired during the exercises of Experiment and the playing of roles.

This exercise in Voluntary Suffering is very easy to state but it is by no means so easy to accomplish. We are continually meeting those who, if for no other reason than type and physical polarity, are objectionable to us, as well as those who, although otherwise entirely acceptable, for some currently automatic reason provide a disagreeable confrontation. In such circumstances the pupil or candidate, even if angered and indeed boiling within, is to present an equable and pleasant outward appearance. For some this is easier than for others but for no one will it be accomplished without a genuine struggle, provided he has submitted himself to a real provocation. In fact a great deal of self-knowledge and a high degree of real non-identification are required if a perceptible success is to be gained.

In numerous cases such success will soon lead to an automatic modification of one's companion's behavior and thus to a mitigation of the disagreeable stimuli upon which the exercise is predicated. The current opportunity is then lost and another must be sought. For of course the purpose of this activity is neither the pleasure nor the supremacy of one's *vis-à-vis* nor is it the feat of altering the mechanical manifestations of the other person. The sole purpose is the creation of an intense internal emotional friction within the pupil himself, a friction in the heat of which indirect and subjective alterations may occur within him that otherwise are unobtainable. Some of these effects of Voluntary Suffering, such as that of intellectual clarification, seem at first to be unrelated to the activity, until we recall that understanding is a fusion of emotional and mental functioning and that this fusion can take place between them only at comparable degrees of intensity.

For this reason the activities of Voluntary Suffering and of Conscious Labor do not constitute separately successive steps of the Method's second stage but in a general way are to be engaged in simultaneously.

The beginning of Conscious Labor is Pondering. In the literal sense Pondering is weighing; it is the solution of problems by the intellectual weighing of their elements and concepts. Specifically it is *not* the acquirement of the sort of information *or* knowledge that can be gotten from books or from teachers; it is the formation of conclusions that are essentially one's own from all the data that one has, sensory, emotional, mentally associative, mentally formal, and all others. All of these data are not equally valuable to a final conclusion; their relative weighing is an integral part of the process. "Pondering is a self-interrogation which consists in stripping off all the answers of association successively until you finally come to your own essential answer." Pondering is answering questions from essence; and answering them practically. In the Oragean Version it was said: "A normal human being spends half his existence in pondering."

From this it appears that Pondering is quite the opposite of what is now called education, in which latter process hordes of items, some true, some half-true and many false, are memorized, accepted and repeated without any participation of the pupil himself but merely upon the insistence of some outside so-called authority. The results of such a process must of course be temporary and often irrelevant to the victim of them. But Pondering is the making of one's conclusions one's own; such conclusions will be at the least relatively permanent and final, in some cases they can be absolutely final.

The activity of correct Pondering is not easy nor is it a pleasant pastime; it is not random speculation nor is it haphazard daydream; it is serious and it is a very energetic activity. In this connection it was also said in the Oragean Version: "When the tempo of the third centre has been raised by a period of active pondering, then there must be a rest in order to allow the other centres to adjust themselves to the increased tempo."

As regards the first stage of the Method the subjects of the activities were persona; the results impersonal. In respect of Pondering the subjects of the activity are impersonal, the conclusions personal. What then are the proper subjects for Pondering? Here it may be of illustrative value to set out a list of headings, together with some hints and notations, proposed by Mr. Orage to one of his groups which was just beginning to engage in the activity. These will be presented just as they were taken down at the time:

"Subjects for Pondering"

1. Man
2. Sex
3. Consciousness
4. The World
5. The Universe
6. Nature
7. God
8. The Three Foods
9. The Three Bodies
10. Hypnotism
11. The Three Centres
12. The Method
13. Religion and Religions
14. Art
15. Science
16. Knowledge and Belief
17. The Three Forms of Reason
18. The Law of the Octave
19. The Law of the Three and the Law of the Seven
20. Individuality, Consciousness and Will
21. Essence and Personality
22. "I" and It
23. The Three Yogas
24. Force, Matter, Energy, Radiation, Emanation
25. Electricity
26. The Bible; and other Sacred Books
27. Good and Evil
28. Time
29. Incarnation and Reincarnation
30. Spiritualism
31. Objective Reason, Objective Conscience, Objective Art, Objective Science
32. Laws of Association

Some of the subjects here presented as items for Pondering will not be familiar to the reader and the list is given as an illustration of the kind of material that forms the subject-matter of the exercise of this function. In general anything can be the subject of Pondering which constitutes a human problem; all the items to be discussed in the chapter entitled The Greater Map offer opportunities for the activity now considered.

The complementary activities of Voluntary Suffering and Conscious Labor begin to produce the second conscious shock discussed in the preceding section, the final shock which permits the food octave of impressions to progress through its own obstacle-gap at the note, 'mi,' and to complete its evolution, the result of which is the formation of the third, or mental, body.

Correct Self-Observation of emotions, including negative ones, is the non-identified observation of their organic symptoms in one's own body. In respect of negative emotions it will be found that such Self-Observation in fact leads to the alterations of the symptoms and very shortly to the disappearance of the emotion itself. But negative emotion *per se*, considered without reference to the particular person who at the moment may be actualizing its organic symptoms, is an objective force of finite proportion existing at a given time and place; for instance, there is so much of it—no more and no less—within a given community or within a given nation at any selected time. This force must produce effects; in other words it must be expressed in the organic symptoms of the human beings composing the given group. Such expression does not diminish the quantity of negative force present which, when the energies of one personal victim have been exhausted in expressing it, moves on to another whose energies can be utilized in the same way. Over a reasonable period the quantity of negative emotion remains constant and its successive victims, far from possessing the self-justifications so eloquently urged in their later rationalizations, are in fact merely the instruments of an objective force that shakes them for a time and then passes on to another conveniently potential tool.

That the force of negative emotion does indeed remain relatively constant is to be seen with more than usual ease in wartime, when domestic conflicts sink to an unaccustomedly feeble level and most of the anger and hatred is turned away from the community itself and projected toward the common enemy; there is as much of it as ever but its victims are now manifesting it in a different direction.

However, there is quite another possibility than these mechanical ones for human beings and even for those who are so far only candidates for a human status. The Self-Observation of the organic symptoms of negative emotions not only alters the symptoms but destroys the emotional force itself. Every time this is done successfully by anyone, some portion of negative emotion is destroyed forever and its total quantity is by so much the less. This was the origin of the old Scottish term, sin-eating, originally a technical Christian term. Sin in this sense equals negative emotion; sin-eating equals the Self-Observation of the organic symptoms of negative emotion and thus the destruction of a unit of the negative emotion itself.

The deliberate and conscious suppression of the symptoms of negative emotion, especially in the presence of others, is an advanced exercise related to the above but to be distinguished from it. Its purpose is not the destruction of negative emotion but instead it is the utilization of the negative emotion for the purpose of creating an internal emotional friction of use and value to the candidate himself. In this way, when quite automatically he becomes the instrument of this objective force in his vicinity, he may gain a personal, human advantage and become the beneficiary of an impersonal objective phenomena rather than its victim. This is precisely the sort of way in which a correctly instructed human being can cleverly turn otherwise injurious objective phenomena, of a scale far greater than himself, to his own advantage.

The suppression of the organic symptoms of negative emotion is the beginning of Voluntary Suffering; Pondering is the beginning of Conscious Labor. Neither of them constitute the end or the completion of their respective exercises. But they do constitute the end of the discussion and of the subject so far as concerns the Oragean Version.

Two facts are responsible for this circumstance and no apology is offered for it, since a factual occurrence requires no apology. It might have been different but in fact it wasn't; and the two elements of the upshot should be taken in conjunction with each other. The first is that during the winter of 1930–1931 the groups conducted by Mr. Orage in New York City had not progressed beyond the point where any further instruction regarding the second conscious shock could be given to them; the second is that at this very time M. Gurdjieff personally disbanded the Orage groups and subsequently did his best to destroy the information previously imparted by Mr. Orage together with any results it may have had. Taken together, these two happenings provide an obviously adequate explanation as to why the Oragean Version stops at this point. It is not because there is no more to be said. It is because there was no further opportunity to say it.

The Method, however, had been formulated and its general outline was complete. This chapter concludes with that outline:

The Method

Stage I.   1. Self-Observation: a) First Centre, Sub-centre #1
b) First Centre, Sub-centre #2
c) First Centre, Sub-centre #3
d) First Centre, Sub-centres #1, #2, and #3

2. Participation: a) First Centre, Sub-centre #1
b) First Centre, Sub-centre #2
c) First Centre, Sub-centre #3
d) First Centre, Sub-centres #1, #2, and #3

3. Experiment: a) First Centre, Sub-centre #1
b) First Centre, Sub-centre #2
c) First Centre, Sub-centre #3
d) First Centre, Sub-centres #1, #2, and #3

Stage II.   1. Voluntary Suffering: a) suppression of symptoms of negative emotion
b) etc. ——————————

2. Conscious Labor: a) pondering
b) etc. ——————————

IV. THE GREATER MAP

To return to our simile of the maps of new continents of knowledge, we have now made some examination of the Local Map, the constitution of Man and of individual men, both in their present distorted and abnormal, essentially undeveloped condition and in the normal state of development which it is natural for men to attain. In the chapter entitled "The Boat" we outlined a practical method for the kind of practical work which will permit of the metamorphosis being at least begun from the first state to the second. This Method has not been carried through to completion, for its full and complete formulation does not exist in the Oragean Version, but enough has been stated to indicate the nature of the Fourth Way from the abnormal through the ordinary to the normal, a Way which offers a *possibility* to those candidates for fully human status who may be unable to proceed along any of the first three more usual paths of the yogi, the saint or the ascetic. It remains, of course, that to the reader the Fourth Way is now closed; should he attempt it by and for himself assisted by no more than the verbal information set forth in this treatise, he must *inevitably* go astray and end perhaps by losing all future possibility of his own advancement by this means. His only hope in this regard is either to discover for himself those who already are far ahead of him on this Way and who, for their own purposes, are willing to accept him as a pupil or else to await the most unlikely circumstance that such an opportunity may be offered to him. An instructor, objectively and correctly informed and competent, is absolutely necessary, and a group of others with whom to work, only a little less so. If he should search for these, his only safeguard against error and thus against irretrievable failure will be an unshakeable skepticism. These considerations are exceedingly unpleasant; they are also exceedingly true.

Meantime we may now consider some further aspects of the Local Map and then come finally to a preliminary consideration of the Greater Map, the outline of the Universe quite literally *sub specie aeternitatis*. For just as the pupil is informed ahead of time as to some of the specific novelties of perception in the state of Self-Consciousness, so some information as to the nature of Reality as perceived in a state of Cosmic Consciousness must be given in advance. Such items of information are merely descriptive, they are guide posts along the roads of a *terra incognita*, above all they are subjects for the activity here called Pondering. They are formulations not to be believed but, instead, later to be confirmed, when and if the reader is ever in a position to confirm them.

These aspects of the Greater Map are part of the Hidden Knowledge of genuine Schools and, as such, they derive directly from those who have *normally* experienced Cosmic Consciousness and have been able to report without distortion concerning it. But of course no one can properly know for himself that this is possible until for himself he is able to experience the same, and thus for the latter they must remain at present hints and suggestions only. Moreover, although the truths expressed are undistorted, the means of formulating them must itself contain a measure of distortion because they must be so put as to be at least partially intelligible to those who are still literally asleep, i.e., to those who as yet are at or in a lower state of consciousness than that in which such items are fully and immediately perceptible. What this means is that they are true but can be only partially true in the terms in which they must now be put.

So for the present the value of such statements does not lie in any dogmatic "truth" allegedly inhering in them. The value is twofold: first, that they present formulations deriving from a viewpoint unaccustomed to us and that they thus present us with novel information; and second, that they supply us with data concerning which our own conclusions, deeply pondered, are worth our own individual efforts to us. It is this last aspect that renders their presentation genuinely important to each of us, without the slightest prejudgment regarding the final opinion we may entertain in respect of any of them at the end of our pondering. No matter what their (as yet undetermined) validity, they offer us an authentic opportunity.

But before we come to these larger and more universal matters, let us consider a number of further details of the Local Map, items concerning mankind and men on this planet.

2.

As previously remarked, what we know today as the science of psychology can deal with human beings only as they in fact are now, for it has no other specimens to examine. Moreover, to such an extent does it lack any concept of the human standard or paradigm that it often miscalls the distorted, the undeveloped and the abnormal, the normal; for it reaches this unscientific self-contradiction by the tabulation of averages or medians from the actual laboratory subjects with which in fact it must deal. In such circumstances manifestly we cannot look to the modern psychologist for correct information in regard to the nature of the human being as such.

The A-type knowledge deriving from genuine Schools does not suffer from the above inconveniences but instead possesses information concerning the standard pattern or design of that being or creature which is called human; and thus it can both describe the characteristics of the normal or fully matured man and can also distinguish in what respects any given man may depart from the normal of his kind. Quite a number of such propositions are open to immediate investigation. That no efforts are made to examine them with a view to possible confirmation by ordinary means, certainly does not demonstrate that these propositions are incorrect; it merely shows that at the present time we have no psychological science competent to examine even its own fundamental subject matter.

For instance, it is stated here that the human being, in his normal state, comprises a trinity of three equally active forces, the positive, the negative and the neutralizing. These may be specified as the positive factor—experience; the negative factor—the end products of neural functioning in a physical body; and the neutralizing factor—consciousness or the pure ability of awareness, which by its patterning transformation of the negative factor creates the positive factor. Then what or who am "I"? This word, "I," denotes the ultimate subjectivity associated with the threefold integration just described, "I" am not a soul, even potentially, for "I" can never become a soul; the word, soul, is properly to be applied to a potential body, just as physical in its own terms as the biological organism with which we are even now vaguely acquainted. Such a soul-body can and does exist, but not in the cases of the sort of undeveloped human beings we customarily meet on this planet; and naturally it cannot be acquired by means of mere emotional aspiration or solely by religious fervor. It is to be noted that no doctrine of any one of the original Religions has ever stated that ordinary men possess souls; and the demonstrable absence of such a possession is sufficient evidence of any given man's abnormality, for normally and fully developed men do and must have souls.

But we can go further and show more clearly from the preceding analysis in what way men as we know them here, are abnormal. Investigation suggests that the positive and negative factors constituting them are more or less active in varying degree but also that the neutralizing factor of consciousness is almost totally passive, responding only sluggishly, incompletely and mechanically to the stimuli furnished by the end products of the physical organism's neurology. In the fully literal sense these human beings are asleep; they are in the sleep-walking, sleep-talking, sleep-experiencing condition somewhat ludicrously known to us as the waking state. It is basically the unnatural passivity of "I," reflected accurately and minutely in the neutralizing factor of consciousness, which renders the ordinary man an abnormal human being.

It is these same three forces that in a practical sense permit us to distinguish between a normal human action and an abnormal one. A normal action of this kind must serve three purposes simultaneously, an intellectual, an emotional and a practical purpose. In other words it must express the proper and equal functioning of the three sub-centres of the First Centre: it must subserve a correct mental judgment, it must mediate a normal emotional response and it must accomplish a practically valuable end. It must do all of this at once. The candidate is first instructed to observe how far short his own actions fall from this norm and later to experiment in attempting to perform at least some actions approximating to this definition of normal behavior which, it will be seen, has only a partial reference to any ethical standards.

Moreover, in the normal case there is a defined sequence in the behavioral appearance of these three factors, which the pupil will soon observe to be reversed in his own case as well as in those of the persons about him. The human standard of action is to come first to a correct conclusion, then to reinforce this conclusion by the relevantly normal emotion and finally to perform successfully the act so initiated. But our actual sequences are quite the opposite: first we mechanically act in some automatically predetermined way, then we experience some or other emotion which itself is the result of the action already performed and finally we go to sometimes great lengths in order to rationalize what has in fact occurred and so to justify to ourselves what may seem at first glance—and what really is—unjustifiable. Our performances, thus observed, no longer seem to be normal even to ourselves.

It has been said that the way to the normal is *from* the extraordinary *through* the ordinary. Let us see what this means. Our planet is plentifully supplied with extraordinary persons—the frenetic maestro in the field of art, the egregious prodigy of science who recurrently claims that no more than ten other living men can understand his tremendous thoughts, the overpowering athlete who excels all others in half a dozen different sports, and that greatest monstrosity of all, the distorted societal dictator. But all of them, sanely considered, are monstrosities; even in the fields where their activities are entirely legitimate, the intense exaggeration of one kind of ability is gained and exercised only *at the expense* of those other properly human abilities whose total and mutual balance is the natural characteristic of man. The geniuses, and in general all extraordinary persons, are not superior to ordinary men but instead they are twistedly and abnormally inferior.

Can we then say that the ordinary person is a normal man? No, this can no more be said than can the same statement be made of a person of forty whose intellect, emotions and physical development are arrested and fettered at a five-year-old level. What was altogether normal at one stage, is no longer normal now that that stage has been passed; the ordinary man is "more" normal than the extraordinary because in his case there is at least a semblance of functional balance; but the development of the typical human functions remains at an infantile stage. First there must be integration and balance, then there must be functional development while at the same time the mutual balance is maintained. The ordinary man is not only the luckier but as a candidate for humanity he is far the more likely to succeed, for in his case the first step is at least partially completed and phantastic life-purposes of competitive "ambition" need not be uprooted and overturned.

But the ordinary man has more than far enough to go, for he experiences sympathy rather than compassion in his emotional life; he possesses personality rather than individuality; in place of conscience there is a vacuum; and his behavior is determined rather by suggestibility than by conviction. These matters, too, merit a brief exposition.

Although sympathy and compassion have the same philological meaning, the one being derived from the Greek and the other from the Latin, in this Version they are respectively and technically defined as feeling-with and feeling-for. Thus when one experiences sympathy toward an unfortunate or injured companion, there is manifested a high degree of identification with the other person and the fright and suffering thereby stimulated are preponderantly not toward the injured person but toward oneself, through the imaginary assumption of what one would oneself feel in the same or similar circumstances. Incompetence is typical of sympathy and little remedy results from it for the actual misfortune that has occurred.

Compassion is feeling-for and in this experience the attention is directed fully upon the other person with little or no introspective awareness of self. Compassion is the adequate stimulus to action; one then does not place oneself in the other person's position but instead one uses all one's ability in order to devise some plan, and then to carry it into execution, to ameliorate the situation. Sympathy is impractical, compassion is practical; with the latter, even if no complete solution be attainable, at least the possibility of one arises. Sympathy, which is really a form of self-centred sentimentality and which is at the bottom of much of the "liberal" degeneracy whereby societies are destroyed on behalf of the poor, the weak and the incompetent, is representative of the emotions of the abnormal ordinary man. Compassion, whereby a distress is clearly and *coldly* seen and a truly practical remedy put in train, is sympathy's normal counterpart. For this reason surgeons, who know themselves to be ordinary men, customarily ask others to operate upon their near relatives, lest an abnormal sympathy for the patient under the knife cause a hand to tremble and disaster to take place; but a surgeon, caught in the desperate situation where only he is available and who then can competently extract a bullet from close beside his young son's heart, has shown that he is capable of compassion.

Personality is abnormal, individuality normal. The greater and the more outstanding the personality, the less the genuine individuality. Personality is what has been done to us by environment, by those external circumstances that have no particular relation or relevance to ourselves; it is what was once expressed by the wailing (and very popular) song entitled You Made Me What I Am Today, I Hope You're Satisfied. Individuality is what we ourselves are. Essence is the beginning of individuality. But essence is arrestedly childish, it is overlaid, encrusted and buried by personality, and only when it has been freed and has grown and normally matured, can individuality be attained. When a fully developed individuality has destroyed the counterfeit of personality, a human being emerges.

Conscience is one of the most basically misunderstood words in our language. Its relation to the feeling of guilt is indirect and in the main incorrect. A feeling of guilt, or of "sin," is not conscience; it is merely the substitute for conscience which occurs in those incapable of the authentic experience. Conscience is the simultaneous experience of all one's emotions. But in the case of the abnormally ordinary man it is not realized, until Self-Observation has been carried forward to a considerable extent, how self-contradictory and mutually destructive are whole hordes of these emotions; even with regard to the same subject or toward the same person mutually very incompatible emotions are entertained. To experience these all at once and at the same time would instate an unbearable suffering that literally cannot be borne, and so all sorts of automatic stratagems (such as differing personalities of one's own) are employed so that the discordant emotions may each have their own day, as it were. These successive appearances and re-appearances of unreconcilable emotions are exactly and by definition the *absence* of conscience. And the feeling of guilt is no more and no less than the result of the inadequate suppression of emotion A while its opposing emotion B is holding the stage. Far from connoting any human virtue a sense of "sin" is one of the best evidences of human abnormality. It is also a stigma of the ordinary man, for the latter, with all his self-contradictions boiling within him, must be the victim of correspondingly dissident emotions in respect of which the only supportable possibility is to keep them successively separated. That this cannot always be done with entire success, results in the arising of that surrogate of conscience, a feeling of guilt. A genuine conscience can no more be achieved directly or by wishing for one than can a soul-body; it can be only when the human being has so far and so normally developed that his emotions are already *in fact* harmoniously human, that he can be able to experience their concord simultaneously. That is conscience, a symptom of human normality.

From personality and conscience the matter of objective dream is not so far distant. The Waking state, in which personality manifests (and conscience does not), is itself a kind of dream state, for only in the condition of Self-Consciousness is a man truly awake. All one's experiences of everything exterior to himself as well as interior come to him in fact through his bodily mechanism and only in the self-conscious state is he sufficiently aware of what is actually going on in respect of his body, to be called properly awake. But in the so-called Waking state itself a man is indeed, even though vaguely, in contact with an objective external reality; this distinguishes his experiences from those of nocturnal, purely subjective dream and thus the waking state may be denoted as being characterized by *objective* dream. The manifestations of one's own personalities, as they currently replace each other, form parts of such objective dream.

But so do the manifestations of other persons, themselves objectively different from the subject. And this circumstance, in the very course of an abnormally restricted consciousness, presents an opportunity for valuable work in connection with the Open Secret. For these other persons, although objectively disparate, are not in fact so utterly different from oneself and in the state of objective dream they may be seen as exterior objectifications of oneself, as portraying now one and now another of one's own personality complexes. Mr. Smith (when you see him) may be acting out in public one of your own multiple-personalities and, a little later, Mr. Jones may be manifesting for you—and for everyone else in the vicinity—another. In this way other people create for you an objective mirror in which may be seen concretely, in the reality of objective dream, the actual portrayal of one after another of your own personalities. It requires a certain shrewdness and a certain degree both of experience and of non-identified impartiality to be able to select the instances accurately, but there are more of them than you at first suspect. It is not "there but for the grace of God go I"; but instead it is "there I go, once yesterday and maybe twice tomorrow." For objective dream is circular and, within your own limited range of personalities, you may be sure that they will repeat and repeat and repeat. The ordinary man does not change inwardly; he follows faithfully his own small repertoire of automatic roles from so-called maturity constantly till death. Only an evolution of consciousness can alter our automatic roles by the gradual technique of changing them into conscious roles and, if one begins this work as an ordinary man, he can count upon his personality-characteristics remaining constant for a long, long time. This matter of objective dream, however, demonstrates again the value of other people to us, a value so great that nothing else can take its place successfully.

To return to the contrast between the ordinary and the normal man, the former is continually influenced by personal suggestibility whereas the latter's behavior is governed by individual conviction. With an undeveloped essence and a personality formed by haphazard circumstance the ordinary man lacks the possibility of his own firmly rooted realizations achieved by his own efforts alone and thus he comes more and more to rely upon outside suggestions furnished by other people. Here is a case wherein others are *not* valuable to one. Moreover, the tendency toward outside suggestion has been reinforced since earliest childhood by the abnormalities of what nowadays is mis-called education, in which the student is required to learn by rote all sorts of information, and of misinformation also, and is passed along from grade to school grade by reason of his successful repetition of this so-called learning. The scandal is such that an instructor becomes famous if even a few of his pupils have by chance (and in opposition to the general trend) learned to think for themselves, whereas the acquirement of such an ability is one of the simplest and most taken-for-granted elements of any genuine education at all. But under the ordinary conditions of the ordinary man there is seldom a trace of it to be found; as in youth he repeated the admonitions of his teachers, so in later life he repeats those of self-serving politicians and propagandists of the most outrageous nonsense and he lives in an intellectual atmosphere of (to him) plausible suggestibility. No standards, no morals, nothing of this kind is his own; all his views on little subjects and on great are the accumulated and often slyly provided property of others. The contrast is the normally developed human being, who has made the happenings of his own experience the subjects of his own pondering and thus has come to his own conclusions concerning their significance—who has welcomed information, to be sure, but who has pondered that information both as to its truth and as to its falsity, never accepting what may not be knowledge at all, in capsules or in tin cans or in predigested form. Such a man is insusceptible to suggestibility; he possesses tested and ultimate convictions.

In this connection I remember an experience of my own, very relevant to the present topic. Having taken dinner one evening with Mr. Orage and then proceeding with him in a taxi to one of his meetings, he suddenly remarked: "It is necessary to make these things your own, so that you may never need to rely upon others for them. You must be prepared, for example, to hear Gurdjieff himself deny the validity of the Method." As the taxi just then deposited us both upon the curb, I contented myself with a rather smug smile, since I had then been acquainted practically with the Method for quite a number of years. As it turned out, although very much later, this was one of the almost unheard-of occasions upon which my smugness was justified; eventually Gurdjieff did repudiate the Method, but without causing the slightest alteration either in my own understanding of it or in my complete assurance both of its validity and its effectiveness. About the latter I really knew; and it was perhaps my first experience of a final and authentic conviction.

Since the question of morals has been raised shortly above, this may be a good place in which to mention morality and the attitude of the Oragean Version toward it. As to all forms of current morality, Christian or any other, they are considered to be purely subjective, to be distortions of the original and genuine doctrines in every case, in short to be the productions of the abnormalities of the undeveloped ordinary man. The instances of the various anti-moralities are of course only the worse. The stigma of all these codes is their ingrained relativity, showing us plainly that none of them can be a genuinely *human* code; for in them what is moral here, is immoral there, and that which is good or bad at one time, is found to be alternately bad or good at another. To the other hand there is such a thing as Objective Morality, valid and true for all human beings at all times; and it is to this alone that a normal human being owes his allegiance. This code of Objective Morality comprises five moral principles but of them Orage could never be brought to say very much, being of the opinion that his pupils were not far enough advanced to be able to refrain, if verbally acquainted with them, from distorting them subjectively. Only the first of these principles did he ever formulate exactly, to the best of this writer's knowledge. The first principle of Objective Morality is this: Keep your physical body in its highest degree of health. That is the first duty of a normal human being.

Closely allied with this subject is the admonition: Do not permit your brain-systems (mind) to be soiled. How does one soil one's mind? The two chief means are through phantasy and sentimentality. Not through the admission of phantastic or sentimental data, for that is inevitable under our conditions and cannot be avoided; but by the reinforcement of such data from within, a reinforcement deriving from some personal distortion of our own. The delusions of Christian Science, the phantasies of bugaboo Psychoanalysis, the sentimentalities directed toward the lazy, the thriftless and the ill-disposed are cases in point. To these and other data like them it is not well to accord a comfortable and self-calming welcome, for they soil the mind and distort its operations. Against such incursions a normal man remains naturally on guard, for how shall his body be healthy when his mind (brain-system) is malfunctioning?

Aside from the specific subject of morality and in regard to religion in general the viewpoint of the Oragean Version is that of a much earlier organization, which formulated its attitude thus: There is no religion, there is only one God.

No discussion of the ordinary man can be adequate without some mention of the Comfort Bed. There is an old tale from a lost civilization far older than our own and even more fully equipped with gadgets; and it is related that the utmost triumph of this great culture was the production of the Comfort Bed. It could be purchased at one fell swoop and thereafter the buyer had no further worries. He simply lay down on the contrivance and from then on everything was accomplished for him: all his needs were attended to quite automatically, such as feeding, excretion, an intermittent cleanly washing, sexual requirements and everything else that could be desired, and in the end the contraption even gave him a decent burial. His existence was thus totally passive, without the necessity for any effort whatever, and this ingenious invention permitted its owner to live mechanically in the fullest sense. Depending, of course, upon what is meant by the verb, to live.

We can appreciate this situation the better since in our own time, although we have yet to achieve the completed instrument, we are already well on the way. To add up the number of mechanical gadgets whereby our trip through life is eased, would involve a considerable mathematical sum—electric fans and heaters, busses, trains, private automobiles, mechanical dishwashers, clothes washers, dryers, stoves equipped with automatic timers, oil and gas furnaces, air conditioning outfits, dehumidifiers, power tools and jacks, Flit and DDT, self-opening garage doors, automatic farming machinery of innumerable kinds, to mention only a few of these appurtenances, and as a matter of course those twin conditioners to a tawdry vulgarity, the radio and television set, the former naturally equipped with an alarm clock. Obviously the answer to all this is not some back-to-nature fad whereby the machines are all to be scrapped; they are part of our present environment and the thing to do is not to destroy them but to relegate them to their proper place in our scheme of practical affairs. But the greater the number of these artifices that are produced, the happier is the ordinary man, for are not all of them "labor-saving" devices and are we therefore not gradually approaching the time when no efforts at all will be required? Of the same sort is the ordinary man's craving for "social security" and indeed for security of any and every kind, so that he will no longer have to take care of himself but may rely upon the government to force someone else to do so. Surely all this is about as humanly abnormal as may be and to sane reflection it will look less like a fuller life than a negation of any life at all. But not to the ordinary man, for under the conditions he himself has created for himself the Comfort Bed is actually a serious ideal. It saves his labor. But for what?

Indeed this insane exaggeration of "labor-saving" desires is far closer to death than to life. No corpse works at all. And many more ordinary men than is supposed, are walking about dead while their physical mechanisms still move; not only have they never developed normally either emotionally or mentally but presently in these two respects they have died in unconscious atrophy while automatic bodily habits yet give them a remaining appearance of lethargic, treadmill life. It is possible to die while still "alive" and the man in whom nothing functions or remains even mechanically active except the first sub-centre of his first centre, is literally dead though moving. To our somewhat naïve sophisticates the "undead" or zombies represent a scorned superstition of less literate (but perhaps more knowledgeable?) folk. For the "undead" do not return to Hungarian castles nor are the true zombies parading Haitian jungles; they are right in New York City, on Fifth Avenue, on Wall Street, in Harlem and the Bronx, and especially along Broadway. Have you seen them, with their vacant eyes, their lax lips, their strained and uncontrollable absorption? These are truly monsters.

The superstition is just the other way around, for those who scorn zombies, which really exist, have been known to report ghosts, which do not. It is certain that no one who has died physically returns; even the Christ did not. The latter case is of quite a different kind: it is in fact possible for a fully normal Man, who of course possesses a fully developed and incarnated body Kesdjan (or astral), deliberately to render it perceptible to those in turn far enough developed and close enough to him to have undergone the entirely naturalistic rites of blood brotherhood with him. Such was the phenomenon of the "resurrection" as alleged and as it could quite naturally have occurred; miracle-mongering Christians are mistaken, there was no marvel involved.

But while we speak of death, let us recognize the significance of the fact that we know about it. Animals do not know, they have no hint of the circumstance that inevitably each of them must die; and who among us would be so cruel as to inform them, even were it possible? Yet perhaps for us that means something, even though we strive so earnestly to render ourselves pseudo-animals by concealing our knowledge from ourselves and attempting to forget it by every means at our disposal. So pitiable a strategem is no less than the ultimate cowardice of evasion. We know that we shall die but we do not know when. In the Oragean Version this results in two preceptual corollaries. Do not succumb to the Disease of Tomorrow, i.e., do not put off doing what is to be done. And it's opposite: live every day as if it were your last. Maybe it is.

Let it not be supposed, however, that this is an invitation to useless worry. Worry is one of those negative emotions just so much of which is always around and, if the ordinary man is not worrying about something really threatening, then he does the same with regard to some imaginary threat. But in neither case is the worry justifiable and it is a typical symptom of the ordinary instead of the normal. Worry uses up more energy than does work; a normal human being works but never worries. If the menace is simply imaginary, it is plainly a waste to fret over it, and this is likewise true if the menace be a real one. If the latter be the case, then the normal thing to do is to plan first how to meet it and then at once set about putting that plan into effect so far as may prove possible. To worry, initially wastes your energy and thus renders you the more incapable of reaching a solution but, worst of all, this very worrying substitutes for and stands in place of the practical action that alone can rescue the worrier. There is a valuable exercise to try some day: when you find yourself worrying about something, force yourself to state the problem clearly and do not permit yourself to do anything else until you have taken some practical step to solve it. Both the energy saved and the satisfaction gained may come as a surprise, and also the realization as to how much of both are habitually lost.

Such an exercise, of course, will not accomplish the solution of a problem that in fact is insoluble; and there can be problems of that kind, for which no solution exists. In such a case the problem remains until the sentence, as it were, has been served and Orage used to refer to a person in so unfortunate a position as one who confronted a term of Penal Servitude. But since nothing can actually be done about it, what is to be gained by worry? In this case, too, once the situation has been accurately gauged and the conclusion finally established without any doubt, the best program is still resolutely to dismiss any further worrying about it and thus to refrain from adding a useless energy drain to the misfortune of the case. The passage of time itself may later alter the circumstances and thus a periodic review is advisable, culminating in the exercise last mentioned in the preceding paragraph.

This exercise, which is typical of the emphasis placed upon practical activities by the Oragean Version, is not to be confused with the deliberate suppression of the physical symptoms of negative emotions (which latter is one of the exercises in Voluntary Suffering, a quite different matter). Worry is a negative emotion, true enough, but the present suggestion is not simply to suppress its physical symptoms; instead, the suggestion is to do away with the worry entirely. That is accomplished by utilizing the underlying apprehension for its proper purpose, viz., to initiate such relevant action as will destroy the worry by removing its cause. In this process the negative emotion of worry is transformed into the positive emotional motive for action, its negativity being manifestly destroyed by the transformation. Thus, getting rid of worries by doing something about them affects behavior, but only indirectly, whereas the direct suppression of its physical symptoms (an altogether differently aimed exercise) can never remove the original cause. Except as a conscious and fully non-identified experiment or exercise, behavior should never be changed deliberately; watch it, observe it and let it alter of itself; all other change is spurious and self-destructive because for any but a completely normal man it will involve inevitably the taint of reform and will bring with it more dangerous, since unrecognized, ills than the original behavior itself contained.

Among the threefold functions of human beings there is a trinity possessing both normal and abnormal aspects, the latter as usual being due to premature or undeveloped activity. The names given to this triad are Faith, Hope and Love; they are basic human functions and of course, along with their normality, there goes their distortion in the instance of the ordinary man. In an allegedly ancient document written by a Saint of times long past these functions are analyzed in accordance with the degree or level of their manifestation; the excerpt is part of a longer formulation entitled "The Terror of the Situation" and runs as follows—

The Faith of Consciousness is Freedom
     of Feeling is Weakness
     of Body is Stupidity

The Hope of Consciousness is Strength
      of Feeling is Slavery
      of Body is Illness

The Love of Consciousness includes the same response
      of Feeling includes the opposite response
      of Body depends merely upon type and polarity

In more modern times we might transpose this formulation for clarity as follows:

Conscious Faith is Freedom
Emotional Faith is Weakness
Physical Faith is Stupidity

Conscious Hope is Strength
Emotional Hope is Slavery
Physical Hope is Illness

Conscious Love evokes Love in return
Emotional Love evokes Hatred in return
Physical Love is a function of physical type and electrical polarity

From these analyses it will be seen that the mentioned functions are not, as they are often supposed to be, merely of an emotional character; they are more complex and emotion is but one aspect of their full scale, by itself an abnormal aspect. Here again we observe the abnormality of the ordinary man, for he is ordinarily confined to the lowest level of such functions and, when sometimes he rises to the middle level, he remains not much better off. Faith as Freedom, Hope as Strength, Reciprocal Love, these are for the normal, the fully developed human being.

Because we are not normal but because, instead, we are ordinary men, all these three terms are vague and little understood by us. Even to appreciate that physical or practical faith is credulity, is often difficult for us and of the kind of faith that is legitimate, normal and conscious we have no experience nor with it any acquaintance. The same may be said of hope but with love perhaps we can come to a little better understanding.

It is not impossible for us to realize that the yearning to possess another's body and our delight in such possession is a case of infatuation rather than of genuine love and that then the focus, as in the similar example of sympathy, is upon ourselves and not upon the other person. Here, too, we can see without too much difficulty that the whole thing is stimulated by a mutually compatible balance of internal physical secretions and that it results from

IV. THE GREATER MAP

the physical circumstance that two or more physical organisms are attuned to each other in a complicated but nonetheless no more than an electro-chemical fashion. For this kind of love we shall not be surprised to learn that the Moon is a powerful ally, a fact that has been recognized in story, song and poetry for ages past.

The case in regard to emotional love is by no means so clearly under-stood; and indeed by those who affect to be above the merely physical va-riety, love is frequently applauded as the highest of all emotions. There is a confusion here, occasioned by a misty realization of the nature of conscious love, which enters into the concept the emotionalist is trying to express and, mixing in with the basic emotional connotation, imports a final contradic-tion into his idea. There is, however, no question as to the practical conse-quence of emotional love, for we see it before our eyes all the time. People, who speak of love being akin to hatred, are in fact referring to emotional love and in fact, in that respect, they are quite right. Of that sort of love jeal-ousy is an inevitable counterpart; and although typical of the ordinary he-man and she-woman and often a vaunted characteristic, jealousy is among the most abnormal and degraded emotions experienced by undeveloped hu-mans. In it the entire attention is upon oneself as possessor and this totally unbecoming and disreputable possession of another person's body or simply of another person's attractive personality becomes a force motivating false-hood, treachery and crime. A jealous man (or woman) is, without qualifica-tion, an emotionally diseased creature. This is perhaps the worst aspect of emotional love, but there are others; and the sign and stigma of all of them are self-love masquerading as the love of others. Thus arise those parodies of genuine love called altruism and sentimentality, in which the poor, the weak and the unfortunate are coddled ostensibly for their own benefit (although coddling has never benefitted *anyone*) but really for the self-glorification or for some other purely selfish advantage of the sentimentalist. Emotional love is somewhat unlovely.

Yet once in a long while and probably to most of us there comes at least a glimpse of Conscious or Objective Love. Occasionally there is a lover who can give up the beloved for the latter's own benefit, even though this may cause the lover almost unbearable suffering—and we have caught one such glimpse. Most unusual, to be sure, and for most of us ordinary men such an action is literally beyond our undeveloped powers; for us what little experi-ence we may have of genuine, i.e., objective, love comes from our relations with our animal pets, with Rover or Tabby or even with a pet canary for whom we may perform services without any hope or the slightest intention of obtaining either personal reward or recompense. It is another glimpse. Orage used often to repeat the exchange between the man who said, "I love you!" and the girl who replied, "Strange. That I feel none the better for it." Women better than men intuitively know this difference, for Conscious Love is always giving, it is never getting; and the extent of the giving is limited only by the degree of the love.

Having just seen how an undue preponderance of emotion can vitiate Objective Love, let us consider now the nature of Objective Art. A tremendous number of ordinary men and women are engaged in art, either as practitioners or as gallery; and what is art? If we would think for a moment of the plain meaning of our words and of the roots from which they come, there would be much less confusion on this, and other, subjects. Art is artifice; it is the production of an effect or the conveyance of a meaning by deliberately invented, artificial means. These means include everything such as craftsmanship and the manipulation of materials from wood and stone to sound, and on their higher reaches they include also the detailed knowledge that can produce a designed, predictable and effective result upon other human beings.

Self-expression has nothing to do with art, for there is seldom any self involved worth expressing; in any but one case out of a hundred thousand self-expression is mere impertinence, not art. Nor has emotion anything to do with art except as the arousing of emotion in the observer may be an intended (and effective) aim. An emotional artist is a contradiction in terms, for the legitimate purpose of genuine art is the illumination of truth through the emotional experience *of the recipient*, not of the artist. And above all, art is not sensory tickling which, carried to a sufficient length, becomes something else entirely, no matter upon what sensation it is focused; it becomes masturbation. Sensual enjoyment is no more a function of genuine art than is a false emotional happiness.

The-universality-of-art is not a meaningless phrase, although its meaning is often turned upside down. Its correct significance is that, for humans, art must be human art; in other words it must be such as to affect human beings by reason of their membership in the human species and for that very cause it must be able to affect *all* beings who, even though undeveloped, may still be called human properly. The state of development will naturally determine the degree of effect but there must be *some* of the *intended* effect upon everyone. In order to qualify as a work of genuine art it is not enough that Mr. Jones should "appreciate" Tchaikovsky or that a portion of the inhabitants of Paris should applaud Matisse or that the citizens of Scandinavia should give their approbation to modern "functional" architecture. None of this renders any of the productions examples of real art. And in general any so-called artistic production which depends for its understanding upon the previous necessity of learning some factitious code in connection with it may be said to be spurious in relation to genuine art. It is not necessary to learn anything—nor is it necessary to be a Chinese or a Caucasian or a Negro or an Indian—in order to realize that one has been slapped in the face. Objective Art is just as objective as that.

It will now commence to be seen how great a human being the true artist must be. He must know the human organism so minutely as to be able to guarantee the effects (and that there shall be no other than the intended ones) of the sensory stimuli with which he proposes to confront it and he must know how to arrange those stimuli in a design, both simultaneous and progressively continuing, such as will produce the emotional result he wishes; finally he must know how to *re*-mind his auditor or observer by these means, not of some personal whim or distortion of his own which only some of them may share, but of a missed fact or a forgotten relationship that is universally and humanly true. And for that purpose he must be of such stature as already to have realized this truth for himself. The genuine artist is much greater than the scientist, because it is demanded that he must have been a genuine scientist first. Real and detailed knowledge is only a prerequisite of his profession and part of its technique; he need also be a human being so far developed normally as to have achieved some realization of those truths which it is the function of art to illuminate.

Are there any extant examples of art as great as this, i.e., of Objective Art? The Great Pyramid is such an example in architecture. No human being of any race can stand before it and remain unaffected, unless of course he deliberately withholds his attention in order to score a debating point. It is necessary actually to be in the presence of a work of art in order to receive an impression from it but, with this exception, all humans will receive from the Great Pyramid what their own degree of development may permit them to receive; and as they develop further, they will receive more. Even now to the architect it is a marvel of construction, to the mathematician a compendium of true mathematical relationships, to the astronomer an atlas of the heavens, to the psychologist who can read it, a handbook of correct human function, even to the aesthete it is not just a void. To the undeveloped human being it can give the hope engendered by its record that development has been once at least achieved and to the normal man it can present a comprehensive review of his struggles and his path. It is indeed a work of Objective Art, universal in its effects.

About us, in the creeds, the sects and the distortions of modern Christianity, lie the fragments of another work of Objective Art—the life of Christ, so it has been said. According to that account the story of the Christ, a messenger of God upon this planet, was and is Objective Drama, played not on a stage but *in life* by the Essene initiate, Jesus. This play had its origin far earlier, in ancient Egypt, as the drama of the life, death and resurrection of Ausar (Osiris), the God-in-Man; its function was to present ultimate human truths through the medium of consciously acted roles. For centuries, we are told, the later Essene Brotherhood, a School itself deriving from Egyptian origins, had held the aim of presenting this drama in life rather than as a prescribed mystery play and for generations had trained its postulants to that end. Eventually the cast of thirteen was complete with Jesus, who had been sent to Egypt for temple training there, cast as the leading actor and Judas, who must play the next most difficult role, that of the betrayer, fully prepared for his part. With the necessary modifications demanded by the local scene and times, the action began.

It is difficult for us to appreciate the magnitude of such an undertaking. The immediate audience is also, without knowing it, the unconscious part of the cast and the conscious actors must not only fulfill the requirements of their own roles, thereby objectively demonstrating the truths they have self-selected themselves to manifest, but in addition they must consciously and deliberately so affect their unconscious counterparts (the priests and money-changers at the temple, Pontius Pilate, the Jewish mob, the Roman soldiers, and all the rest) that the latter are forced to enact their own roles, too. Even with all possible preparations made beforehand, it may well be imagined what hitches in the performance unforeseen and unpredictable circumstances must threaten and what consummate ability must be required in order to meet these difficulties and keep the drama upon its course. No comparable type of acting, the playing so successfully of conscious roles upon the objective stage of real life, has ever been reported. This was Objective Art.

There is said also to be some very ancient Chinese music of an objective kind and likewise some remnants of color-work and sculpture still surviving, in the Near East; but to most of us these are inaccessible. The only survivals in our own Western civilization are again architectural, the original or earliest medieval cathedrals, Notre Dame, Reims, Chartres. According to tradition a genuine School stood behind these, initiated their conception, planned their design, directed and utilized the actual constructional work as a training of the postulants. The earliest cathedrals of this kind are symbols in stone, serving many associated purposes among which not the least is the architectural formulation of true and objective information not itself concerned with architecture but rather with cosmic characteristics of the Universe and of man. Thus each of the gargoyles, for example, originally had a specifically descriptive reference to particular emotional distortions or negative emotions to be found in man, and the level of the building upon which they appeared as well as their individual and collective relation to the whole structure was of objective significance.

Such detailed knowledge was later lost, although even today in minor and mostly insignificant ways Christian churches still retain certain crude survivals of symbolic design in transept, nave, and so on. When normal development is lost, so is correct knowledge and its representation; modern churches are our degressed reminders that in the original medieval cathedrals it was meticulous, detailed and accurate. For certainly that kind of art is not produced today in a civilization regulated of, by and for the ordinary abnormal man and in which the normally developed human being has no part. Perhaps it is not surprising that our "artists" are so "sensitive" and that they raise so loudly self-approving an uproar; they are ordinary men frantically pretending to a greatness so far beyond them that the very definition of Objective Art is inconceivable to them.

Nevertheless we have today what passes as art among ordinary men; how shall we characterize this product and place it in a purely objective relationship to what genuine art has been and may be? For this purpose it will be illustrative to take Literature, which is accepted to be one of the arts, and for the sake of simplicity to consider only Prose Literature.

Objectively this art may be divided into three main categories, respectively scripture, prose and journalism. The lowest category is Journalism, which is no more than the report of facts; if the report is accurate, it is good journalism and if inaccurate, it is poor or bad. To skip now to the highest form of Prose Literature, this may be analyzed into Major Scripture and Minor Scripture. Both take as their subject and content the relation of man to the Universe and the aim of the first is to produce intellectual illumination and an ecstasy of understanding while the second takes as its object the evocation of cosmic emotion. As to Prose, it too, is separated into Major and Minor forms which together are concerned with the relation of man to man and of men to men, Major Prose being characterized by reflection and Minor Prose by sentimentality. Here it will be seen that the analysis is made on the basis of subject-matter and treatment, as affording us an objective foundation for judgment respecting any given piece of writing; and on such a scale it must be admitted that very little contemporary Prose Literature ever rises above the levels of Journalism or of Minor Prose and that any kind of Scripture is manifestly absent.

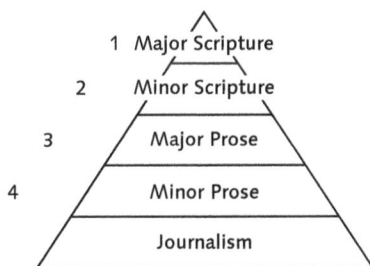

Figure 15. Prose Literature.

Legend: 1) *Relation of man to the universe* — *intellectual illumination ecstasy of understanding*
2) *Relation of man to the universe* — *evocation of cosmic emotion*
3) *Relation of man to man* — *reflection*
4) *Relation of man to man* — *sentimentality*

One of the adjuncts of Objective Art is the objective symbol, in which relationships are set forth with visual directness. An objective symbol is simply one that refers to objective fact, in contrast to the subjective symbol referring only to personal phantasy or subjective imagination. Of the latter we have a surfeit—such as the subjective nightmares of Surrealism and the like—in modern art but there are many examples of the former that have come down to us and remain as genuine symbols of Objective Art, even when their correct significance has long been lost and their correct interpretation has vanished. The interest in such symbols does not reside in such anthropological superstition as may now be associated with them but rather in the genuine knowledge to which originally they pointed. The art of objective symbolism begins with the posing of questions concerned with objective (not personally phantasied) figures. A triangle is such a figure whose basic relationships can be perceived equally by all who can perceive any relationships at all. Thus a triangle has three points:

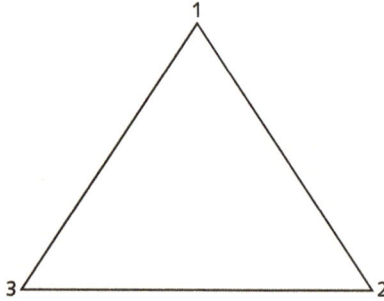

Figure 16. A Triangle, of three points.

Where is the fourth point of this triangle? It is here:

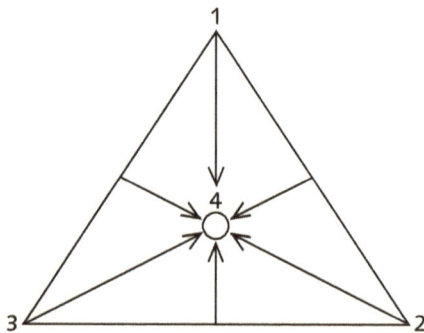

Figure 17. A Triangle, of four points.

When this fourth point is dimensionalized, i.e., when it is as equally removed from the first three points as they are mutually removed from each
other, a further dimension of space is required and we have a pyramid:

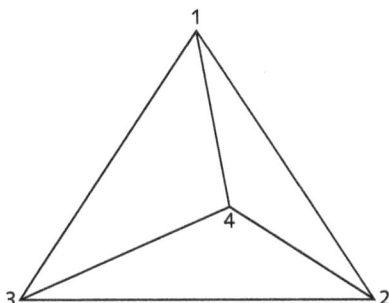

Figure 18. A four-pointed triangle dimensionalized; a Pyramid.

This distinction of the fourth point, and its independence, from the other
three has a correspondence in the distinction of the Fourth Way from the
usual three Ways relevant to the three chief types of men: the Fourth Way is
equally a factor in the triangularity of human function but it is neither an
additive sum nor any other combination of the three fundamentally human
factors, although it is still related to them as the fourth point is related to the
triangle or as the apex of the pyramid is related to its base.

Of course the figures just given are a kindergarten illustration of considerations taken for granted as long since appreciated by both designers and
perceivers of objective symbols, for the fourth point of a triangle is there,
naturally, whether labelled or not and whether seen or not. We may now
proceed to two instances, and their explanations, of objective symbols that
have appeared many times in human records:

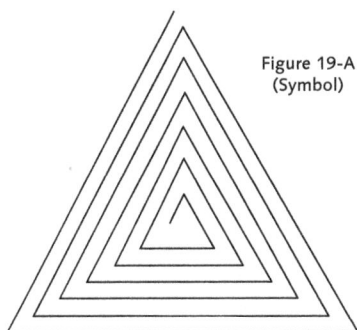

Figure 19. Octavic symbol and its derivation.

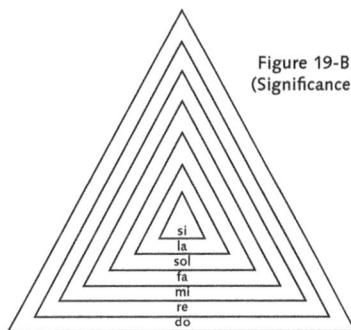

An octave may be symbolized in many different ways, the present one being designed to show forth the presence of the three fundamental forces throughout each of its notes. By altering the spaces between the triangles correspondingly, it can also be made to exhibit the relationships between the different octavic intervals, which do not appear in the present illustration.

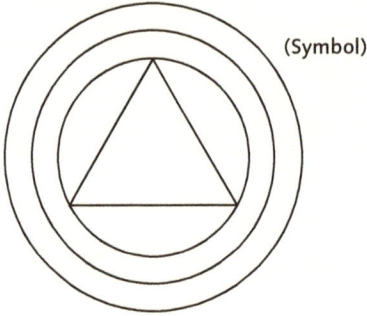 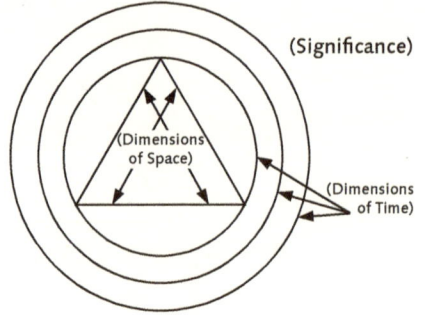

Figure 20-A   Figure 20-B

Figure 20. Symbol and Significance.

The bearing of this symbol upon the relations between Space and Time will become clearer when we later discuss the dimensions of the latter.

There are, of course, a great many objective symbols like the foregoing scattered over the surface of the earth, fragmentary hints of the knowledge of earlier civilizations, even the names of which are now lost in oblivion. It is often the crude fashion of the present to dismiss them as meaningless or superstitious scrawls; but one must fear that it is our anthropologists who are the victims of a pseudo-scientific superstition so literal that in a triangle they can see just a triangle and that the originators of such now mis-called "primitive" symbols were really expressing certain entirely objective relationships.

Among the relationships portrayed in the symbols of Objective Art three of the simpler derive from the following formulation:

The presence of two opposing forces gives the BINARY;
>   of two opposing forces including the struggle between them gives the TERNARY;
>   of two opposing forces including the struggle between them and also the result of the struggle gives the QUATERNARY.

With this formulation as a key the significance of a large number of ancient symbols is readily disclosed. For instance, the simplest form of the old

Hebraic symbol often known as King Solomon's Seal, is an expression of the binary relationship, with the two interlaced triangles, one pointing upwards, the other downwards, thus indicating the universal tension engendered by the forces respectively striving toward the Positive and Negative Absolutes.

There is another symbol of this kind, not ordinarily encountered, since it is part of a tradition kept secret, or in any case closely guarded, for hundreds of years if not for millennia; in fact it is of such high importance that it is said never to have been published.* This symbol provides a representation of the two primary laws of the Universe, the Three and the Seven, and of their interrelationships. It furnished the principles of design for the original and earliest medieval cathedrals, already mentioned as the products of a genuine School, and although it never appears itself in the actual construction, all its elements can be discovered there by one who knows what to look for.

The single lines within the circle represent the Octave and by following them from any selected point where they touch the circumference one of the recurring decimals of the fraction, $^1/_7$, is obtained. The double lines represent the free Triangle of Being, lying behind all Manifestation (the Octave); and they designate those special points of the octave where interrelationship takes place, viz., at the origin and at the two gaps or intervals that permit the reciprocal feeding process of the Universe to occur.

This figure also illustrates well one of the basic principles of passing on knowledge by means of symbols, the principle of embedding the items desired to be preserved, in anomalies. The result is accomplished by devising a figure, outwardly either appropriate or familiar, but in which some deliberate alteration of detail has been made. When such a discrepancy has been noted and its significance appreciated, the information is thereby disclosed.

* The statement is no longer true, this symbol having been published lately: *In Search of the Miraculous, Fragments of an Unknown Teaching*, P. D. Ouspensky, Harcourt Brace, NY, 1949.

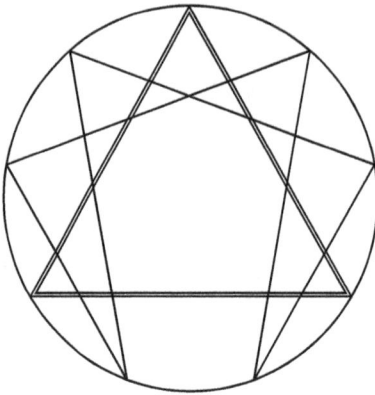

(Symbol)
Figure 21-A

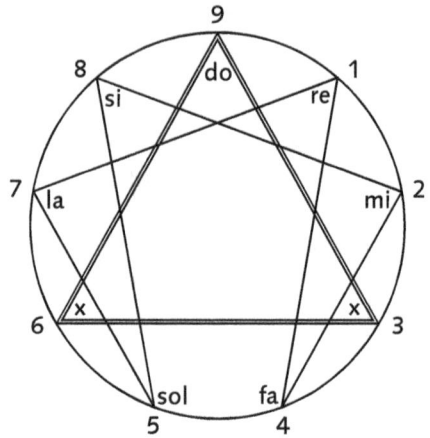

(Significance)
Figure 21-B

Figure 21. The Enneagram, "Asymmetrical Asymmetry."

The reader will quickly notice a discrepancy in this symbol, namely the displacement of the second gap or interval from its correct position between the octavic notes, si and do. The occurrence of the discrepancy was used as a test in certain of the Orage groups, the student being invited to work out its explanation for himself. Since that is impractical here, the derivation of the Enneagram is given below.

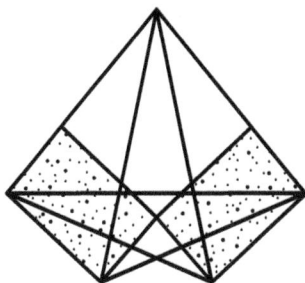

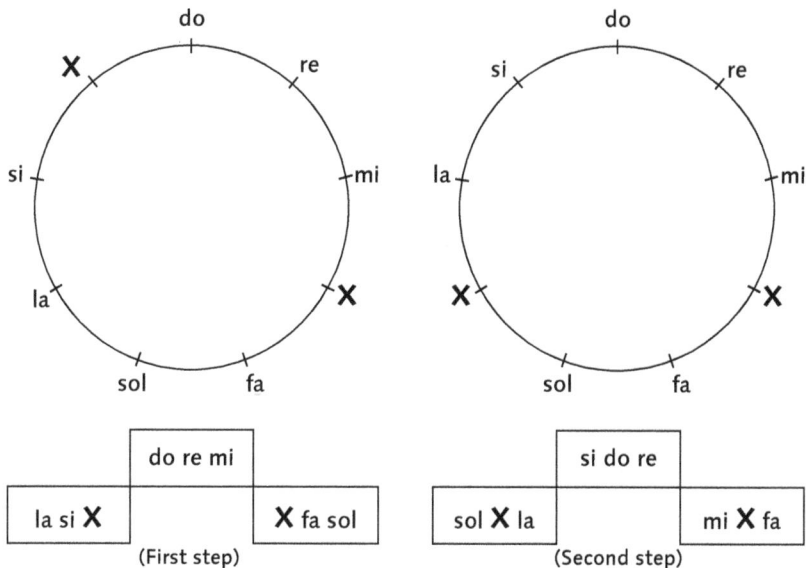

Figure 22. The Derivation of the Enneagram.
(By means of the two successive steps noted above, the symmetry of the
relations between the Triangle and the Octave is reduced to symmetry.)

We have now wandered a little, however, from our subject, which in this
section is man—man in relation to the Universe but with the emphasis upon
the former rather than the latter. We must now come back to the main line
of discussion.

The Gurdjieffian system analyzes the components of the Universe from
the point of view of the Cosmic Ray, which gives us in descending order the
primary octavic composition as follows: Galaxies, the Milky Way (a single
galaxy composed of stars), the Sun (a single star), the Planetary System (surrounding the Sun), the Earth (a single planet), the Moon (a satellite of the
Earth), and finally Anuleos (a second satellite much younger and smaller
than the Moon). This Anuleos, apparently unknown to modern astrono-

my (a circumstance that by now will perhaps not arouse in us too much negative credulity), is alleged actually to be there; moreover, along with the Moon, it represents the growing end of the Cosmic Ray, toward which energies are drawn intensively from the levels immediately above it. The name assigned to it is derived from a somewhat dissimilar word, Kemespai, which means that-which-does-not-permit-to-sleep-in-peace. Each of these stages (or notes) of the primary octave is again composed of second-degree octaves, and these in turn of third-degree octaves, and so on. Upon such an objective scale it is possible to identify the location of an individual man with remarkable exactness:

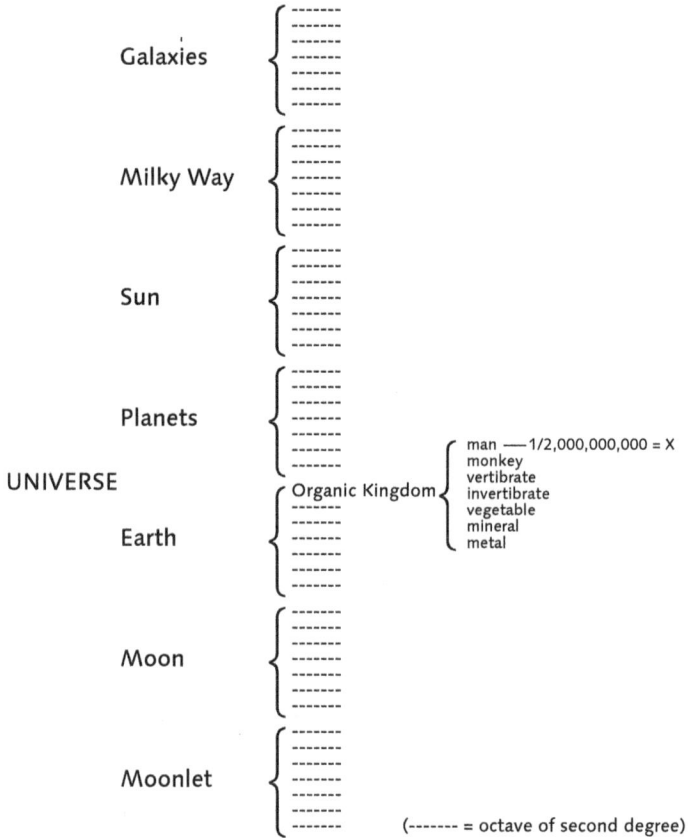

Figure 23. The Position of an Individual Man in the Universe.

An interesting point appears in this connection with regard to the human population of the Earth. Nowadays it is generally agreed that that population approximates some two billion persons *in toto*, of all ages, both sexes and all races; but what seems to be overlooked is that throughout the span of known history and for the foreseeable future the number has been and will be the same. With the outlook confined to a portion of the planet's surface and in the absence of any sort of accurate census of the whole it has often been supposed that the human population of the Earth may vary within rather wide limits and over relatively very short periods of time. With a short-term and small-area view it is not realized that when, for example, the European peoples are multiplying at a rapid rate, there must be a corresponding decrease somewhere else that is not seen, perhaps in the interior of Africa or of Asia; and that when the populations of the western cultures decrease, a balancing increase must occur elsewhere. Such a conclusion is by no means *ex cathedra* but rather is dictated by the common sense integration of a few obvious circumstances immediately before us.

The first of these is that the primary components of the universe are closely and inevitably interrelated in law-conformable ways that they do and must interact in fashions that can permit only of the most minor exceptions, that the lesser elements are in fact parts of the greater. The concept is of an immense and smoothly functioning machine, each one of whose subdivisions is meticulously related to the others and to the whole; and incidentally this is a basic assumption upon which modern physics also rests. The second matter to be taken into consideration is the respective sizes, and especially the respective ages or life-spans, of the different components. Plainly a galaxy will endure far longer than a sun; the suns, or stars, that make up a galaxy, are born and die but the galaxy was there before them and will be there after them individually. Similarly with the other basic units of the universe; a planet cannot endure as a planet for as long as a sun endures as a sun for presently, if it continues to evolve, the planet will in turn become a sun with its own satellites as its surrounding planetary system. All this, of course, is contrary to the deadly mechanical, scientific view which, because of its own limitations, is forced to look upon the universe not as living and upon its parts as dying and disintegrating even in their mechanical aspects. The present view is quite opposite and regards the universe as living and growing, with each of its Cosmic Rays representing a trunk of evolution from which branches spread out in increasing numbers the farther from the origin we proceed; the actual growing end of our own cosmic ray we have already identified as the Moon and Moonlet, or Anuleos. In this process of growth or evolution the human race, as the most complex portion of the organic kingdom on this planet, fulfills an energy-transmission function which, if the human population were to wax and wane beyond the smallest limits, would have the most astonishing effects upon those units lower in the universal scale than is the Earth itself.

Thus we have come back to the interrelatedness between the various units, which integration in connection with their differing durations determines the constancy over long periods of the human population of our planet. As we shall see later in this chapter when we consider the temporal relations of the Universe, an average human life of eighty years corresponds only to a day in the life of the organic kingdom and to no more than a breath in that of the planet. It is then manifestly impossible for the human population to alter more than very slightly over periods of time that must be measured successively in millions of years; otherwise the whole functioning of the machine must be drastically upset and the evolving growth of our own cosmic ray interrupted and destroyed. That the undeveloped human beings whom we know here, carry on these objective functions blindly and automatically without in the least knowing and even less understanding the cosmic purposes they serve whether they know of them or not, has already been pointed out earlier.

Such information is available, however, under certain conditions and part of it is available right here. To conclude the present section let us return to our previous analysis of A-knowledge, B-knowledge and C-knowledge and show just where in the human economy these various sources of information either actually do register or potentially may register:

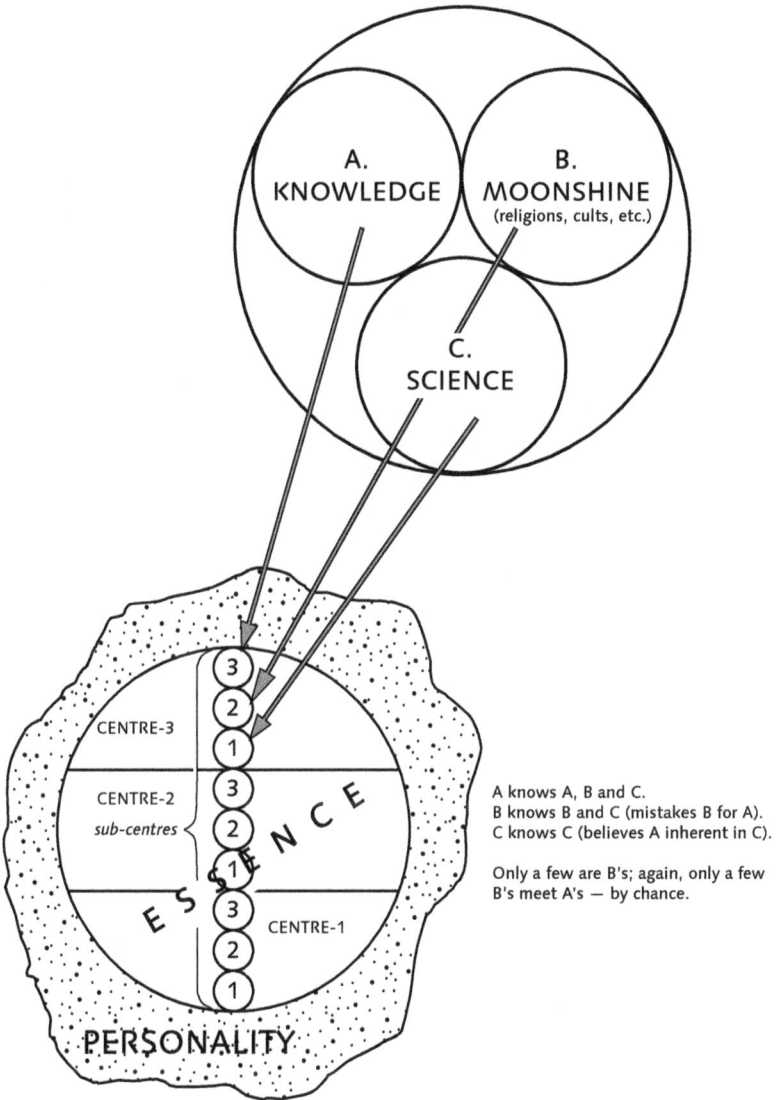

Figure 24. Relation of Sub-centres to Information Sources.

We now come to so much of the Greater Map proper as is presented in this Version. Orage's period as representative, chief instructor and head of the Institute in the United States was not of a duration sufficient to proceed further; as has already been noted, his formulations were interrupted and his groups disbanded at the point where this Version concludes, by Gurdjieff himself. Thus it is not only incomplete but it is not even as complete as it might have been, for in the three or four remaining years of Orage's life he could assuredly have carried matters considerably further, had he been permitted to do so; and it should be stated unequivocally that it was not Orage who was responsible for the degree of incompleteness that in fact prevails.

Nevertheless, a good deal remains to be said, for the outlines of the Greater Map are here, and even some of the details as concerns the larger organization of this Universe and the interrelations among its primary components.

First it may be well to say a word about the terminology to be employed, which will consist often of technical words, strictly defined and used consistently in the significance arbitrarily assigned to them in the Gurdjieffian system. Thus, if elsewhere they are used with different meanings, the latter must be disregarded in respect of the present discussion and only those definitions used in the reader's thought that are likewise used in these formulations. As to the propriety of some of the terms there can be differences of speculative opinion naturally but what in fact interests us, are the concepts involved and not the sounds of the terms by which they are labelled. Moreover, the specific reasons for the selection of these words have never been fully explained to the writer and we are not in a position, when approaching these subjects for the first time, to judge of the full appositeness of the terms later, when a greater understanding of such matters has been attained. In any case the meanings are rigorous and must be adhered to, if the discussion is to be followed properly.

To begin with, we shall consider the Cosmoi (or, if it be preferred, Cosmoses) that make up the Universe and in these cases each of them has a technical and exact name. The Universe itself comprises all Reality, that is, everything of which we are or can be aware. Such a statement does not, of course, exclude the possibility of other universes besides or beyond this one; and indeed it is said that such other universes do exist but of them we can have no knowledge nor any relation with them, although it may be that our own Universe is so related.

The first Cosmos of this Universe is God or, as Gurdjieff sometimes put it, His Endlessness. The latter term derives from the Gurdjieffian account of the creation of the Universe and of the reason for it, the latter being as follows. We are told that, before the creation, God found Himself existing upon the Sun Absolute, the correspondence here being on the one hand between God and what we call "I" and on the other between the Sun Absolute and what we know as our bodies. The position in regard to God is the same as that in regard to the Universe: behind the God of this Universe there is another, and beyond that one another, and so on, but of those we can have no understanding whatever since they are outside the only Reality we can know.

Our God, then, existing comfortably enough in the Sun Absolute, noticed that the place of His abode was gradually shrinking and that, if this continued, it would presently disappear, leaving Him, presumably, with no other place to go. He constated that the circumstance was due to a particular aspect or quality of Time, and specifically to that aspect which in the end deteriorates and destroys all physical substances; and He directed His full intelligence upon a solution of the problem. The solution turned out to be the creation from the Sun Absolute of the now existing Universe, which is essentially a gigantic reciprocal-feeding apparatus and which, due to the slight alteration effected by His Endlessness in the fundamental cosmic law of Heptaparabarshinokh (the Law of the Seven), by means of this reciprocal feeding can maintain indefinitely not only the Sun Absolute but also itself. The two fundamental laws of Triamasikamno (the Law of the Three) and Heptaparabarshinokh, being defining characteristics of the God of our Universe, functioned on the Sun Absolute before the creation of the Universe, the alteration in the latter of the two, which now permits the manifestation of the reciprocal feeding process, having been the introduction into the originally uniform octave of the two idiosyncratic intervals or gaps existing between the notes, mi and fa, and the notes, si and the superior do.*

The name of this first and original Cosmos—i.e., of God including the Sun Absolute, as we include our bodies—is Protocosmos.

The entire Universe, including the Sun Absolute and also all of the Cosmoi resulting from the creation and noted below, is called the Megalocosmos.

The first of the latter Cosmoi to come into being as a result of the creative process was the Galaxies or Milky Ways (of which there are seven) taken as a whole and to this totality the name is given of Ayocosmos.

A single Galaxy—our own Milky Way, for instance—is called Macrocosmos; and any single Sun, a part of such a Macrocosmos, is named Defterocosmos. Next in the order of descent is the Planetary System surrounding any Sun and this is called Messacosmos, while a single Planet within such a system is called a Tritocosmos. Upon the Tritocosmoi there at last arose those smallest units which still preserve a similarity to the Megalocosmos and which are ordinarily called organic cells; here their name is Microcosmos. And finally we have a term for any composite mass of Microcosmoi that forms a relatively independent unit; such a unit may be a biological

---

* The full Gurdjieffian account of the creation of the Universe is to be found in the chapter entitled Purgatory, in: *All and Everything; First Series, An Objectively Impartial Criticism of the Life of Man, or Beelzebub's Tales to His Grandson*, Harcourt Brace & Co., NY, 1950.

organism including all its aspects, conscious as well as mechanical, but the term embraces more than that for it can refer also to such a larger organization as an Organic Kingdom. This term is Tetartocosmos.

We then have the following list:

Megalocosmos	—	the Universe, including God in the Sun Absolute;
Protocosmos	—	God or the Sun Absolute;
Ayocosmos	—	all Galaxies together;
Macrocosmos	—	any single Galaxy;
Defterocosmos	—	any one Sun or star;
Messacosmos	—	any Planetary System;
Tritocosmos	—	any single Planet;
Microcosmos	—	any single cell;
Tetartocosmos	—	any organic whole, composed of "cells."

Having made this brief but broadest of all possible surveys of the Universe, we may now consider in more detail the phenomena of its operation. We have already described and discussed its two basic laws, that of the Three applying to existence or being and that of the Seven, which determines all phenomenal happening. But the results of these two fundamental laws are many indeed and they give rise both to other derived laws and relationships and to numerous different orders of being.

For purposes of orientation it should be repeated that this Version, like all the Gurdjieffian system, claims to be "more materialistic than Materialism." This means that it considers everything in the Universe to be material, everything including dreams, all other experiences, emotions, thoughts, all such things as ESP, intuitions, and whatever may be vaguely and inaccurately termed "subjective" by contemporary viewpoints. In all Reality there is but a single genuine subjectivity, that which is called "I" or the Ultimate Subjective and which by definition can never either observe or know itself; but by the same token there is no separate or unrelated "I" and the Ultimate Subjective is itself a part of Unreality except when comprised within a larger whole of which all else is material. Without qualification the Universe is objective and by objective is meant, without hedging, material.

All materialistic philosophies, examined sufficiently closely, are qualified in some way or another and the qualification usually derives from the arbitrarily limited field assigned to physics in our present organization of the sciences; this in turn is occasioned by the limitations in instrumentation and technique that result both from the meagre time-span over which scientific work has been prosecuted and, more basically, from the predicament that even the best scientists themselves are ordinary, undeveloped human beings, therefore inevitably shut off from the type of intrinsic concept that alone can provide the basis for fully genuine investigations.

A physics and a chemistry that can deal adequately with the phenomena of universal Reality, both terrestrial and cosmic, must therefore be of a different sort than those branches of modern science now called Physics and Chemistry. One premise shared in common is that the Universe is objective, i.e., that it exists independently of the investigator and that its characteristics, correctly understood, do not derive from the investigator's subjective dream. Another, lately mentioned, is that all the phenomena of the Universe are law-conformable, that they occur in ways which, correctly understood, do not vary capriciously. But other matters do not stand in so nice an agreement. In the Gurdjieffian system, as in this Version of it, it is not considered necessary to make any real distinction between physics and chemistry; they are both concerned with the same kind of phenomena and any attempt to draw a meaningful line between them results in a meaningless line.

But the greatest distinction is this: the scientific premise is that only organic substances are alive whereas the premise, and indeed the assertion, of Gurdjieffian physics is that all matters, organic and inorganic also, possess and manifest different degrees of life. The Universe is living and so are all of its functioning parts; only at the final end of the scale, at the point denoted as Negative Absolute, does real deadliness—the lack of all potentiality—reign, and matter in this condition is not available to investigation in our portion of the Universe. Thus a sun, from the present point of view, is not an inertly flaming mass (or whatever astrophysicists may now presume it to be); on the contrary it is a highly complex organization, in fact an organism possessing not only a high order of being but a relevant consciousness also. Similarly with a rock or a solar system or an atom of lead: all these, and all other relatively independent units, possess not only physical characteristics but those of being and consciousness likewise, ranging respectively from a very high to a very low degree. It is the task of an objective physics to distinguish accurately between all these, and particularly in respect of their different vibration-rates, the higher the vibration-rate the lighter and more vivified the matter, the lower the rate the denser, heavier, slower and less vivified the matter. It is a corollary of this view that the Universe is both living and growing, in contradistinction to the scientific implication, sometimes plainly stated that it is mostly dead and in other respects dying in accordance with the so-called second law of thermodynamics.

A further distinction must be made in the matter of terms, especially of two most important terms, both of which are familiar to almost everyone nowadays and which unfortunately bear very different connotations in the Gurdjieffian and scientific terminologies respectively. These terms are 1) atom and 2) hydrogen. It will be necessary to make it perfectly clear just in what lies the difference between the respective concepts.

Scientific usage confines the word, atom, to the smallest part of any of the chemical elements which still retains all the characteristics defining it as such an element. But in the case of a compound substance, such as water, the scientific term for its smallest, further indivisible unit is molecule; and below the atom (which stands on the border separating scientific physics and chemistry) we have such terms as electron, positron, neutron, meson, and so on, signifying different physical particles characterized by mass and velocity. Also we have the electromagnetic fields, sometimes considered as functions of the relationships between these physical particles and sometimes just vice versa. On account of the incompatibility between particle and field physics—one placing the emphasis on one side, one on the other—the concept of matter itself has tended lately to become vague and unstable.* That whole situation is contrary to the precise clarity of the Gurdjieffian position, in which matter and materiality are basically fixed concepts.

But to return to the term, atom. Scientifically this word signifies the smallest part of any of the *chemical elements* still retaining all the defining characteristics of the element. But in Gurdjieffian physics the term, atom, signifies the smallest part of *any relatively independent unit or substance* that still retains all of its own defining characteristics; and this latter use of the term is therefore not confined simply to the case of the chemical elements but possesses a far broader application. Thus we speak of an atom of water as well as of an atom of lead or of boron; there is also such a physical entity as an atom of electricity, an atom of man, and atoms of specific thoughts and emotions, for these latter are physical matters also. This use of the term, incidentally, is in strict accordance with its correct derivation from the Greek, for "atom" simply means indivisible and there is no implication in it such as to confine it arbitrarily only to those substances that compose the periodic table of the chemical elements.

The second term, hydrogen, is assigned by scientists to a chemical element, found usually in the gaseous state and possessing defined chemical characteristics. The same is true of the terms, oxygen, nitrogen and carbon, except that the last occurs ordinarily as a solid. But in the Gurdjieffian system the use of these words is entirely different, for they can refer, under appropriate conditions, to any and all substances, no matter how different chemically the latter may be respectively. In other words, these terms do not now identify specific substances but instead they designate the various conditions in which any substance may exist or in which it may manifest. Thus the Sun at one time may be a carbon and at another time a nitrogen, an oxygen or a hydrogen, and so may an atom of water or a number of such atoms; indeed the hydrogen of scientific chemistry can also be a carbon, a nitrogen, an oxygen or even a hydrogen in this Gurdjieffian sense. So also

---

* The cause and reason for this scientific inefficacy (whereby both at the top and the bottom of the scale scientific calculations tend to disappear into satisfactory symbols for infinity) has been brilliantly laid bare by Ouspensky: *In Search of the Miraculous*, op. cit., 1949, pp. 208–213. That discussion, however, is not a part of the Oragean Version.

with electricity, or man, or an organic kingdom, or any other substance recognizable by reason of its particular physical, chemical and cosmic properties. To understand this position is not a difficult matter but to hold to it consistently throughout the discussion is much more troublesome, for one must continually remind oneself of the rigorous meaning of these terms, quite other than either their usual or their scientific significances. Perhaps the greatest quandary consists in considering such a body as the Sun to be a substance in its own right rather than as being merely composed of numerous other substances; but it is plain to a rigorous consideration that the Sun, as sun, possesses cosmic and even just physical properties as a whole which do not inhere in its constituent parts and thus that, strictly speaking from the viewpoint of an objective physics, it does in fact represent a determinate kind of substance not to be found with these full characteristics in any cases except those of suns. The same is true of that further substance denoted as all-suns-taken-together either as Macrocosmos or as Ayocosmos, which possesses both physical and cosmic properties lacking to any single sun taken by itself. To put it otherwise, substances may be not only simple, as lead, or compound, as water, but they may also be both complex and compoundedly complex, as in the case of a sun or of a galaxy; in all these cases they are still material *substances.*

Having described these differences between the ordinary scientific and the Gurdjieffian views as to physics, we can now formulate what those conditions are which are here denoted as carbon, nitrogen, oxygen and hydrogen. In all manifestations there are present three forces and any substance whatever may at different times be mediating any one, or none of them. When it is mediating the positive force, any substance is called a carbon; when it is mediating the negative force, it is named an oxygen; when it is mediating the neutralizing force, it is a nitrogen. And when it is mediating none of them or, for the purposes of discussion, is to be considered apart from the specific force being mediated, then it is denoted as a hydrogen. The chief impediment in this case, aside from the employment of the terms in an unfamiliar way, is the necessity always to remember that the terms are variable, i.e., that because copper or a sun may be a nitrogen at one time, this does not at all prevent it from filling the role of a carbon, an oxygen or a hydrogen at another. The terms denote not a constant but a variable characteristic of a substance, and the hydrogen numbers identify the *relative* vibration-rates by which the various substances are differentiated.

From these considerations the Table of Hydrogens of the Universe is derived. This will be presented only for our own Cosmic Ray, the one in which we find ourselves, but obviously, with the necessary variations apposite to any other cosmic ray, similar relationships will exist in all of them. It will be seen (in the table to follow) that a series of four overlapping triads exists between Positive and Negative Absolutes, these triads consisting of positive, negative and neutralizing elements and providing the four fundamental concentration points of the Cosmic Ray. Note that the Milky Way, a nitrogen for the superior triad, becomes equally a carbon for the inferior one. Between the four basic points stretch three octaves and it is the recurrently overlapping triads of these octaves which determine the fundamental hydrogens of the Cosmic Ray, distinguished in accordance with their relative vibration-rates. The table is given below:

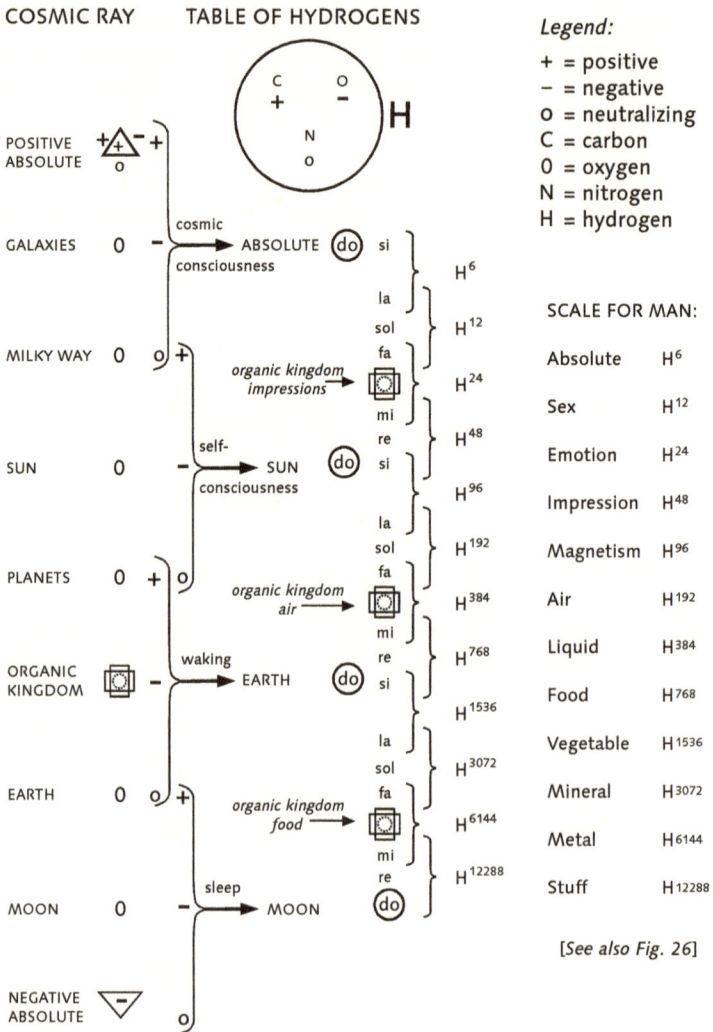

Figure 25. Derivation of the Table of Hydrogens.

It will be observed that the scale referring to Man commences at H^{24}, which for him constitutes his own Absolute or H^6. This means that in the Universe, and of course in this Cosmic Ray, Man represents and is H^{24}; whether he is a carbon, an oxygen or a nitrogen, depends upon the circumstances of the moment. And of course also these statements apply only to fully developed man; a less than fully developed and functioning man does not have the defining properties of H^{24} but in such a case represents an incomplete cosmic H^{24}. But since Man cannot be more than human and still remain human, his complete development represents his own Absolute and therefore this completeness becomes his own H^6 upon his own specific scale of hydrogens.

In Man also there is a Sun, an Earth and a Moon as well as the complete development which is his Absolute; and these again establish four basic concentration points between which reach three octaves. Man, being the cosmic H^{24}, is a replica in miniature of the Universe and contains within himself its fundamental interior relationships. The overlapping triads of his own three octaves in turn establish the range of hydrogens for a fully developed man, and these are set out in the table below in respect of Man only.

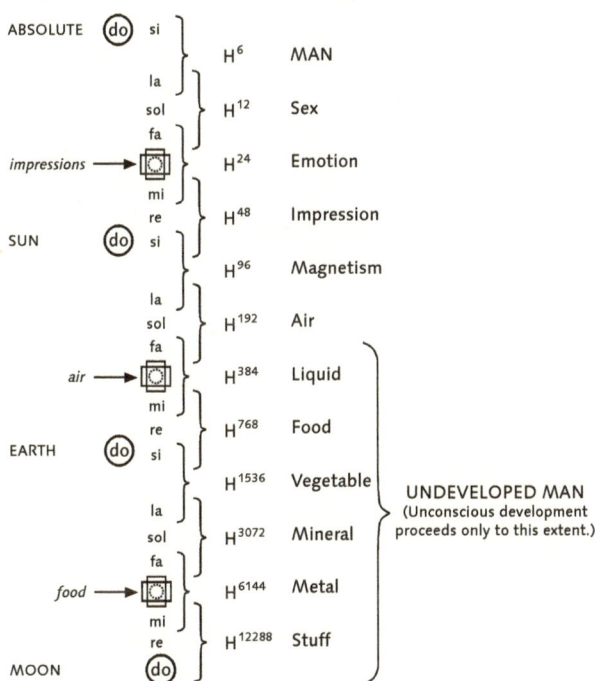

Figure 26. Table of Hydrogens specific to Man.

In connection with the hydrogen Tables just given, there can be found one of the many applications of the Enneagram, which was presented a number of pages above. Being so basic a symbol, the Enneagram is applicable to any and all phenomena that follow the two primary laws of the Universe and of course the more fundamental the phenomena in question, the more clearly does the Enneagram provide a graphic symbol of them. In the present case it shows the progressive relationship of food values, their products and the corresponding stages of development resulting from their active digestion, now set out in terms of the hydrogens listed in the preceding Tables.

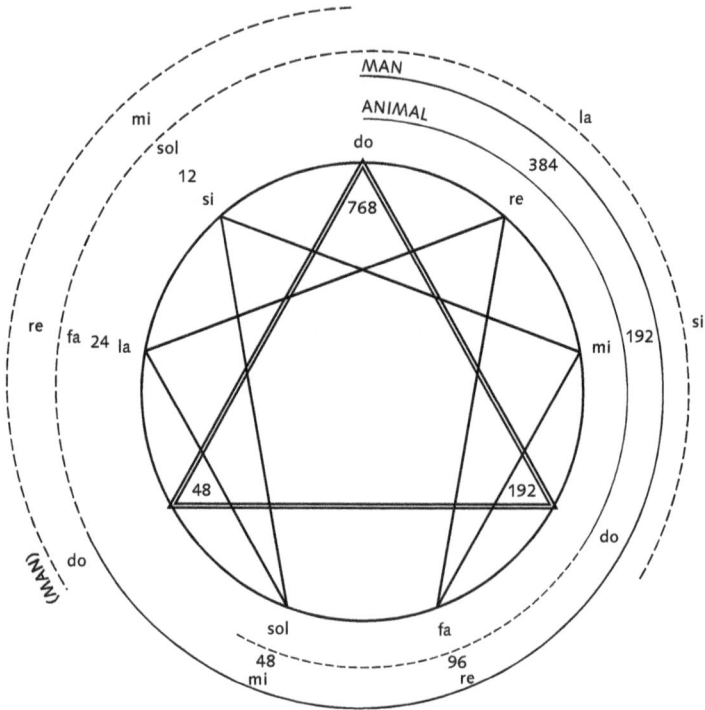

The numbers relate to hydrogens.

Animal: no reflection.

Man: 96, 48 = points of actual reflection.
24, 12 = points of potential reflection (when full development is attained).

Figure 27. Food Values, Products and Corresponding
Development as represented in the Enneagram.

Naturally there is considerably more "food for thought" in the above diagram than has been noted in the legend beneath it. But if all its indications were to be made explicit, the reader would be deprived of such inherent possibilities for his own Pondering; and a long study of the further applications contained in the figure will well repay the time spent.

It will now be seen to what an extensive range of connotations the term, hydrogen, may be applied. It has just been used in connection with various kinds of foods and it can also be employed with reference to different grades and degrees both of Being and of specific beings. And indeed these two employments are not so diverse as they might appear at first sight, for one grade of being in fact stands to another in the relation of a source of nutriment. Plainly one must not interpret the statement in the literal sense of food-intake through the mouth; but we have long since seen that both air and impressions also constitute perfectly factual varieties of food for man and the definition of food in the present sense is a very broad one, denoting anything that either does or can provide nourishment for the use of any type of being in the Universe. The subject, of course, is identical with that reciprocal feeding process which maintains the constancy of the Universe in the face of the deteriorating aspect of temporal succession and of even further dimensions of Time.

The reader must also be reminded once more that, from the viewpoint of a living and growing Universe; there are far more degrees of real Being than would be derived from the more usual scientific position. Thus a tree very plainly possesses Being; but so do many other organizations of substance that from a less mature point of view are customarily dismissed as manifesting a mere lifelessness very far from being the case. There is a tabular diagram representing this situation from the top to the bottom of the universal scale, which is known as the Ladder of Beings and which will be shown next below:

1. GOD	2. SERAPHIM & CHERUBIM

3.
MANIFESTATION

H^{24} MAN	H^{12} PLANETARY GODS	H^{6} SOLAR GODS

H^{48} VERTI- BRATE

H^{364} MINERAL	H^{192} VEGE- TABLE	H^{96} INVERTI- BRATE

H^{768} METAL

H^{6144} ANULEOS	H^{3072} MOON	H^{1536} STUFF

H^{12288}

NEGATIVE
ABSOLUTE

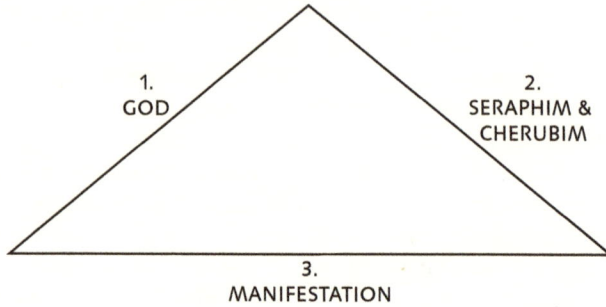

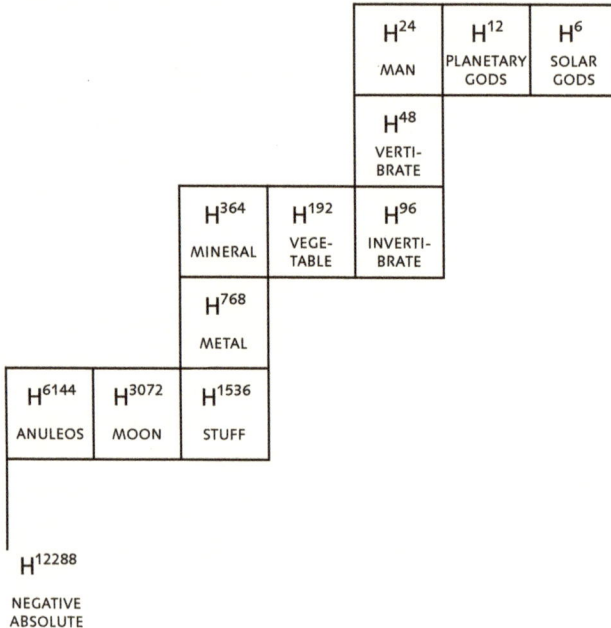

Figure 28. The Ladder of Beings.
The hydrogen-numbers designate the relative degrees
of being as between the various Beings listed.

On previous pages we have several times discussed the problem of "I" or the Ultimate Subjective. Let us see now if, in relation to the Greater Map and its universal relationships, we can come to a further understanding on this subject. Here, so far as the Oragean Version is concerned, is the final conclusion respecting the vital question: who am "I"?

But the preliminary question is this: with what am "I" identified? There exist several partially incorrect answers to this and one wholly incorrect answer. There are those who say: "I" have a body; "I" am a soul. The error here lies in the circumstance that in such cases there is in fact no soul and the identification is a false and phantastically imaginary one; moreover, in the potential case where a soul-body may be in the process of construction, the correct statement, once that body actually exists, must be: "I" have a soul. Only during the process of acquiring a soul-body, may there be an identification of "I" with such a body and even then the first statements above are at least partially incorrect, for the identification can be only a temporary one.

Those statements, however, are far better that the usual one, viz., "I" am a body, meaning an ordinary physical body, for that is wholly incorrect, being no more than the name-and-address fallacy whereby one misidentifies oneself completely in saying: "I" *am* Mr. Aloysius Smith, for instance. The more excusable series of errors proceeds as follows: when one has nothing except the first physical body, one identifies with the incomplete Body Kesdjan (or astral) and says—"I" have a physical body; when the astral body is developed, he identifies with the mental (or soul) body and says—"I" have an astral and a physical body; and when the third body is developed, he then says—"I" have those three bodies (if the first one is, or the first two are, still alive). What demonstrates that all these statements are only partially correct is that, when the last one is reached, one is still confronted by the unanswered query: who am "I"? For the truth is that, no matter how far back the question is pushed, "I" can never either observe or know "I."

In regard to this Ultimate Subjectivity there is a mantram; it will be recalled that a mantram is a series of words for repetition, to each of which the fullest and most specific meaning possible is consciously attributed as the words are pronounced successively, either vocally or subvocally. The mantram:

> More radiant than the sun,
> Purer than the snow,
> Subtler than the ether,
> Is the Self,
> The spirit within my heart.
> I am that Self;
> That Self am I.

One use of this mantra is to assist in establishing non-identification with the first physical body but, although it consists of positive statements and although its mental, emotional and practical effect is helpful (if properly performed), it still does not provide a fully satisfactory intellectual reply. There still remains: who am "I"?

In this difficulty we may seek to discover what assistance there may be in the concept of the Cosmic Ray—whether, for instance, it may permit us to discern the origin of "I" so far as concerns ourselves and thus to orient ourselves more accurately in relation to the question. For this purpose we reproduce below another diagram of the Cosmic Ray with notations apposite to the problem.

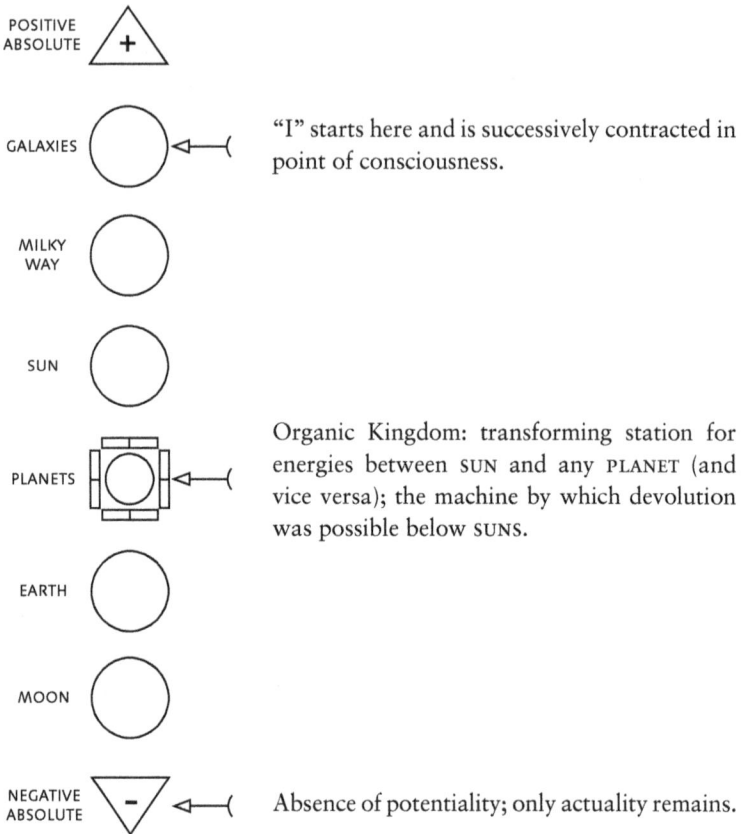

POSITIVE ABSOLUTE △ +

GALAXIES ◯ ⟵ "I" starts here and is successively contracted in point of consciousness.

MILKY WAY ◯

SUN ◯

PLANETS ▣ ⟵ Organic Kingdom: transforming station for energies between SUN and any PLANET (and vice versa); the machine by which devolution was possible below SUNS.

EARTH ◯

MOON ◯

NEGATIVE ABSOLUTE ▽ − ⟵ Absence of potentiality; only actuality remains.

The Universe is the form brought about by the reaction between the POSITIVE ABSOLUTE and the NEGATIVE ABSOLUTE.

Figure 29. A Chart of Universal Relationships.

Let us disregard the notations on the diagram for a moment and take up a larger question. The Universe, i.e., the range from Galaxies through and including Moon and including also, of course, all other Cosmic Rays in addition to the one charted, can be considered as God's physical body and in a relationship to God corresponding to the relationship between our physical body and ourselves. From such a viewpoint, then, God's "I" originates and remains in the Positive Absolute. Moreover, the upper half of any Cosmic Ray represents the extent of it to which God can be consciously related directly; His consciousness does not extend directly below the note, sol, of the cosmic octave. At this point a mechanical device, which we know as an organic kingdom, had to be devised in order to carry devolution beyond the cosmic order of Suns; but this device provides also for the particularized consciousnesses of the units composing it and, by such a means, the consciousness of God is carried *indirectly* below the note, sol, of the cosmic octave.

The highest element in any organic kingdom is its human component, the human race, and such a race exists on most planets, although naturally of a very different exterior form than our own. Exterior form is a function of planetary environment; the definition of a human being is that creature which can think, feel and do, and any creature of such a character is by definition human. Humanity, in the broadest possible sense and throughout the Universe, fulfills a most important role in God's indirect consciousness below the cosmic order of Suns. Of course we must realize that the statement applies only to normally *conscious* humanity and it will occur to us immediately that the situation upon our own planet cannot be very favorable in this regard. But indeed this planet, called by us Earth, has been and is considered an abnormal one by every genuine School known to the present Version; its abnormality originates from and inheres in precisely that portion of its organic kingdom which is the human part of it and which by its mechanical, lethargic and unconscious manifestations denies the definition of its own being. None of this alters either the functions of organic kingdoms or of their human components upon normal planets.

In connection with this large view of the above diagram there is an incorrect assumption generally held among us (when any assumption on the subject at all is held), as follows: that the forces striving upward toward the Positive Absolute are holier or more sacred than those striving in the opposite direction or, to put it differently, that evolution is more praiseworthy or valuable than devolution. Such an assumption is a mistaken one, for not only are both processes equally valuable in the reciprocal feeding mechanism of the Universe but it will be seen also upon reflection that those devolutionary forces proceeding downward are in fact proceeding directly from the Positive Absolute whereas those proceeding upward on the return journey are by so much the farther removed from their original and sacred source.

Let us now return to our own situation as shown still in Figure 29, above. Here we see that, for us, "I" or Ultimate Subjectivity originates at the level of the Cosmic Ray representing all the Galaxies taken together or as a whole and that this entity of being thereafter is contracted in point of degree of consciousness down to the level at which we find ourselves, i.e., to the level of the highest component of an organic kingdom. That is taken to mean that supreme development, for us, might theoretically, conceivably and eventually permit of our return, in relation to consciousness, to the level of the origination of our own type of "I." Such an outcome is naturally altogether beyond our present comprehension; but it is also plain that a beginning must be made here or nowhere and indeed "now" or never.

In order to make such a beginning a graphic representation of our situation as it now exists, may be advantageous in keeping our concepts clear as to the nature of our problem. One of the first necessities is to establish a real non-identification with our bodies and in order to do so it is well to understand just where the false identification occurs which it is required to break. Actually this identification of "I" with "it" is cemented fast at the point of our main weaknesses or Chief Features; it is with this point in ourselves, so sore that we dare not even recognize or look at it, that our false identifications are held. Chief Feature, as we know, is part of Essence; and the following diagram distinguishes our point of false identification in relation to our actual body and to our potential bodies or Centres.

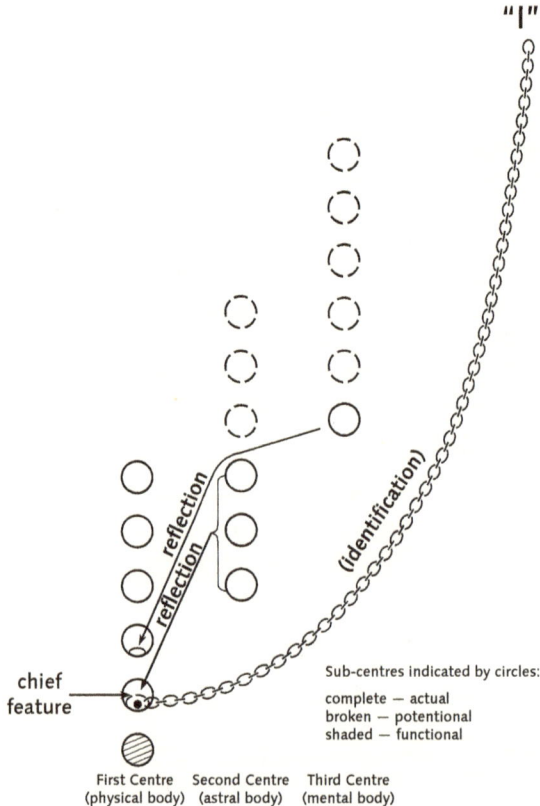

Figure 30. Relation of "I" and false identification to centres and sub-centres.

Together with the situation just pictured there goes a restricted degree of individual consciousness, because of its lethargy and incompleteness quite improper to a normal human being. This is a concomitant of our undeveloped and non-functioning series of centres and sub-centres, as shown in the preceding figure, and is indeed an inevitable accompaniment of the abnormal conditions there disclosed.

Accordingly another diagram may be presented here, to show the relation of the fully developed and functional centres and sub-centres, both lower and higher, to the different states or degrees of consciousness possible for human beings. (It will be remembered that the distinction between higher and lower sub-centres is a valid one during the course of development; later, in a certain sense they coalesce and it may then be considered, for appropriate purposes, that each centre is composed of three sub-centres only.) The diagram, as it stands, will be self-explanatory at the present point of the discussion.

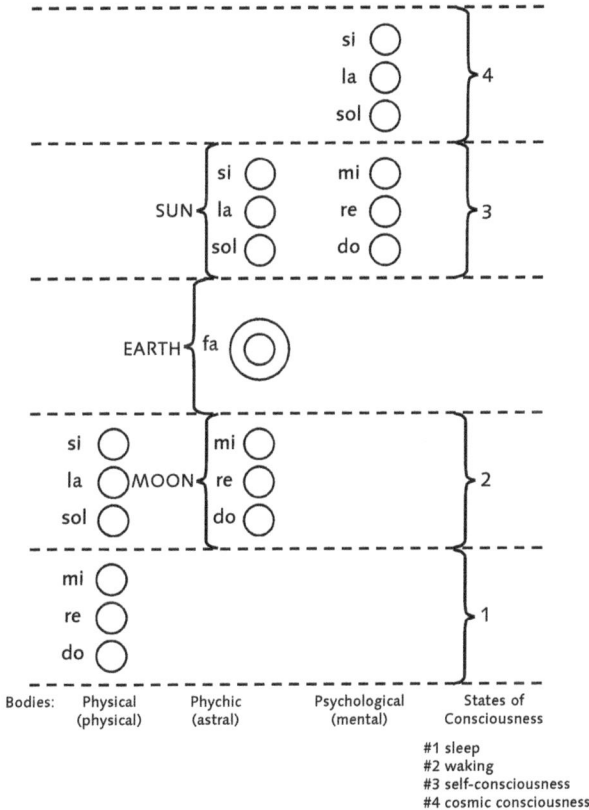

Figure 31. Relations of Centres and Sub-centres to Conscious States.

Figure 31 represents diagrammatically the functional aspects of the human economy in respect of the different possible states or degrees of consciousness; in regard to the threefold analysis of the problem of biological organization discussed several times earlier, that diagram is concerned with the third, or field, force involved. The first, or negative force consists in the chemical constituents of the given bodies and this force is taken account of in the description of the respective centres and sub-centres, both actual and potential, so far as the situation applies to men on this planet; the totality of such organized entities comprises the total first force in the case of human beings. But man's body and bodies operate functionally by means of the transformations of various energies supplied originally from outside and transmuted internally by the metabolic processes of such organisms and here we have the second, positive force, analytically denoted as that of the thermodynamical energies involved in the human organization. These energies originate from different points and different levels of the Universe; in Figure 32, below, we have a schematic representation of the sources of the various kinds of energies required for the full operation of the total human economy.

At the left of the figure the three octaves of our own universal Cosmic Ray are noted, divided into upper and lower halves, and the respective varieties of energies deriving from these sources, together with their terminal functional locations in the human organization, are identified by the arrows originating from the respective octavic levels and ending in the boxlike rectangle to the right. The latter part of the figure represents the original analysis of the organism into lower and higher centres and from that point of view may be taken as denoting the first centre (or body) with its lower and higher sub-centres. But such a view is only partially correct, for in the first, or earth human body all of these energies are not in fact actually available, since the organs for their utilization are not fully developed; and the three storeys of the box are properly to be considered as representing the three bodies of fully developed man, the physical, the astral (or Kesdjan) and the mental (or psychological).

At the upper left of the figure these bodies are identified by number and their energy sources are shown to derive from the opposite levels of the Universe. The names given to these kinds of energies are technical terms of the Gurdjieff system:

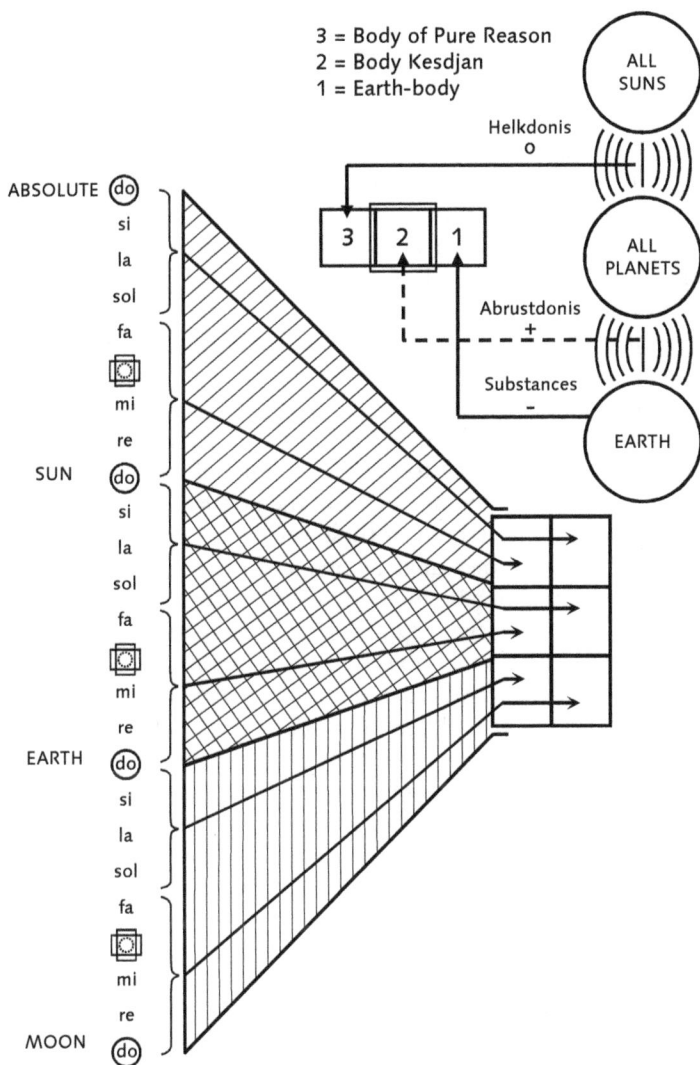

Figure 32. Man's Energy Sources.

It will be noted that in the above Figure the third or psychological body is called the Body of Pure Reason. That is neither a misprint nor an error, for the kinds of reason that a human being may possess, are to be analyzed into three varieties, corresponding to the succession of three bodies that he may develop.

The first and lowest form of reason for human beings—the kind which can be, and is, exercised through the functions of the physical body—is here called Verbal; and we are all accustomed to its use, and to its fallacies. Its shortcoming lies in the circumstance that it is entirely subjective and thus entirely personal; it is obvious that our modes of Verbal Reason are determined by the languages our nurses taught us. For example, it is not possible to entertain thoughts in English that are easily represented in more grammatically complex languages: if it be said that a lawyer travelled with a companion, the expression itself does not tell us whether two men, a man and a woman, or two women were taking the journey together. Similarly, there is no dual number in English, and very many other instances could be cited of its vagueness and lack of specificity. When we think in English, all of these deficiencies become part of our thought; and other verbal languages, although perhaps superior to English in some of these respects, are inferior in others. But even this is not the worst aspect of the matter, for besides the general deficiencies of any language, each person thinking in it attributes an essentially private meaning to the verbal units of his thought. The ideological use of terms like "democracy" and the political use of words such as "liberal" demonstrate how both of these verbal symbols can come to have almost exactly opposite meanings at one and the same time. Nor are the victims of such confusion able in any wise to guard against it, since the associations that in turn determine the significances of the verbal labels, have nothing to do with intellectual objectivity but instead are the result (for the given person) of merely haphazard external events. Thus the relevant associations are, and must be different in the cases of different persons and the consequences are not only a failure of correct verbal communication between them but a comparable subjectivity, a lack of proper distinctions and a high degree of intellectual incompetence in their verbal thought-processes. Under these circumstances it is more surprising that people come out as well as they do in their mental undertakings than that as many mistakes are made as do occur.

The second or intermediate form of reason is called Formal. Insofar as it takes place among us, it results from the partial and unconscious organization of the second or astral body, for it is this organization by means of which it can function. Formal Reason is just what the words imply: it is thinking by means of and *in terms* of forms instead of words. To us the best known example is the mental manipulation of mathematical symbols; and their superiority to verbal labels has been recognized ever since they were first heard of. The meaning of such symbols is not private but instead it is public and in order that all human beings capable of it should understand what a given equation signifies, no agreements upon definitions are required beyond the selection of the visible symbols themselves. There are other symbols of this sort (among them the ones we have briefly mentioned earlier) but in the declining civilization of our times most of them have been lost, together with the ability to think in their terms. Plainly they show us the possibility of a more accurate sort of thought-process than the verbal kind and, in the case of mathematics, the universality of agreement upon the propositions disclosed by them and the absence of serious controversy about them upon the part of all competent mathematicians sometimes has led to an over-exaggeration of their virtues, as if Formal Reason were the highest and final variety of reason open to mankind.

Such, however, is not the case—there can be, and are, occasional fundamental disputes among competent mathematicians—and there is potentially a yet higher and genuinely final type of thought-process for human beings, which is here named Objective Reason. In this case there can be no disagreement or dispute between different individuals and everyone capable of reasoning objectively must come to the same conclusions, for the process itself is based upon an immediate perception of universal data as in fact they are. Objective Reason is a function of the developed and operating third or mental body and it is for that cause that the latter is sometimes called the Body of Pure or Objective Reason.

But there is a greater and more basic distinction between Objective Reason and the two lower forms of thought-process than the fact that they are functions respectively of the three different human organisms. This difference is very simple to state but very difficult to explain, particularly in view of our automatic verbal conditioning in regard to all thought-processes and the way in which we have been taught to assume that they operate; probably it would prove entirely impossible to bring almost any contemporary psychologist to a comprehension of it for, like all experts, they (who should be the most competent to understand this matter) are prone to suffer from the Pauper's Fallacy. Thus it will be necessary for us to do only as well as we can.

The first two types of reason, the Verbal and the Formal, are functions of the apposite physiological structures, brain systems, in the operating physical and astral bodies respectively. In order to function, and thus in order that these two kinds of thought-process may occur, it is necessary first that there be present a supply of the relevant thermodynamical energies for the organism to use and second that by either a passive or an active process of digestion such energies be actually taken into the body or bodies and there transmuted in the required ways. To all of this the only objection that can arise is that many of the details of such processes are not scientifically known at present; but there is nothing outrageous or even unusual in the general picture as presented.

The third type of Reason, however, is not of the same character, i.e., it is not a function of any operating brain system but instead it is the actual, material output of such a system. In other words, objective thought is a physical substance, having its own specific vibrational centre-of-gravity and what would correspond to its own "atomic weight," and it will now be seen why genuine thought, as thought, has its own number in the Table of Hydrogens for Man. Thus a supply not only of certain thermodynamical energies but also of certain specific chemical entities is demanded in order that it be produced, both the energies and the chemical substances of course being assimilable only in the third or mental body. From this fact also, viz., that objective thought is the physical output of a higher brain system, comes the circumstance that such substances, being uniform in kind, cannot form the basis for antagonistic or contradictory conclusions, as may naturally be the case when more restricted, subjective conclusions are drawn only from the *functioning* of personally different brain systems of the two lower bodies. Another distinction will likewise occur to the reader: objective thought is unchanging and permanent up to the limits of the substances composing it.

As frequently reiterated, these statements are not offered for credulous acceptance or belief; they are made to serve as guideposts set up on the new and presently unknown continent of knowledge described by the Greater Map. Also they are for eventual confirmation in a personal sense when such an opportunity may offer, but plainly no ordinary man can be in a position to obtain properly any such confirmation now, since he possesses no actual third body through which to obtain the necessary validating data. When and if he ever does possess such a developed and functioning third body, he will no longer be an ordinary man.

But such is the destiny here asserted as *possible* for man, as man. These possibilities are inherent in him and in the organism with which he is born, within which—provided he encounters accurate information and responds to it with his own active potentialities—first the astral and finally the mental bodies can be developed. All the bodies are purely and completely material and the two higher ones possess successively longer durations corresponding to the increasingly finer substances of higher vibration-rates of which they are composed. In general the durations of the two lower are sufficient for the next higher to develop within them before they die; if this were a normal planet, eighty years would easily suffice for the establishment of the astral body and its continuation into an independent maturity when the first or physical body had been worn out. Of course it is not a normal planet and our own situations are not so fortunate; but in like fashion, given normal conditions, the astral body in turn will endure for a sufficient time to permit of the development within it of a functioning mental body capable of independent survival when at last, after a much longer period than the life of the physical body, it too dies. A mental body, being composed of substances from the level of all suns, is indestructible within the limits of this Universe and will therefore endure for as long as the Universe does.

These pleasing prospects are not, however, open to us as a mere matter of undeniable expectation. In the first place there is the question of the time at our disposal in respect of our physical bodies, the only ones which we now possess; but this is a very complex and difficult question and we will deal with it where it more appropriately belongs, in the following section. Meantime the position of the Gurdjieffian system and of the Oragean Version is that we have only a single physical life at our disposal and that, if anything is to be done, it must be done now—a rather desperate formulation, all things considered.

But in this connection all is not entirely black, for what might be accomplished during a leisurely lifetime in the natural course of events upon a normal planet, can be compressed into a much shorter period under the lash of desperation. How long, it has often been asked, does it take to become self-conscious in the strict and technical sense of the word? The reflective inquirer must soon realize that such a question is unanswerable. How long does it take to become a thoroughly competent higher mathematician, or to master Sanskrit, or to overcome any other formidable task? That depends, naturally, upon the amount and degree of effort put into the job; and no two people will ever accomplish it in precisely the same period of duration. It is stated in the Oragean Version that anyone who can be fully aware of all his manifestations for a period of one day, will have achieved the permanent ability of Self-Consciousness at will. But only those who have really understood what Self-Consciousness is and have attempted to maintain it for one minute in respect of a single category of their behavior, can realize how tremendous the actual task is. In the end it depends upon the existence of an irresistible drive upon the part of "I" to accomplish it.

The situation for us, however, is even more awkward than these considerations would suggest. Upon this particular planet external forces, relating not at all to ourselves as potential individuals, must prevent all except a very small minority from any successful participation in such activities. Indeed so small must the number remain of those who achieve a success of this kind that it can pass unnoticed, as it were, in the general economy of the planet; for otherwise measures must, and will, be taken by far superior forces to conclude the attempt.

It is not difficult to see why this must be, upon an abnormal planet. Nature always strives to achieve and maintain balances and in the present case the balance to be maintained is a relatively uniform human output to the Moon, varying only within small limits; this output is not mystical or imaginary but instead is entirely chemical and the technical name of the output-substance in this Version is *askokin*. In accordance with a secondary or even tertiary physical cosmic law quality and quantity vary inversely, i.e., the less the quality the greater the quantity, and this law applies to human beings as well as to everything else. Consequently, as the quality of being of men on this planet has decreased, their numerical quantity has risen to the quite unnecessary (upon a normal planet) number of some two billions and we have already seen that this circumstance is one impossible of alteration over what are, to us, very long stretches of time. If any large proportion of persons, therefore, were suddenly to fulfill their genuine human potentialities in the sense of acquiring higher bodies and higher levels of consciousness, the subhuman population of the Earth would have drastically to be reduced. Of course this is exactly an eventual goal to be attained but the point is that, on a cosmic time scale, it cannot be done except over very long periods; the application to us is that it cannot be done quickly now and that therefore, now, very few of us can be permitted to achieve a truly human status. It should be emphasized that these considerations do not derive from human intentions and are not subject to human decisions; they are, instead, matters of cosmic law and cosmic necessity which are far more powerful than the entire human race, let alone its abnormal component here.

But as usual there is a counterbalancing element in this case, too. Those who have taken part in this sort of activity will soon realize that, among ordinary men, there is very little interest indeed in it. Even as regards the tiny minority who ever hear of these ideas, "many are called but few are chosen" can easily be read as "many may encounter them but few indeed will respond." This is not the disaster which it is sometimes assumed to be. Also it accounts for the fact, often remarked with indignant surprise, that those who are genuinely acquainted with these ideas seldom proselyte for them.

The practical measures taken under competent instruction by the very few who are actually capable of improving their own human status have come to be known as the Work. The term includes everything of a practical kind suggested in connection with the attempt to develop human potentialities upon the part of the human candidate; it comprises the work of the Open Secret as well as of the Hidden Secret, it comprises the efforts of the instructor as well as of the pupils—for the instructor is simply a pupil who has advanced to the point where his own further progress demands the presence of pupils of his own, only by assisting whom can his own increased abilities be exercised and further extended. It comprises also all activities concerned with either the publication or the suppression of these ideas when such purposes are demanded by external or more subtle conditions. In the Gurdjieffian system the Work includes *everything* of a practical kind associated with that system.

For a given person the Work is never finished. Although, if he is to attain his own human development, this must be done within the span of a single lifetime of his physical body (for he has no other lifetime), it is practically impossible for him to do this. Yet he must, it is his only chance. That would seem to conclude that matter and for a good many, indeed, it does conclude it, for they abandon the quest and discard any further interest in such ideas forever. But they have given up too soon. Despite its hopelessness it is not hopeless. For a resolution of that paradox the discussions of the following section may provide some light.

4.

This section will be devoted to Time, first to its real nature and then to its relation to the human being in connection with his attempt to become fully and humanly developed.

Time cannot be sensed or felt or thought. Cosmically it is the Unique Subjective. But also it is a cosmic reality, and indirectly responsible for the creation of this universe, which took place precisely through the effort to overcome the Heropass, which is the name for the destructive aspect of Time. The success of that effort, in turn, is the reason that God, the creator of this Universe, is termed His Endlessness in this Version. Time is not therefore destroyed; indeed it everywhere penetrates this Universe, as it were, and its relation to our bodies and to our ultimate hopes is close and decisive. What is the real nature of Time?

No more than in the case of space can time be understood without recourse to the concept of dimensions. This concept lends itself easily to mathematical representation and in modern times mathematicians have experimented geometrically with kinds of space involving far more dimensions than the Euclidian three. And some of them have manifested the not unusual error of taking the products of their mathematical imaginations rather more seriously than is justified, for the only real—objective—space in this Universe is that of three dimensions and all other kinds are purely and finally fantastic. More lately physicists, whose experimental results have not happened to gee with theoretical expectations, have seen some hope of a better outcome if they should employ in their calculations equations representative of spatial dimensions higher than three and have even been known to assert that the improvement in the conformity of their results with their new calculations argues the objective existence of this or that multidimensional space. Obviously the argument is entirely circular and in no way alters the tridimensionality of space in this Universe. It is merely an example of what M. Gurdjieff often called "Greek games." But as a result of such speculations, taken overseriously, physics just now seems on the verge of becoming a veritable madhouse of mathematical delusion.

Strangely enough, these concepts of dimensionality have not been extended to the treatment of physical, or objective time; the Einsteinian four-dimensional continuum (three of space, one of time) remains still fashionable and physicists of the writer's acquaintance even display a sort of horror of considering the possibility that time may correspond to space in its real tridimensionality.

Such, however, is the case. But before analyzing the nature of time in this way it will be well to discuss briefly a difficulty that seems to arise almost inevitably when time is being treated. Thus the objection is frequently raised that the description of it derives from our personal experiences and that consequently we are not speaking of the objective time of physical reality but instead of some kind of private or "psychological" time. Of course the objection is invalid; the case in respect of time is no different from that in respect of space, for in both these instances the origins of our recognition are exactly the same, namely experiential. Indeed in the matter of space the situation is rather more doubtful than in that of time, for our original acquaintance with space is purely sensory and only later are our conceptions of it extended by mathematical manipulations, leaving us with a foundation that, at least theoretically, can be attributed as much to the character of our sensory equipment as to the nature of the real Universe in which that equipment functions. Time, which we experience directly, has no such one-to-one correlation with the functioning of our sense organs; but one can go too far in this direction also, for although we do not know the location or manner of operation of our "time-organ," there might conceivably be one or, alternatively, our perception of time may relate to the general functioning of our organism-as-a-whole. But the point to be made here is that the objective nature of time neither depends upon nor necessarily corresponds to our modes of perceiving it and indeed we shall soon see that, with our presently undeveloped organic equipment, we are not in fact capable of being directly affected by the full characteristics of time. The assertion of the position here, however, is perfectly definite, and it is this: that the following description of the nature of time is not derived either from psychological sources or from personal or private experience but refers instead to the characteristics of time as it exists objectively and entirely apart from anyone's apprehension or non-apprehension of such characteristics. To make this clear we shall call the time to which we here refer, physical time, the time that interpenetrates this physical Universe.

Such objective time comprises within itself three dimensions, not just the single one of which we are most directly aware. This latter we will call the first dimension of time, the usual verbal label for which is succession or duration. The first dimension of time can easily be, and often is, represented diagrammatically by a straight line, points along such a line being marked off at intervals to indicate relevantly numbered years or any other restricted periods of duration that may be under treatment. This is the customary date-line of history, upon which may be represented the durations of wars or of some specific human life or of the average relative lengths of infancy, childhood, adolescence, maturity, senility, and so on. The name given here to this first dimension of physical time is Succession, and although we are directly aware of it in our own experience, we are not accurately so, since some hours are much longer to us than others and a lapse into complete unconsciousness does not inform us of its duration. What this means is that the regularity of our own experience is not as uniform as the functioning of the larger components of the Universe, such as suns or solar systems; and already we must make a distinction between objective, physical time and our own "psychological" times, which last phrase refers actually to our personal inabilities to perceive time accurately as it is in its physical functioning.

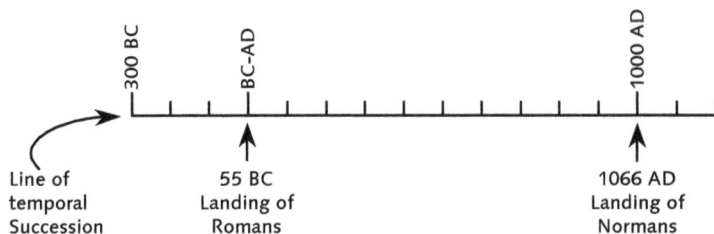

Figure 33. Single Dimension of Time.

This is a relatively simple diagram but it is not quite so simple as it looks, for there is something in it—or rather there is the absence of something in it—which is most significant in respect of our understanding of time and which indeed lies at the bottom of much of the intellectual confusion regarding the nature of time that is manifested in the speculations of modern physics. This element absent in the diagram is what is usually called "Time's Arrow," a short spear or javelin lying parallel to the line of Succession with its barbed end pointing to the right, to indicate the direction of progression from past through present to future. This arrow is not included in the diagram because it is not in fact an objective characteristic of physical time, being instead an attribute of our own (and the physicist's) subjective "psychological" time and really referring not to time itself but to the inaccurate time-perceptions of ordinary, distortedly undeveloped men. Time's Arrow is an illusion issuing from our own lack of development and in turn it leads to many theoretical delusions concerned with the "irreversibility" of various natural phenomena, which irreversibility exists only in respect of the inabilities of ordinary men to perceive the reversibility of such phenomena by means of their sense organs but does not exist either with regard to time itself or to the phenomena themselves. Time's Arrow is an artefact of our restricted type of consciousness; it is not an objective characteristic of physical time. Right at the beginning it is very necessary to recognize this first instance of the distinction between the real nature of time and the way in which we happen to perceive it, i.e., inaccurately.

Still confining ourselves to the first dimension of time it is possible not only to construct diagrams relating to it but also tables whereby the temporal durations of different grades of beings may be set out and compared with each other. The following table of this kind was devised by M. Ouspensky and was not originally a part of the Gurdjieffian system but it was included in the Oragean Version as first formulated in New York. The constant involved is more exactly 28,800 but for convenience and since only approximately round numbers are required, it is taken as 30,000.* The ordinate divisions of the table are units of unilinear, or successive duration; the abscissae give us various universal components.

	Man	Organic Kingdom	Earth	Planetary System	Sun	Galaxy	Universe
SENSATION	1/10,000 second	3 seconds	24 hours	80 years	2.5 million years	73.8 billion years	2.25 quatrillion years
BREATH	3 seconds	24 hours	80 years	2.5 million years	73.8 billion years	2.25 quatrillion years	66.5 quintillion years
DAY	24 hours	80 years	2.5 million years	73.8 billion years	2.25 quatrillion years	66.5 quintillion years	2 sextillion years
LIFE	80 years	2.5 million years	73.8 billion years	2.25 quatrillion years	66.5 quintillion years	2 sextillion years	60 octillion years

Constant — approx. 30,000

Figure 34. Time Table.

This is the table to which reference was made earlier, when sudden alterations in the human population of the planet were discussed and also when the question was considered regarding the natural limitation upon the number of persons for whom a normal development, even through their own efforts, could be permitted. From the last Figure it will be seen that eighty years, the natural life of a man, represents no more than a breath in the life of the planet, that the conditions respecting the latter's most important component, the organic kingdom, cannot alter appreciably in so short an interval, and that consequently the general balance of the human race on Earth, which in turn is the most crucial unit within the organic kingdom, cannot change radically over periods of this order of duration of unilinear time.

Let us now advance to a much more difficult question, that of the second dimension of physical time. The dimensions of space will serve us in this connection as a convenient analogue; but, although our diagrams will be

---

* For the derivation of this table which, in its full form, includes units below and smaller than Man, see *In Search of the Miraculous*, op. cit., pp. 330 ff.

put in terms of space and many of our descriptive words will be drawn from the same source, it must never be forgotten that this is for illustration only and for ease in the transmission of the relevant concepts and that in fact we are discussing temporal relationships and dimensions which are only similar to, but not identical with, their spatial counterparts.

Now the three dimensions of space are sometimes spoken of as being Length, Breadth and Depth, and they are represented diagrammatically by three coordinates mutually at right angles to each other. The first of these ordinates or axes defines the first dimension of space or its unilinear aspect, the first two together define an Area and the three coordinates together define Volume. In the case of time we do not have terms corresponding to Breadth and Depth but have one term corresponding only to Length, namely the term, Succession, which is both the first dimension of time and the word defining its unilinear extension or duration. In the case of two-dimensional time we have no word for the included second dimension but we do have a term for the Area thus defined; and that term is Simultaneity.

At once we must be extremely careful to understand just what this term signifies, for otherwise there will be no possibility of understanding the corresponding characteristic of physical time. Its usual significance is that of togetherness at a single point upon the time-line of Succession: if two events occur at once, they are said to be simultaneous; of course in advanced physics of the relativist variety simultaneity of this kind is alleged to be impossible or, to speak more accurately, unascertainable but the foregoing is the usual acceptance of the word. However, that is not precisely *the present use of the term*, which at first glance will seem almost the opposite, for events occurring in Simultaneity can be far, far distant from each other upon the line of Succession. Thus the landing of the Romans upon the shores of Britain and the landing of the Normans close by are separated by an extensive length upon the date-line of history but in the area of Simultaneity they exist together. How can this be and by what process do we realize that in this case two dimensions of time are involved instead of one?

In the first place we must understand that the fact that we personally do not perceive either of these landings through our sense organs—this fact being represented in our language by our use of the past tense in connection with them and in our thinking by the assumption that they have occurred in the "past" and are "now" over and done with—is an attribute not of the objective Universe but instead that it is a characteristic of our own subjective limitations. In the matter of space, for example, we do not make such hasty and ill-founded assumptions.

For instance, when we take a train from New York to New Haven, we pass through many towns and cities, among them Bridgeport. As the train rolls along its elevated structure through Bridgeport, we can obtain a considerable view of that city and we are then (indirectly) aware of it through the mediation of our own sensory equipment. This is what we account our personal evidence that Bridgeport exists and it also informs us of specific characteristics of the place. Later, as we come into New Haven, none of this evidence is any longer present to us but we do not therefore make the false assumption that Bridgeport (or New York either) has occurred in a "past" space and is "now over and done with." To the contrary we recognize properly that, although we personally are not looking at it, Bridgeport with all its specific characteristics is still just as much there as ever, that it is a continuing physical event in the universal continuum. Indeed we can reassure ourselves upon this point by stepping into a telephone booth at the New Haven station and calling up one of the Bridgeport hotels, a matter which we take so fully for granted that it would scarcely occur to us to do so. Yet it is just our inability to make a telephonic (i.e., a sensory) connection with the "past" that produces our doubts and reinforces our false assumptions concerning it; and this despite our knowledge, when challenged, that there has certainly been an era, and one which most of us can remember, when no such connection could have been established between New Haven and Bridgeport and when, just the same, we entertained no doubts as to the latter's objective existence. Moreover, we do of course make *phonographic* connections with "past" time.

For a "past" event is never "over and done with"; it exists, and all "past" real events exist, eternally in the universal space-time continuum, just as do all "future" real events also; and in this formulation the term, exist, means exist physically. The past, the present, the future, all these are attributes of Time's Arrow, that is, they are attributes of our own subjectivities but not of the objective Universe of physical space and of physical time.

An important corollary of this is that *all* physical motion, not only of our own bodies but also of all other physical entities, is an illusion. All motion is subjective, i.e., it is the motion of subjectivity, ultimately the motion of "I"; this purely subjective motion produces first the *changing* relationships that only apparently take place between external objects and then in turn is projected upon the objects themselves by the really moving subjectivity or "I." The objective, physical Universe is completely static, all motion of whatever kind inheres in "I," and for the physical Universe there are no such realities as past, present or future or any objective distinctions between these purely subjective divisions. In discussing the questions of a genuinely objective and real physics* only the deletion of all motion can permit us to see those other

---

* Here is a crucial instance of the inability of modern physics to deal objectively with its subject matter. So long as physicists postulate the concept of fundamentally objective velocities (let us say if only of that of light, although today they still postulate many others), they will always be considering a subjective-objective mixture but never the purely *physical* Universe. All velocity-calculations refer ultimately to physicists, not to the physical world. Velocity does not characterize any physical system or its parts.

aspects, especially temporal, of physical Reality that are actually the correct ones. We shall have to return to this matter of the real origin and locus of motion later in the discussion, so it should not be forgotten.

To continue with the bidimensionality of physical time, the area of Simultaneity so produced is to be defined by two time-axes at right angles to each other, as in the corresponding case of space. As has been mentioned, no term in the Oragean Version is known to the writer to apply to the perpendicular axis taken by itself but obviously this axis is one of extension or of physical duration in a direction at right angles to the duration set up by the motion of subjectivity. It represents a real dimension of potential measurement applicable to any real physical object or event (i.e., a relationship between or among objects) and is a fully genuine characteristic of objective Reality. As a consequence it will be seen that, whereas the location of an event upon the line of Succession of unilinear time may be made by a point placed at the proper position upon the line, in the case of the area of Simultaneity such an event can only properly be located by the placing of a line across the area in the apposite position. It will of course be understood that in the following diagram the situation is reduced to its barest elements for the sake of simplification and that the actual physical reality is considerably more complicated.

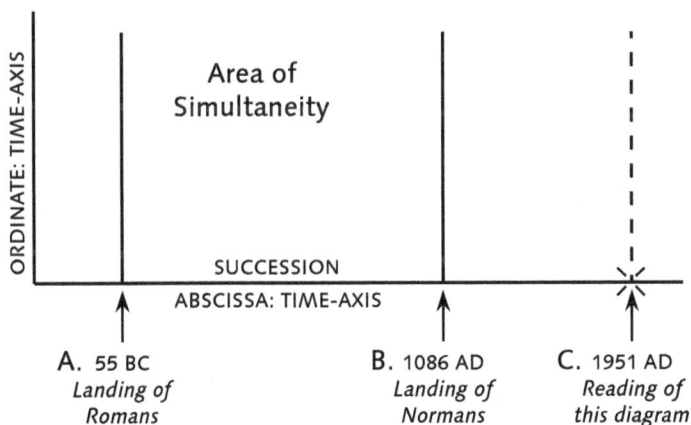

Figure 35. Two Dimensions of Time.

In the diagram just given, the three located events are represented by the three perpendicular lines, which indicate not only their relations to the date-line of history or unilinear temporal Succession but also their physical extensions or durations in the temporal area of Simultaneity. The third of these lines is broken in order to distinguish it from the others, since this last event, as well as being a physical one, is for us an experiential occurrence also. As a physical occurrence it possesses its own duration in Simultaneity just as do its two predecessors but in experiential terms it is confined to the small cross at its base, for we are not aware of the Simultaneity-aspects of our bodies which accompany the event simultaneously and are restricted in our further limited awareness to the small cross-section existing only upon the line of temporal Succession.

The physical relations in the diagram, however, permit us to comprehend how it is that we find ourselves in a position not only to experience at one remove each of the "previous" events located but also to have cognizance of both of them at once and thus to compare them in various ways. For this kind of experience and of experienced comparison is likewise a fully physical event. And obviously, if Reality were comprised solely within or along the line of temporal Succession, it would prove impossible for us to be so related to events of the "past," even of the "past" of our own bodies and history; and memories, which themselves are physical events, could not contribute to our experiential content. For how can one look along a line and perceive beyond one of its points another in exactly the same direction? The first in line would obscure, as it were, the second. Indeed, in order to view any except the very "last" moment upon such a line of succession it is plainly necessary that another dimension outside that line be involved. The following modification of the previous diagram can suggest a way in which our memories are possible, although the simplicity of the previous diagram must now inject serious distortions.

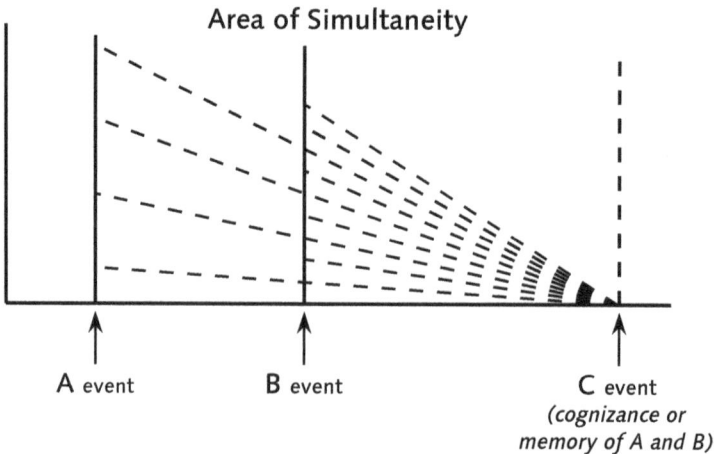

Figure 36. The Relation of temporal Bidimensionality to Cognizance or to Memory.
(This diagram was not included in the Oragean Version.)

This sort of demonstration, alleged to be an argument from our own subjective abilities to the nature of the physical Universe in respect of its temporal characteristics, has sometimes been held improper because of its assumed direction, viz., from ourselves to physics. However, the situation (only crudely) diagrammed above is not an artefact of our cognitive or our mnemonic abilities but to the contrary it is just the opposite.

The fact that by a mental activity we can be aware of such two (or more) happenings at the same moment, derives directly from the prior fact that they do in reality so coexist within the temporal continuum of the objective Universe. The circumstance that we can perceive an area of space through the mediation of our sense organs, by no means implies that the objective existence of the given area depends upon or is created by those organs or their functioning; and in the same way neither does the circumstance that we can collect together in memory two or more events which themselves are successively separated, mean that the simultaneous existence of these events depends upon or is created by our own ability to be aware of them at a single moment. In fact, it means just the reverse, as is likewise the case in regard to space. To exist in the physical area of Simultaneity is to exist simultaneously, because in that area there are no objective distinctions corresponding to the past, present and future of subjective experience.

But if three-dimensional spatial events exist in the area of Simultaneity as well as upon the line of temporal Succession, their time-aspects are not yet exhausted. Along with the two foregoing ways they exist also eternally. Eternity, as a technical term of this Version, does not bear the customary and quite incomprehensible significance of either an indefinite or an infinite extension along the time-axis of Succession; Eternity does not mean infinite duration but, rather, it means time-*volume*. In this sense it is obvious at once how Eternity can and must be here and now as well as everywhere and everytime else. But before we discuss this matter further, let us observe the diagram illustrative of it.

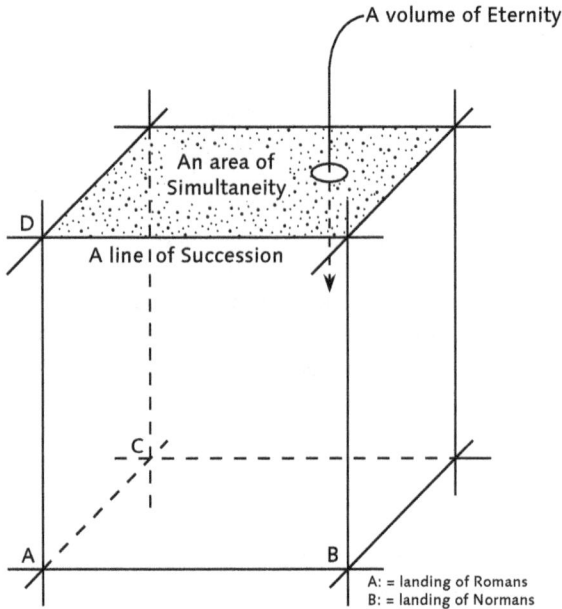

Figure 37. Three-dimensional Time.

It is seen that a three-dimensional time-volume is constructed by erecting the three time-axes, A-B, A-C and A-D, at right angles to each other at the point, A; and of course any other point would do as well. Each of the time-axes is a line of Succession or an extension of durational time and with them as a basis a cube is constructed, each of whose edges comprises another possible line of successive time. Each side of the cube represents an area of Simultaneity; and both the lines and the planes so set up are continued beyond the limits of the cube in order to show that the latter is merely an arbitrarily selected and arbitrarily bounded volume of Eternity out of the total Eternity-volume of the Universe. Finally, any line traversing the cube in any direction will constitute a line of Succession and any plane cross-section intersecting it will constitute an area of Simultaneity; these latter are omitted in the drawing in order not to clutter up the diagram. It should be repeated that this analysis of the objective nature of time is unconnected either with consciousness or with experience but is instead a formulation of the purely physical characteristics of time as manifested in the purely physical Universe. The successions and the simultaneities created in this continuum by experientiability are only special and limited cases of the potentialities inherent in the whole continuum. It should also be noted that, whereas we have a partial and crippled awareness of objective simultaneity (in our memory-function), we have no similar awareness of Eternity in our present condition.

Here, then, we have the time-continuum which, together with the corresponding three-dimensional space-continuum, creates the total Universe-continuum of Reality as formulated by an objective physics. Naturally it can be asked: what are the limits of the time-continuum? And this also can be asked in regard to space. There is an answer to these questions, although such an answer cannot be diagrammed upon a plane surface such as one of these sheets of paper. The total universal space-time continuum is finite but unlimited, just as, in three spatial dimensions only, the surface of a globe or ball is finite but unlimited. Since we have here a three-dimensional time-continuum combined with a three-dimensional space-continuum, their common containment is within a seven-dimensional continuum comprising them both together. The finite but unlimited boundaries of this last seven-dimensional continuum are also the finite but unlimited boundaries of the Reality of this Universe. It is within such a seven-dimensional continuum that our own actualities and our own potentialities as human beings are manifested.

Before we advance to a consideration of our own confined temporal situation, let us discuss briefly the matter of Relative Time as it affects all the beings in our Universe, ourselves of course among them. For every different type of being in the Universe time flows differently, which is to say that the lines of Succession along which their experiences proceed are different lines; and the bearing will thus be seen of all the different possible lines of this kind that may traverse a given Eternity-volume. In the language now of experience instead of physics it means that for a being with a relevantly constructed organism a "day" or a "life," comprising a full content of daily or lifetime experience, may be and is of an entirely different duration than our own. From our subjective point of view such a full and complete life, including all its experiential stages from birth through growth and maturity to death, may be either so short as to appear miraculous or impossible to us or so long as to exceed the bounds of our subjective real imagination. This is exactly the situation portrayed in Figure 34 where a tabulation of such experiential divisions was set out respecting beings of greater durational extension than ourselves; and as mentioned, this table could be carried in the opposite direction also, to include cellular and electronic phenomena and thus the types of beings whose experiences are so conditioned. But for all of them from great to small a sensation, a breath, a day and a life are approximately the same in experiential terms although varying through extremely wide degrees in respect of the time-space continuum of the Universe. The only exception to this statement occurs in cases like our own, in which retarded and only partial development itself decreases our experiential potentialities and in which circumstances naturally a full and normal lifetime cannot therefore be experienced. But for all normal beings from galaxies to electrons a lifetime, no matter how widely different in temporal duration, is approximately the same in experiential data. In the Oragean Version this circumstance is subsumed under the heading of Relative Time, which has its repercussions in our own subjective experiences also, as has already been noted when we alluded to the differences in our experiences of quite similar physically objective durations such as an hour or a week.

But there are other matters, too, as to which our hopes, our phantasies, our delusions and our real expectations are related to the nature of time. For instance, there are those among us who entertain the fancied hope of Reincarnation. This for us is either miracle-mongering or an instance of the Gratuitous Heaven Fallacy, for how can a man reincarnate who has no notion as to the process or else, like a New Deal reliefer, expects someone else to accomplish it for him? Indeed the idea is even sillier and depends upon no more than a plain misuse of words. Can one re-enter a house or anything else which he has never previously entered? Of course he cannot; the prefix, re-, has the precise meaning of repeating the action or doing it again, and this carries the direct implication that already it has been done at least once. Since almost all of those who speak of Reincarnation have never yet incarnated, they cannot now be in a position to repeat the latter action. We say "almost all" because Reincarnation is in fact a real possibility in this Universe but certainly it is not one for such undeveloped and abnormal persons as ourselves. Only after a genuine Incarnation can any real possibility of a genuine Reincarnation arise.

The act of Incarnation was held in the early Christian religion to be one of the major Mysteries, by which it may have been meant that it could be understood only through the logic of *solvitur ambulando*, that is by means of actually doing it and thus becoming acquainted with its nature through one's own experience of it. The exact information as to how to incarnate was a secret doctrine of the Christian Church and today is unknown to any Christians either in or out of that Church, from its highest dignitaries to its lowest and humblest members.

That information, however, was never the private property of the Christian or of any other religious sect and all genuine Schools have always known it. In the present Version Incarnation is defined as a *correct and objective identification* with the physical body, which can only occur long after our present incorrect and *subjective* identification with its Chief Feature has been destroyed by means of a correct and *objective non-identification from* the physical body. Non-identified Self-Observation first permits the now distorted functions of the physical body to re-align themselves more normally, the further steps of the Method (called Participation and Experiment) increase the normality of function and eventually Chief Feature is destroyed, by observing it but *never* by attempting to alter it directly. When Chief Feature has been destroyed, the last link of the chain of falsely *subjective* identification with the physical body has vanished and only then can there be any possibility of the correct and *objective* identification with it which is called Incarnation. This Incarnation is also related to the coalescence of the lower and higher sub-centres that takes place at a stage of development later than its beginning and no genuine act of Incarnation is possible until after such coalescence has occurred. But that is what Incarnation is and, no matter in what terms it may be or may have been described by religious organizations or for what emotional motives it may have been advocated, it always was and always will be the same essential act. That act permits one to be one's physical body (without losing the further attributes of one's being) and involves a far closer association with it than is possible in our present subjectively identified state.

Reincarnation involves more than that, for it means the ability successively to incarnate *different* physical bodies existing between different points along the line of Succession of temporal dimensionality. It means, for example, that "I" can have the physical body of Pocahontas at one durational period of the date-line of history and the physical body of General Ulysses Sampson Grant (or, if a change of sex is not desired, of his wife) at another, different durational period—unlikely as we should be to find either of these possessions an agreeable one. But such an ability implies more than the capacity to incarnate and then to reincarnate for, no matter how small it may be, there must always be some temporal interval between the existences of the selected physical bodies; and where do "I" go or where am "I" then? Without a body there is no "I," which is a way of saying that the subjective can occur only in relation to the objective, and "I" (as an actual aspect of Reality) vanishes unless and except in association with a body of some kind. What all this means is that a prerequisite of Reincarnation is, at the least, a body Kesdjan with which "I" may be associated during the time-interval intervening between the objective existences of successive physical bodies, if by Reincarnation is meant (as it is) the successive incarnation of different physical bodies by the *same* "I."

Two corollaries of this situation will occur to the reader. The first is that, although Reincarnation is a mere phantasy on the part of those who talk most about it, it is a real potentiality for a fully and normally developed human being and perhaps even for one not yet fully developed but at least normally developed up to the stage of possessing an astral body in good operating function. This first corollary is quite correct but the second one, although often entertained, is not; the second corollary is to the effect that, once a persons's physical body dies, he himself (the "I" associated with it) will vanish and that thus no further worries can plague him, since worries are a part of experience and all experience must lapse. Such a one may now *think* so but in fact, as we shall soon see, his position is by no means of so favorable a sort. "I," while eventually destructible, is in no wise so easily destructible.

If, then, both Incarnation and Reincarnation are real human potentialities but in our own cases are actual phantasies, what may be our circumstances as stated here? Our circumstances are those of an automatic Recurrence. At the death of the physical body "I" cannot proceed further along the line of temporal Succession previously traversed because "I" has now lost that association with a physical body which alone permits of successive experience along that line. Moreover the "I" now considered possesses no other body than the one which no longer functions.

However, not only does "I" have the attribute of extantness but also the association between "I" and even an undeveloped and abnormally functioning physical body is a close one, not easily to be broken. So where does "I" go at the death of the physical body? Where else but to the other (functioning) end of that body, which we call its birth and which, as a physical event in the physical space-time continuum of the Universe, has vanished only as a datum of our subjective experience but not at all as a factual physical event? The physical body, like any other physical event, is always there, in Succession, in Simultaneity and in Eternity, just as the events of the year, 55 BC, and of the year, 1066 AD, and of any other year or of any point along the line of Succession, are always there. We may not be experiencing them "now" as we say but they are there, they exist and they present always the potentiality of experientiability, in the same sense that Bridgeport is spatially where it is even when we don't happen to be looking at it. The birth of a physical body is as much an enduring event as its death or as any happening in respect of its lifetime. That is the physical fact; the experiential fact is that the point of death is experientially adjacent to that of conception, for of course, to speak strictly, experientiability "commences" prior to birth, at conception. And until "I" vanishes completely, which is the goal of certain sophisticated diabolist cults but which will not happen "as yet," "I's" association with a specific dying body must be succeeded, in terms of experience, by "I's" association with the same specific body at the point of that body's "origin." In the Greek myth it is during that transition that memory is wiped out, the symbolism being, immersion in the waters of Lethe.

Perhaps it will now be well to introduce a diagram of the situation, which will be a modification of Figure 33 for a single dimension of time.

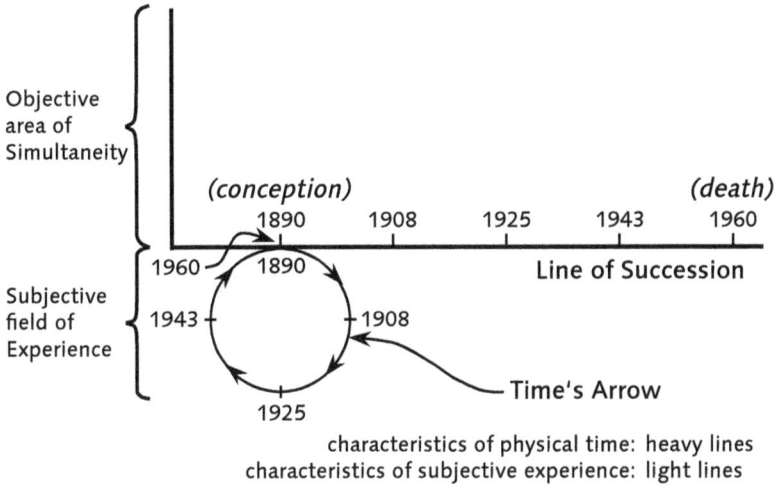

characteristics of physical time: heavy lines
characteristics of subjective experience: light lines

Figure 38. Relations between Objectivity and Subjectivity in a given Lifespan.
(This diagram was not included in the original Oragean version.)

The diagram represents primarily a typical lifespan of seventy years of an undeveloped human, from the date of conception, 1890 AD, to the date of death, 1960 AD; this is shown in a heavy line. Immediately below the durational extension in successive time is shown the circular lifespan of subjective experience, the lighter circle from 1890 AD back to 1960 AD being of the same length as the corresponding black line above it. Time's Arrow is included in the lighter circle, since this is a characteristic of subjective experience, but is omitted from the heavy line where it is not a characteristic of physical time. The area of temporal Simultaneity is noted to the left, only to contrast the upper portion of the diagram to the lower subjective portion; it has no other significance in the drawing.

As has also been noted, several of these diagrams were not offered in the original Oragean Version and are not to be attributed to Mr. Orage. But the formulations accompanying them were made by Mr. Orage; the reader will recall that otherwise they would appear in italics, as does this explanation. Some of these diagrams, however, as will be noted in each relevant case, have been invented just now by the present writer under the impression and in the hope that they may serve to clarify a rather difficult exposition.

Another diagram of this same sort, approaching in another way the situation portrayed in Figure 38, is given below.

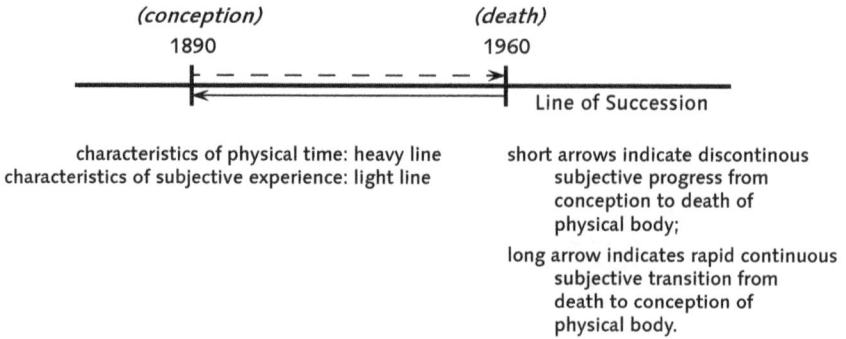

Figure 39. Another Representation of Relations between
Objectivity and Subjectivity in a given Lifespan.

Figure 39, above, is only another way of representing the circle of Recurrence and the fact that 1890 AD (or any other unilinear time-point upon the date-line of Succession) is always there in objective Reality and that, if "I" be associated with a physical body of the above durational span, it is not only possible but indeed unavoidable to revisit such a temporal location and to re-experience subjectively all the objective events related to it. It will be seen that those are not new events but in every respect the same events; and our experiences, as they proceed successively, may appear novel to us only because we have "forgotten" them. It might be, for instance, that this is the millionth recurrent occasion upon which the reader has read these words but in great probability he will not be aware of it. Sometimes, though, that is not completely the case, as is testified by the well-known subjective phenomenon of *"déjà vu,"* in which an apparently novel scene possesses a striking familiarity to us and we may even know full well what our companion is about to say, and which has never been very satisfactorily explained by the Gestalt-like and other assumptions of psychologists. Numerous writers have also experienced the equally strange and uncomfortable phenomenon of *"déjà écrit,"* a comparable subjective happening.

In the last diagram a further feature of subjectivity is encountered, the discontinuous nature of our subjective experience, represented by the broken line of arrows extending from conception to death. This is not an objective characteristic of physical Reality but instead it is a feature of our trancelike state of consciousness, in which our bodies only momentarily and intermittently emerge into our clear awareness from the nebulous fog of our so-called Waking state.

How can we ever truly wake up from such a dream-state and escape from this one body to which we are bound by the Chain of false Identification, as well as from always the same events related to that body and which must recur to our subjective experience over and over again in the same predetermined way? Only when one is completely aware in detail of that entire circle of recurrent events making up the full lifespan of the physical body, can he ever leave it, and the foregoing is only the first of the necessary conditions. Do we remember the motion picture exercise mentioned much earlier, in which only one day out of a life was taken and the attempt made to re-experience it visually? In the practice of that exercise the student will soon realize that the portions of the picture that stand out most clearly are just those during which he had successfully performed the act of Self-Observation with impartial non-identification. And just one of the purposes of Self-Observation is eventually to bring the whole lifespan into full and clear awareness; that is why there is no special time or place for its practice and why also the attempt is to make the activity as long and continuous as possible.

Now let us consider the situation in greater detail. In the first place it is plain how and why our experiences are predetermined, since they derive exclusively from our association with a specific physical body. But that body, from beginning to end, is an objective, non-moving and immovable event in the space-time continuum of physical Reality. Let us take it for the present purposes as a four-dimensional object, comprising three dimensions of space and one of time, the successive or durational dimension of time. As such a four-dimensional object the body appears to go through many and intricate motions but actually it remains immovable; the illusion of motion arises from the subjective movement of "I" along the body's durational extent bit by bit successively, and this motion is then at once projected upon the successively perceived three-dimensional cross-sections of the body, very much as the successive frames of a motion picture film seem to be filled with motion if they are thrown upon the screen at the proper successive intervals. There is no actual motion within the confines of a motion picture film; it is merely a linear arrangement of completely still pictures. Similarly there is no motion in a four-dimensional physical body; it too is merely a temporally linear arrangement of completely motionless three-dimensional cross-sections, *existing simultaneously* but *seen successively* by "I" due to the motion of subjectivity along this arrangement.

This concept will also solve a non-existent problem over which modern physicists plague themselves unduly, for all physical objects are in the same situation as a physical body. It is not that the physical "future" is inherent in the physical "past." The physical "future" is not only inherent in but *is* the physical "future"; it exists "now" and unchangeably in the area of Simultaneity and in the volume of Eternity, as it is and not otherwise. Our ignorance of the "future," as well as the very concept of the "future," derive from our *subjective* limitations and has nothing to do with the realities of the "future," which will not be altered by any imaginary "free will" inherent either in us or in the physical world.

It has been suggested that a quite simple model can be made of the four-dimensional physical body which is accessible to the awareness-ability of "I." Such a model would take the approximate form of the kind of cigar known as a panetela, one end of which tapers nearly to a point while the other end is cut off bluntly. The smaller end would represent the point of conception where two sex cells combine to form the beginning of the body; then the shape rapidly "grows" to its maximum diameter and its length will correspond to the durational extent or lifespan of the given body; the larger end, cut off abruptly, represents the body's death. Along the entire length very small cross-sections must be imagined next to each other in succession and each of these will represent a single slice or "frame," corresponding to the motionless physical body in many different successive positions. "I" may be imaged as passing through the centre of the cigar, becoming aware of its arrangement of cross-sections or "frames" successively and thus receiving the illusion of motion as between those cross-sections due to their varying configurations. Finally, the cigar must be imagined as bent about in a circle so that the blunt end lies adjacent to the tapering end; this will represent the four-dimensional physical body as it exists in the subjective field of experientiability.

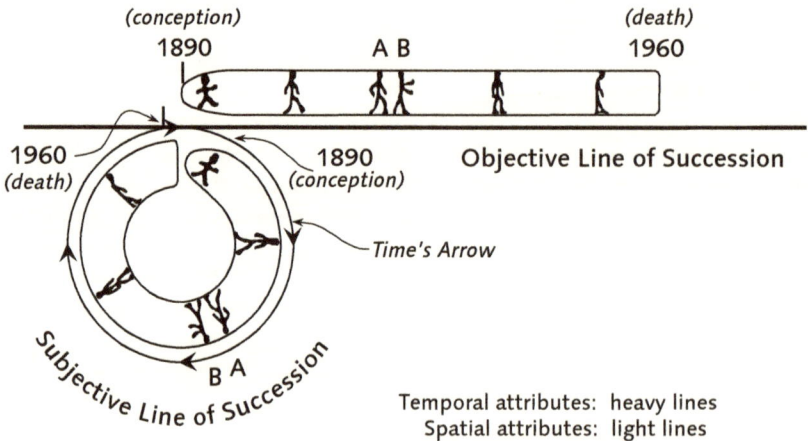

Temporal attributes: heavy lines
Spatial attributes: light lines

A and B: two immediately successive three-dimensional cross-sections or "frames" of the four-dimensional physical body.

Figure 40. The four-dimensional Physical Body in relation to Objective and Subjective Time.
(This diagram was not included in the original Oragean Version.)

It is to be understood in the above diagram that, although there appear only a few little symbolic figures (three-dimensional cross-sections of the four-dimensional body), the entire cigar-shape is to be considered as crammed full of them, each one representing a potential instant of awareness successively upon the part of "I." "I" is not represented at all in the diagram; the reader who looks at it may be thought of as taking the place of "I" in the simile. If he looks at the diagram slowly from left to right and slowly clockwise around the circle, he will be representing "I" as now functioning successively moment by moment in the single durational dimension of time. If he regards the diagram all at once (as no doubt he will do), then he is, as it were, seeing the entire lifespan at once, as if in the two-dimensional area of Simultaneity. What he will have to do with his actual physical body is to experience all its actual events simultaneously in this way over the full range from conception to death to conception before he has fulfilled the first requirement necessary in order to free himself from it.

But there is still a third dimension of time, or rather there is time's three-dimensional volume, which as yet we have not taken into account. And to do so will slightly change the formulation of Recurrence so far presented. Here it may be well to have the diagram first.

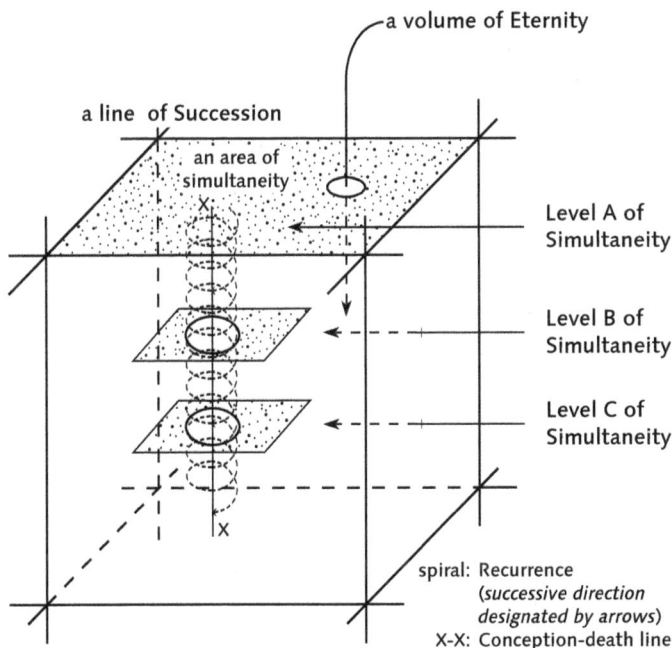

Figure 41. Recurrence in Eternity.

In this diagram it will be seen that the circle of Recurrence in the area of Simultaneity becomes a series of circles in different areas of Simultaneity and thus a spiral down through a part of the total volume of Eternity. In the same fashion the point of adjacent conception-death or death-conception becomes a line in the three-dimensional time continuum.

One thing which the diagram attempts to show is that, in an objectively temporal sense, Reality possesses a kind of perpendicular structure; each area of Simultaneity is as it is ("predetermined") in Eternity but, as between immediately adjacent layers of Simultaneity, there may be slight differences. In the subjective experience of the ordinary man this means that he cannot continue to recur in *exactly* the same way—that his experience during the circle of his Recurrence cannot be exactly the same—indefinitely. Subjectively he must either be going up or going down. The circular cigar to which he is bound by Identification, is not just a single cigar but a series of them, and in far enough separated areas of Simultaneity it possesses gradually altered characteristics. Nothing is changed in respect of the determined series of events he must experience but, after a sufficient degress, the events themselves must alter because they constitute successive cross-sections of a different part of the total cigar-spiral than that at which he started. In this sense it is said that there is already a lag between ourselves and our proper objective time-line of Succession, since we have dropped below that area of Simultaneity upon which we began.

This degressing spiral of Recurrences is shown in the drawing and it forms the original basis for the later superstition of Metamorphosis and the Transmigration of Souls, in which the subject is supposed suddenly to be transplanted, as it were, into a different, usually a lower, kind of body. But this can really happen gradually and over what we would now call "long periods" of time. If one lives always in a passive state of consciousness, without any of that kind of effort whose first form is here called Self-Observation, then slowly, Recurrence by Recurrence, that consciousness becomes more passive still, until at last all real potentiality of a genuinely human type of consciousness is lost. At such a point in the cigar-spiral the organism becomes correspondingly animal; and "later" it assumes the organic forms of lower orders. To these the degressing "I" is bound one after another until, in the final conclusion, it may descend to the level of being of metals and at last to the Negative Absolute, thereby losing all potentiality forever.

But if one can go down simply by never expending any truly human effort, he can also go up, by the correct expenditure of such effort. The lower limit of the cigar-spiral ends, as we have said, in the Negative Absolute; but its upper limit is the human Positive Absolute, the fully developed and functioning human being, the Hydrogen[24] of the Universe. Such a progress upward from our present condition has, however, serious obstacles to pass, including the decisive limitation, for us upon this planet, that only a very few may do so within an approximately similar time-period.

There is then the further difficulty that, when one advances upward, another must take his place. At all sections of the spiral, i.e., upon each recurring level or area of Simultaneity, there must be an "I" associated with that cigar-circle or recurring organism. Without an organism there is no "I"; and equally without an "I" there is no organism. Thus subjectivity is always the undiagrammed feature of the spiral and no section of it can be left "I"-less. Who, then, is to take your place, if you go further? In the work of the Method, as in that of all genuine Schools, this is provided for by the hierarchy of candidates and pupils, the candidate becoming a pupil and introducing other candidates, the pupil becoming an instructor and assisting other pupils, the instructor becoming a teacher, and so on, thus imaging upon a small scale the same process of Reality whereby at last an ordinary man may become a complete human being.

In this progress upward there are also the mi-fa and the si-do intervals of the octave, where outside assistance is required without fail, if the point is to be passed. And these also exist with regard to a downward degression (although in this case we probably would not regard the external force as one of assistance), so that the diabolist goal of nonentity is not either entirely easy of access or immediately accessible.

For the sake of simplicity and in order to discuss an associated topic let us now confine our attention to a single level or area of Simultaneity in relation to our own planet and let us further confine this area to a portion bounded along one side by a line of Succession of approximately eighty years' duration, the length of an average human life. Within this small physical-temporal portion of eternal Reality we shall consider the situation respecting a single man and respecting all men existing on this planet during the given temporal period.

The first thing to be said is that practically everyone so involved is an ordinary man and that his life-path, made up of the potentialities actually realized and constituting his experience, is limited by reason of his state of human undevelopment. Nevertheless, these potentialities are vast in number. The second thing is that every life-path is manifestly different and that so must be the train of experiences which comprises it. This must be true merely from spatial considerations, for no two bodies can occupy the same points in space and the experiences perceived simply by reason of the occupancy of different spatial locations are different experiences; moreover, despite every equalitarian lie ever uttered, no two persons ever are, or ever can be, the same. Thus every single person does, and must, travel a life-path different from that of everyone else. Obviously this refers also to identical twins who, no more than others, can occupy the same spatial locations.

But there is also the life-path of the entire planetary human race during the given durational period. This life-path is the sum of all the life-paths of the separate members. It must at all moments fulfill the total potentialities really possible to human beings in their then condition, limited only by the number of separate units available, which in the present case is about two billion. What this means is that someone at every moment—at this moment now—must be experiencing one of the facets of human real possibility and that all such facets must be included. The darkest depths of ignorance and the utmost possible clarity of thought, the most profound and hopeless despair and agony as well as the summit of possible bliss, failure and success and all the intermediate degrees between these opposites are being experienced by someone *now*. Every three seconds, every time that on the average we draw and expel a breath, someone experiences the birth-struggle, someone else the death-struggle, during the latter of which that chemical substance called askokin, the accumulated result of his passive life-experiences, is released to feed the Moon. Thus is the total life of planetary mankind fulfilled in its complete potentiality. There are a number of implications in this situation, of which we will notice only one. It is that all possible personal life-paths must always be covered in order to make up the complete life-path of mankind; quite possibly this is what was imaged in the ancient Egyptian Schools by the Paths and Highway of Anpu, now supposed superstitiously to refer to something called the Underworld by those who Greekishly term that god Anubis. It is another reason for which you cannot go further, either upward or downward, until some other "I" is ready to take your place.

We have now covered the information in regard to the nature of physical or objective time incorporated in the Oragean Version and with this discussion bring the chapter entitled The Greater Map to a close, with one final word. Let it be remembered that none of these statements is offered for credulous belief. Let it also be remembered that few better opportunities for Pondering could be provided.

V. DESTINATION

1. ORAGEAN APHORISMS[*]

Miscellaneous

1. Buddha, Jesus Christ, Pythagoras and the like were practical workmen.

2. Gurdjieff represents a Fourth Yoga with no school and no teachers, a combination but not an addition of the three Yogas, Raj, Bakhti and Hathi; the wholeness that is something more than the three parts which make it up. You cannot refer to the whole without referring to the parts but the whole is different; this is the difficulty of talking about "I."

3. The normal is not dependent upon the average.

4. A flock of sheep exists for the *objective* reason of wool and mutton. Perhaps we can cheat our fate as mutton and wool, although we shall then serve another objective.

5. The difference between subjective and objective value is that between the sheep's attitude regarding sheep and the sheep's function or purpose. Our herd values have no preferential over our objective value to a superior power, the Moon.

6. The black sheep finds itself very odd among the other sheep; but our interest lies in the individual, the rebel with an inkling.

7. The meaning and aim of existence is the preoccupation of the ordinary man, never the occupation.

8. Discover Chief Feature; never mind what it comes from.

9. Non-identify with your Chief Feature and it will not bother you.

10. Individuality is consciousness (of the possession) of Will.

11. The Potential is that which can be, given external and internal circum-

---

[*] The numerical arrangement is that of the present writer, the quotations are direct.

stances capable of converting it into the Actual. These potentialities are not infinite in number.

On Science

12. Scientists are engaged in anatomizing the corpse of the Universe.

13. If you wish to understand the life of a being, you must approach it not only from the side of its mechanical functions.

14. Modern science reduces the Universe to a series of behaviors and there remain no entities at all. All that we call life is behavior; but what behaves? Nothing.

15. Science is the expression of the third sub-centre of the first centre; it sees everything mechanically, i.e., only to the extent of one-third; it has no answer to human needs in crises.

On Bodily Phenomena

16. Can you correlate certain states with certain ways of breathing?

17. You cannot think clearly unless both nostrils are clear.

18. Vision must be experienced in the back of the head.

On the Centres

19. Centres are not brains; the three brains are the organs of the respective three centres.

20. The interrelation of centres: the art of jiu jitsu as applied to the three centres depends upon the fact that, when any note of any octave is struck, it tends to sound similar notes of other octaves; and thus the similar notes in the three centres are related. Cf. the assistance of intellectual and emotional states by posture, and vice versa.

21. The fourth centre is the synthesis of the three preceding centres.

22. Of nature centre #1 is on the Moon, centre #2 is on the Earth, centre #3 is on the Sun.

V. DESTINATION

On Bodies

23. You must finally be the tutor of your body.

24. Have you the same certainty that you possess a mind-body as that you possess a physical body? Reasoning is the locomotion of the mental body, which is made up of definite organs, e.g., concentration, etc. Logical progression is the ordinary locomotion of the mental body as a whole. Life in the physical body gives sensations; life in the astral body gives emotions; life in the mind-body gives thoughts.

25. Psychological exercises are devised for obtaining freedom of movement for the astral and mental bodies, for these have to be consciously taught to crawl.

26. Conditional immortality is to be contrasted to the impossible immortality of "those who faintly trust the larger hope." The possibility of immortality is a responsibility. What part of us is potentially immortal? Only the third body has the necessary amount of self-maintenance. (A diamond is immortal on this planet because here there is no heat sufficient to destroy it; but that is not so elsewhere.)

27. Purgatory, Hell, Paradise only apply to those that survive the death of the planetary body, that is, those who have an astral body; the soul-body cannot experience any of this.

28. The psychic body is the umbilical cord uniting the two higher bodies with the planetary body. It is confused with the astral body but it is really a separate body, sometimes called the etheric body; it is the least permanent and the most easily dissolved at death.

On Fallacies

29. There must be something to explain why we are all such fools, why we are not self-conscious, why we treat ourselves with such care; this something we call Kundabuffer.

30. Amusement is an accidental blend of emotion and idea and is not a real emotion.

31. Idealism consists in a) wishes that are actualizable and b) wishes that are not. The latter include pursuits which spend the force that might actualize the former.

32. The third centre is not contemplative; this is the Esthetic Fallacy, which is very harmful psychologically.

33. Hypnotism is a matter of building currents; it can be done by stroking animals behind the ears.

34. Spiritualism: there is nothing in it except something trivial. It is a neurosis like Magic. It is the proposal to get into a state of *delirium tremens* in order to investigate snakes.

35. Astrology makes two assumptions: 1) that at the moment of conception the potentialities of experience are precipitated into a being (but it does not differentiate between the seed and the subsequent being); 2) that the fate of the individual is comprised in the elements contained in the seed (but astrology cannot predict the order of the external events which will actualize the seed).

36. Religions were originated by King Konuzion, with the purpose of keeping his subjects from the poppy. They are expressions of distorted essential emotions. "There is no religion, there is only one God."

On Being and Beings

37. Being is the emotional centre but it is only the result of a conflict between knowing and doing. You must try to know and to do in order to be; that is the value of knowing and doing. Man is a superior species on earth because there is a great conflict between knowing and doing in his case. Men among themselves should also be graded in this way. And for the same reason the equal development of centres is necessary.

38. A being is a creature that feels; and therefore is to be graded by the range and intensity of feeling, which depends in turn upon the quantity of knowing and doing.

39. Any attempt to attain superior being directly, leads to a psychopathic state; this is the fallacy of Mysticism, which involves imaginary feelings.

40. Being and Non-being are two absolutes between which is a state of Existence moving in either direction, that of evolution or that of involution. The range of Existence between Positive Absolute and Negative Absolute provides the scale of beings, of which man is the third from highest and metal is the lowest.

41. A being is defined in value according to the degree to which Faith, Hope and Love have become objective in him.

On Faith, Hope and Love

42. Faith, Hope and Love are the growing ends of essence.

43. Faith is confidence, not belief; for example, the way a lion walks through the woods.

44. Hope is effort, not a wish; an effort to make it so and not a wish that it may be so.

45. Of Love the first form is of self and of self in others; the second form is love of others and of self in them; the third form is love of duty or God and the other forms are by-products of it, i.e., it is love of that for which the individual exists.

On Art

46. Objective Art produces the same effect upon the subject as that of Self-Observation. One man's remark upon seeing the Great Pyramid—"I felt my nothingness"—evidenced an experience of non-identification.

47. Objective Art is art with a conscious purpose that is successfully realized.

48. There are no immortal works of art. There is one Art: the art of making a complete human being of oneself, of making an enduring mental body.

On Intellectual Functions

49. The mind is an octopus, a dragon, the devil on the threshold. It will not answer questions clearly. The beast must be slain by making it answer clearly.

50. Belief is a luxury and only those are entitled to it who have knowledge.

51. Instinctive reason we share with the animals but have a higher type of it; associative reason functions according to verbal associations; of objective reason we know practically nothing, it is to be pondered over and acquired.

52. Knowledge is consciousness of external facts; belief is conviction on inadequate grounds.

53. Knowledge and Understanding: The reason of ordinary beings is the reason of Knowledge. The reason of the normal being is the reason of Understanding. Knowledge is a temporary part of the being; Understanding is a permanent part of the being. A man can behave otherwise than his Knowledge; he cannot behave otherwise than his Understanding, which circumstances can never overcome. Knowledge must be repeated often in order permanently to be gained; Understanding is incorporated into essence forever.

54. No statement can be understood without the effort of conscious assimilation; this brings Realization.

55. Man is a passion for understanding the meaning and aim of existence. But we have only instinctive passions and thus fail to understand this. Not one in a million has any interest in man as differentiated from himself; or else he is interested only in some happiness-reform. Being 99% abnormal, the-meaning-and-aim-of-existence means only instinctive advantage; and it is therefore an academic question. We are never on the plane where these questions have any real meaning for us.

56. The method of accomplishing this (genuine) type of Understanding is more and more awareness. The ordinary vibration-rate of 48 prevents real Understanding; a rate of 24 is necessary. 48 = personal understanding; 24 = objective understanding.

On Objective Physics

57. Force, matter, energy, radiation and emanation are all physically distinguishable terms.

58. Electricity: in our usual opinion there are two forms of it, positive and negative; but there is also a third form, viz., the field within which the positive and negative forms are related to each other. Any manifestation of positive and negative electricity implies a fulcrum, i.e., a point of resistance over which they balance. Consciousness is an electrical phenomenon which arises from a state of being which we can feel.

59. The Law of the Three: every existing thing (or being) is ultimately composed of three forces, positive, negative and neutralizing; insofar as the thing is developed, these three are separated into three centres instead of being

blind; thus development is the increasingly separate organization of these, together with the provision of organs for each.

60. The neutralizing force is non-existent except by definition, since it is the field wherein phenomena take place; the neutralizing force is difficult to define because we are third-force-blind. There is the same difficulty in defining consciousness because it is the field of its content.

61. Trogoaftoegokrat: the law of mutual feeding; the law by virtue of which all things (including beings) feed on each other. Trogo = I eat; afto = auto = himself; ego = I; krat = system or government; trogoaftoegokrat = government by mutual feeding.

62. The Law of Aieoua: the highest vibration-rate in any field tends to raise the rate of all others in its neighborhood; cf. catalysis.

63. There is a scale of matters and a scale of beings, a physical ladder and a biological ladder.

64. Evolution-Involution is the process of proceeding up and down the scale; all things partake in this process continually.

65. The Universe is the body of God; it is the neutralizing force of the Sun Absolute, the manifestation of the interaction of the positive and negative forces of God.

66. The World (earth) is the note, mi, in one of the Cosmic Rays; it is the localization in astronomical space of 2,000,000,000 distorted human beings, and thus the lunatic planet; it is a being toward which there are three forms of apprehension.

67. Nature is the evil stepmother, an organic machine whose purpose is the evolution and involution of substances.

68. H^3 is His Endlessness, the fundamental unity, composed of one atom Will, one atom Individuality, one atom Consciousness.

69. H^6 represents archangels, solar gods.

70. H^{12} represents planetary gods.

71. H^{24} represents man.

72. Objective Science is science with the conscious purpose of investigating the meaning and aim of existence.

On Time

73. Time is the Unique Subjective.

74. Time is the potentiality of experience. To experience successively is to experience in a line. Simultaneity is the experience of two or more potentialities at once, thus the experience of a surface. That all potentialities be experienced successively and simultaneously demands a third dimension of Time. The Universe as a conscious being is the third dimension of Time.

On Incarnation and Reincarnation

75. Christianity has always insisted upon the Mystery of the Incarnation, viz., how does a spirit which is the son of God, have the use of a physical body? Self-Observation is only a survey of the body; Participation is practice in making it work; Experiment is seeing what you can do with it; and all of these are the preliminaries of Incarnation. Reincarnation is a problem which can arise only subsequently to the accomplishment of Incarnation.

76. Incarnation is the conscious inhabiting of a body already present. Reincarnation is the conscious inhabiting of a body consciously sought out; Reincarnation cannot take place prior to Incarnation.

On the Universe

77. The Universe consists of seven Hydrogens but each Hydrogen has three parts and the Hydrogen itself has no manifest existence because, as soon as it is manifested, it becomes either Carbon or Nitrogen or Oxygen.

78. The Universe is a being with three centres corresponding to our own; their material aspect is comprised of vibration-rates which appear to us as substances.

79. God is the "I" of the Universe, is termed His Endlessness and is not inferior to Time.

On Pondering

80. Pondering is answering questions from essence; and answering them practically.

81. One-half the energy of a human being must be spent internally in Pondering.

82. Pondering is a self-interrogation which consists in stripping off all the answers of association until you finally come to your own essential answer.

83. When the tempo of the third centre has been raised by a period of active Pondering, then there must be a rest in order to allow the other centres to adjust themselves to the increased tempo.

84. We all have a certain conception of the meaning and aim of existence and it is the Chief Feature of our mental centre; Pondering is supposed to bring this infantile conception to light and let it grow up.

On Man

85. Three centres compose a man, who is a Hydrogen and his number is 24.

86. Man is the mind of God; man is a passion for understanding the meaning and aim of existence.

87. We are victims of the sevenfold tragedy of human life, which includes the sevenfold ecstasy of tragedy; the difference between the old classical drama and ours is the difference between ecstasy and dream.

88. We are also the victims of birth, life, suffering and war, which are cosmic phenomena.

89. Birth is *nature's* way of providing matter for the cosmic transmutation of substances; thus births vary with the efficiency of the machines involved.

90. Life is the expenditure of the small change of potential experience, the trick of a wound-up spring; this wound-up spring = time = potential experience.

91. Suffering comes from the conflict of centres. (Taken consciously upon oneself, when one centre wishes and others dislike, it can become Conscious Suffering.)

92. War is not subject to human control; it was originated by nature to produce certain chemicals of which there is a lack.

93. Because external events which unwind us, do not fit into a recognizable order, we have the illusion of freedom. This is also why we do not learn from experience.

94. Sociological influences: the sum of the external stimuli that unwind the potential experience which constitutes the field of life.

95. The sum of the tunes events have played upon our three octaves, is visible in the forms we now have.

96. Essence is what we inherit; Personality is what we acquire.

97. The harmonious development of man: an "all-around" man according to the original definition is one who is equally at home in all three centres, a man who is really in occupation of his house, i.e., all three storeys of it. To produce such men is the purpose of the Gurdjieff Method, which rules out the three forms of monstrous genius.

98. Quantity and range of consciousness is the ultimate standard of value; and this is a factor in man's history.

On Consciousness

99. We are completely mechanical with the exception of Self-Observation and what that makes possible. Self-Observation is the letter, A, of consciousness; it is the first conscious ability that can be attained; if you cannot do that, you are completely unconscious.

100. Animals have sleep and waking states. We have sleep but not waking. When awake, we are lightly hypnotized.

101. The states of consciousness are Sleep, Waking, Self-Consciousness, Cosmic Consciousness. *Waking* is a pseudo-state of consciousness; there are really only three forms and our waking state is abnormal among states of consciousness. *Self-Consciousness* is consciousness of self; self is that amount of the original conceptual seed that has been actualized and its form is the body; therefore Self-Consciousness is consciousness of our body. *Cosmic Consciousness* is consciousness of the Cosmos, it is the awareness that there exist other planets than our own, other suns and the Sun Absolute, and that they are the centres of a being; it is thus a consciousness of the body of God.

On Psychology

102. Learn to know when you are making effort consciously by your experience of making effort physically. You are making an effort when you are "pushed against the collar." You do this when you try to include more phenomena in consciousness than would be there naturally, a continuously sustained effort to include in immediate awareness more and more that is not there, beginning with your own body.

103. Specific gravity controls the grasping of thoughts. In each of the three centres are depths in which related items lie. All thinking, feeling and instinctive perception is associated; and there are interrelations between corresponding depths in different centres. These interrelations between the three centres compose the total associative psychology of man.

104. Centre of gravity can be compared to absolute pitch. Any variation is a little abnormal. Every form has its own centre of gravity, each substance the same. Permanent dwelling place or habitual centre of gravity of whatever centre you are most often in has to do with Chief Feature.

105. The only real understanding that can ever be acquired depends upon a certain substance which can only be formed in a particular manner. This substance depends upon three factors: the presence of understandings of a like nature which become relatively positive and negative, and the new piece of knowledge which is the neutralizing force. The result of the three is a new understanding. One set of previous understandings says yes and another set denies, and there is a certain friction created; the result of this clash is perceived as a new understanding (which may be either according to knowledge or according to essence and thus either temporary or permanent, and that is decided by whether the individual himself makes effort when the clash occurs). If effort is not made, the new understanding is perceived only according to the specific gravity of the words and this is at random and thus mixed with uncorresponding items; but when effort is made, each direction of the clash is appreciated consciously (through the effort) and the final result will be *directed*. That is why people cannot be told but must first get the necessary substance and then make effort.

106. Thinking round about such items is building around them and giving substance to the deeper levels; it produces a form of understanding that is specifically human.

107. The fusion of similarities results in the grouping of experiences within

the centres; depends upon the attraction of likes or of similar vibration-rates.

108. Laws of association: all things seek their levels in the scale; things heard (when the effect upon the hearer is not involved) are distributed according to former associations; when effort is made, they go to their correct places in the organism.

109. Try to induce a real emotional need to observe yourself by repeating the mantram: I wish to remember myself. This is a psychological trick.

110. Attempt to objectify what has previously been subjective. All of it.

111. The observation of others is colored by our inability to observe ourselves impartially. This is an error of psychology.

112. You can never be impartial about any person or thing until you have been impartial about your own planetary body.

113. "I" and It: in our present state we subtract from It and give to "I," i.e., we reserve certain feelings, states, and so on, and attribute them to "I"; but every scrap must go to It properly.

114. Here is a psychological example of the octave in personal relations:

DO   the first contact with a situation, in which nothing is decided as
          to action and which may last a long time;

RE   the attempt to discover, on the part of the other person, what he
          really wishes to do, i.e., what is his essential wish;

MI   does the practical situation admit of the satisfaction of that wish?
          Not all essential wishes can be gratified within a given time;

FA   in the case where the wish can be gratified, something can be
          done if you are willing to take the responsibility of giving advice
          and then of standing by to see that it is correctly taken;

after FA the other person can go his own way; he has reached SOL.

115. Conscience is a function of a normal being; it is the representative of God in the essence; it is buried so deeply that it still remains relatively indestructible.

116. Playing roles is a form of Experiment. An ultimate aim is eventually to cast oneself for a role in life instead of (as at present) being cast for such a role involuntarily.

117. Anger and hatred are negative emotions only when they are misdirected; never fear to hate the odious.

118. There is a complete protection available to you—Silence.

2. SUMMATION

We must now mount to a summit and attempt to see this formulation wholly. What will be needed is not an intensity of apprehension but a synthesis of comprehension. It is necessary to draw a balanced picture of the data here presented and to view it as a simultaneous whole.

The Oragean Version begins by posing a number of questions lying beneath our temporary problems and difficulties, questions fundamental to our very status as human beings. Who are we? What functions and purposes do we really serve? And if these purposes are not our own, what other interests may we truly have and in what relation do we stand in respect of their accomplishment? It is such matters of which this Version takes stock, to begin with.

To the analysis of our situation there is brought information not ordinarily accessible, consisting of items of knowledge acquired very long ago by men entirely unknown to us; lost long ago, too, so far as ordinary people are concerned, and preserved only as the Hidden Learning possessed by genuine Schools. Regarding such knowledge our attitude should and must be one of complete skepticism, using it as the basis neither of credulity nor of incredulity, accepting it only provisionally and as something to be tested by each one of us personally; that is the attitude of this Version. Certainly there are answers presented, answers to some of our inmost questionings, but these cannot be accepted as true for us until we have confirmed them in the only correct manner in which any truth can be confirmed—intellectually, emotionally and practically, and in our own experience, checked and counterchecked against the similar findings of other and competent persons. As this process proceeds, faith in the sense of confidence may grow; for faith in the sense of belief the Oragean Version holds no place.

How may inquiries of this kind take place correctly, viz., in a self-respecting and rational way? In reply to this perfectly proper query the Version presents a technical and carefully defined Method, a series of activities in which it is possible for human beings to take part, commencing with the simple, though very difficult, attempt of Self-Observation as rigorously defined, and going on to the more complicated and strenuous exercises in

Participation and Experiment. The final steps, to which we are taken, are those of Voluntary Suffering and Conscious Labor. All this may be called the psychology of *solvitur ambulando*, it can be called practical or applied psychology (even though these last terms differ very much from their current scientific usage), it can be called the confirmation of the alleged meaning and aim of our existence through personal experience; it doesn't make very much difference what it is called, so long as it be correctly understood within the strict rigor of its own definitions.

All our difficulties, our really horrible distortions, our lack of understanding of ourselves, of others and of the world in general, can be reduced to or summed up in the abnormality of our usual conscious state, a condition so obviously unnatural that it must seem so to ourselves as soon as we reflect seriously upon it. The Method here presented can be looked upon as a practical means of altering our habitual state of consciousness to one more becoming and natural to triply integrated beings such as we can soon discover we in fact are. And we can also discover for ourselves, without further reliance upon outside allegation, whether or not it be possible to raise our own level of consciousness from that of the hypnotic state called Waking to that of a clear Self-Consciousness. If the latter state be possible for us (as for some of us it is), then assuredly everything—our problems, ourselves, others of our own kind, and indeed all external Reality—must take on an appearance very different from its previous guise, just as all these things are differently perceived by us in the ordinary Waking state as contrasted to nocturnal dream. It is a function and a purpose of the Method to accomplish just this transformation of consciousness in respect of those who are able to follow it successfully.

Following it successfully, however, can never be done simply by reading about it or thinking about it or contemplating it, and least of all can it be done successfully by supposing that one understands it verbally and can therefore put this Method into practice personally for himself. It is not at all impossible to understand it clearly and for the most part correctly from such an exposition as the present one; but that is only a mental understanding and not at all a practical one. Moreover, like all verbal understandings, such an acquaintance with these ideas cannot, and will not, remain permanent and unchanging; to the contrary it will alter at the very first attempt to do something practical about it, it will alter erroneously and it will continue so to alter until, after no long time, meanings that once seemed clear and unambiguous will become increasingly vague and confused, and the solitary student will find himself turned about on his path without being aware of it, unless worse should happen and he become the victim of all kinds of fancies and even delusions of the most serious kind.

That has happened before. And once again the reader is warned with the utmost gravity: *do not try to do these things alone.*

Not only are others necessary to accompany one on a path such as this but, above all, a fully competent and responsible instructor is demanded, lest those who search be transformed into scrabbling lunatics with all hope of their real humanity lost forever. Of these the most hopeless are those who become so convinced of their subjective delusions that they never suspect there can be aught amiss.

And finally this Version has presented certain items of a larger scale, information about the Cosmoses and about cosmic phenomena, most of which are inaccessible immediately to any proper confirmation upon the pupil's part. The features of the Local Map are confirmable, under the necessary conditions of group work, within a reasonable time, sooner for some, longer for others, by means of the procedure called the Boat. But the specific characteristics of the Greater Map—the real nature of Time, its dimensions and the difference between its subjective and objective aspects, the hierarchy of beings of this Universe, the constitution, the levels and the physical laws of the Universe, the true nature of His Endlessness and the relation of that (for us) Supreme Being to genuine Reality—all these and similar items of information can be validly confirmed only by one to whom the state of Cosmic Consciousness is not an abnormally induced and unpredictable experience but by whom such a conscious state can be entered and left at will. The Greater Map is, and only is, a series of formulations to be taken by us for Pondering, certainly never for belief.

And so this Version ends. It might have gone further but, as Actuality ruled, it could not. So far as this writer can see, its importance, as things stand now, has perhaps been lost for practical activity; at least he knows of no instructor competent enough to meet his own drastic need in relation to it. But he thinks also that its formulations are far too important to be lost, as will next appear.

3. THE DESTINY OF MAN

Man in this Universe—Man even on this distorted and ill-starred planet—is not a small thing, but a great one. His potential greatness is as tremendous as his necessity to manifest the mind of God; and his responsibility is of an equal gravity.

For us, who are not yet men, that responsibility is but the weightier by reason of the words, not yet. We are in the desperate position of not manifesting our manhood (because we cannot) but still of being unable to deny it potentially. Well may we cry: wherewith shall we be saved? And only we can answer that question ourselves, for ourselves.

Let it not be supposed that what has been formulated here is the only path whereby a man may fulfill his destiny. For some it is, but for all it is not. That which no human can escape, nor essentially wishes to escape, is his necessity of some path, his need to find himself, his place, his human duty, his ultimate being in relation to that Reality of which he is undeniably a part. That necessity is his and he alone can solve it. Every man must somehow find how he can become genuinely human; and to discover this, he must first find out what "human" really means.

In some of us this final drive is vague (perhaps we are not quite ready yet), in some it is so intense as to betray them to charlatans. Yet finally each one must find his answer in himself, in his own essential humanity after ruthlessly obliterating the personally subjective wishes, fears, ambitions, arrogances and abasements that fetter and surround him with their false deceits. In the end he must judge for *himself*, with the help of those whom he has consciously and impartially selected as able to help him, but with the final judgment and the final decision his own *alone*.

Perhaps that is the greatest characteristic of the Oragean Version. First to prepare one to be able to make his ultimate judgment of the meaning and aim of his own existence, and then to show him that he must make it *for himself*. Only so can he fulfill his own destiny as Man.

RECKONING

What further I have to say, will come as anti-climax; yet it must be said.

As may well be supposed, the preliminary forms of thought existing in my mind when I began this task, I have found changing—sometimes expanding, sometimes contracting—as I have pursued its course. At the last I find it very difficult, and perhaps impossible, for me to judge impartially as to how well I have succeeded in reproducing the essential skeleton of that Version of the Hidden Learning expounded by Orage in New York.

But of what follows, the reader is surely entitled to be apprised. In the first place I know of my own knowledge that what is set down here is incomplete. In a sense it must be so, for the mere number of words spoken by Orage during his instruction of his groups in New York would have filled thirty or more volumes the size of this one, not to mention the many, many more words of explanation and counsel addressed by him to this hearer alone. What I have collected here is, properly speaking, a *précis*, a selection and organization of what seem to me to have been the leading and most important points involved in the formulation of his exposition of these ideas, and I do not think that any of those have been left out. But there was more, very much more, which I cannot devise a means of including.

And there is another aspect of this treatise which no appearance of false modesty upon my part can prevent my acknowledging. As I have proceeded through these formulations, I have become more and more aware of how much more they are mine than Orage's. This does not refer to the content of what is expressed (concerning which I have taken the utmost care that it be accurate) but to the manner of expressing it. What one man may truly illuminate by the brilliance of his exposition, another may becloud by his stumbling, even though painstaking, explanations; and it is the latter position in which I find myself. I do not mean that I consider my formulations to be unclear; I mean that, compared to the brilliance of Orage's, they stand upon another and far lower level of communication and that thus I have been unable to give the reader, at second-hand as it were, the clarity of insight into the meanings of these statements which Orage could and did provide in his own discourse. Because I am not Orage, I cannot in sincerity apologize for this; but I regret it and I consider it the reader's due to inform him of it. It seems to me that the latter must readily appreciate what I mean when he compares my own discussion of some given topic with the succinctness of an Oragean aphorism upon the same subject.

What, then, are we to say of my own version of the Oragean Version, hereinbefore presented? As the Oragean Version certainly differed in some measure from the Gurdjieffian original (and in my opinion to the benefit of the former), how much of what I have written differs from the Oragean Version as presented by Orage himself?

On this score I am prepared to defend myself in considerable measure. I have already disclosed the sources upon which I have relied in undertaking this reproduction; and I consider them adequate. Moreover, I am not entirely inexperienced in self-examination and in the ability to distinguish between what pertains to the subjectivities of C. Daly King and what else is characteristic of the objective experiences he has undergone. That I have been able to exclude all subjectivities is of course ridiculous, and I do not so claim; what I do claim is that, within all reasonable meaning and within, also, the limitations just acknowledged. I have reproduced the content and some of the feeling of the exposition Orage presented to his groups in New York City. If this is not a correct account of what he meant, then I am totally incapable of handling either thoughts or words. I am able to give the reader this final assurance: that no one lives or has lived, including Gurdjieff, who could make me doubt what I have just asserted or, certainly, make me deny it. It has not been done as well as it might be done but within its bounds it is correct.

Having done it as well as I may, I feel entitled to a last observation. It depends, of course, upon my own subjective view and no one knows better than I (although some suppose themselves to do so) how far from human normality I am. Even so, I wish to put myself on record regarding what I have experienced in this work, now that it seems for me to be over.

I do not think that the being of Alfred Richard Orage was as great as that of Georges Gurdjieff, for I have never encountered anyone with a degree of being comparable to that of Gurdjieff. Moreover, it is true that all of us, and Orage too, owe to Gurdjieff's efforts the truly astonishing and altogether invaluable information that the latter somehow collected and later, for a time, formulated to his earlier disciples. But as to Gurdjieff as a teacher, I declare sincerely that he has hindered and not helped me; it is no matter why or how, that is my constatation and I do not consider the fact a recommendation of any teacher.

Upon the other hand and precisely to the contrary Alfred Richard Orage has helped me, not personally but impersonally, to an extent I find it impossible adequately to acknowledge. To him I owe whatever scraps of genuine manhood I have ever been able to gather out of the debris of our automatic and mechanical living. He is not only the greatest teacher I have ever known but one whose greatness I cannot conceive the need of exceeding.

Explicit.

APPENDIX

I have been asked to set down in an Appendix what I know of the Ouspenskian Version.

As to any full and proper critique of that Version, it must be said first of all that I am not adequately qualified to make one. As set forth in the Premises which opened this book, I attended only two or three of M. Ouspensky's lectures in New York City during the years, 1940–1945, and at that time I had a single personal conference with him which lasted perhaps an hour or the best part of one. Later, as also related above, I was invited to attend a series of readings from his unpublished writings, at Mendham, New Jersey, and these readings I did attend, driving to Mendham every Sunday afternoon for the purpose for roughly the period of a year, commencing in the late spring of 1949. At this time I also took part in a ritual dancing class conducted at Mendham by Miss Jessmin Howarth, who had been one of the original instructresses in this type of exercise at the former Gurdjieff Institute. And meanwhile of course I became acquainted with a number of the followers of M. Ouspensky who, up to the occurrence of the latter's death, had received their instruction primarily from M. Ouspensky rather than from M. Gurdjieff and who were undoubtedly well acquainted with the Ouspenskian Version.

The Ouspenskian writings which I then heard (and some of which have subsequently been published*), by no means render a full account of the complete Ouspenskian Version, for the latter involves group and individual work on the part of the pupils, to which there is little reference in the books written by M. Ouspensky. And just as the work of this kind that was prosecuted by the Orage groups, derived from the original instructions of Gurdjieff and from similar activities at the Fontainebleau Institute when it was in operation, so the similar work of the Ouspensky pupils is likewise related to the same source. The difference is that the former depends upon the constatations of Orage, the latter upon those of Ouspensky.

This difference is considerable, in my opinion. It should be stated that I myself have not engaged either in the group or the individual work of the Ouspenskian Version and that I cannot speak with a final authority about it; moreover, during my contacts at Mendham I was in the position of a guest and could not institute very searching inquiries. However, from what

---

* Ouspensky, P. D.: *In Search of the Miraculous*, op. cit., 1950; *The Psychology of Man's Possible Evolution*, Hedgehog Press, NY, 1950.

I heard and encountered at Mendham and from conversations and discussions elsewhere with those who originally and long had been members of the Ouspensky groups I received very definite impressions not only regarding differences of this kind but also concerning the ultimate character of the distinctions between what may conveniently be called the teachings of Orage and those of Ouspensky.

That is scarcely a background permitting one to speak with real authority and manifestly it will thus be possible for anyone with a comparable motive to dismiss what I say as being self-admittedly ill-founded. But I do not think that such a dismissal would be well-advised; what I shall try to formulate is neither a personal prejudice nor is it by any means a snap judgment.

We have discussed earlier the rigorous meanings to be attached to two of the technical terms included in the body of the Gurdjieffian ideas, Self-Remembering and Self-Observation. It will be recalled that Self-Remembering is one of the necessary preliminaries to Self-Observation, the other one being obviously the recollection that one wishes to engage in the latter activity. Self-Remembering consists in the establishment of the dichotomy that genuinely exists between "I" and It, between the at first almost empty reality of the ultimately subjective entity which proposes to engage in the self-observatory activity and, to the other hand, that objective organism to which he is related and which he is about to observe. In short, Self-Remembering comprises the effort of non-identification from the physical body which is essential to any correct or successful practice of Self-Observation. In the Oragean Version these distinctions are clear and final and there exists no excuse for confusing either one of these terms with the other; but in the Ouspenskian Version the distinction is by no means so clear-cut, in fact it is rather fuzzy and at times it even appears that Self-Remembering is actually considered to be synonymous with Self-Observation. When such an attitude is maintained, therefore, no genuine Self-Observation can take place and the very first practical work relating to the Hidden Secret is omitted.

This same fuzziness or lack of rigorous and conclusive definition appears also to me to characterize a number of other concepts closely connected with the Ouspenskian Version, and in particular those involving the work of the pupil upon himself rather than those concerned with the paraphysical, parachemical or cosmic formulations.

It is my impression that in the Ouspenskian Version the individual work of the pupil—which of course is the very heart and core of the whole procedure, being what in the present treatise is called the Boat—is far more introspective than genuinely objective and that it is often taken for granted that the candidate, newly come to these techniques, is in a position to understand both the possibility and the nature of a genuine Self-Observation far more readily than in fact is, or can be, the case. Thus the real crux of the Hidden Secret is missed; and without that revelation, which must always be fully understood *self*-revelation deriving from an actual experience of the difference between introspection and objective observation, no sort of work that is done can in fact lead to the results formulated in the Gurdjieff system.

To be specific, I suspect that the individual work of the Ouspenskian Version consists, either wholly or predominantly, in what I have above called the work of the Open Secret and that the work of the Hidden Secret is either omitted or so inadequately glossed over that it is never really mastered by the candidates concerned. It must be remembered that I do not *know* this to be the case but it should also be stated that the opinion is no mere guess. It has arisen not only from lengthy discussions with members of the Ouspensky groups but likewise from my experiences with them, as well individually as collectively. Never at Mendham, for instance, have I heard the least mention of the kind of constatation that must result from the Self-Observation of a specific organic body but, to the contrary, only the sort of opinion that can arise from introspections relating to subjective states of mind or emotion or from reflections upon the nature of one's habits, and so on. On occasion I have heard ordinary students, much interested in class work in the usual kind of psychology, produce equally shrewd opinions; but the work envisaged here is not at all comparable to class work in ordinary psychology or to the assumed self-interrogations of psychoanalysis.

Now this is an extremely serious point and it ought to be discussed in the light of Ouspensky's own words in regard to it. In his book, In Search of the Miraculous, on page 193 he speaks of the required transformation of that hydrogen in man's body which is here identified as the hydrogen, "mi 12," and of the allusions allegorically made to this transformation by the alchemists. He continues: "Alchemists who spoke of this transmutation began directly with it. They knew nothing, or at least they said nothing, about the nature of the first volitional 'shock.' It is upon this, however, that the whole thing depends. The second volitional 'shock' and transmutation become physically possible only after long practice on the first volitional 'shock,' which consists in self-remembering, and in observing the impressions received. On the way of the monk and on the way of the fakir work on the second 'shock' begins before work on the first 'shock,' but as mi 12 is created only as a result of the first 'shock' work, in the absence of other material, has of necessity to be concentrated on si 12, and it very often gives quite wrong results. Right development on the fourth way must begin with the first volitional 'shock' and then pass on to the second 'shock' at mi 12."

In the words of the Oragean Version the first conscious shock is created by the activity of Self-Observation, the second conscious shock by the activities of Voluntary Suffering and Conscious Labor; and it is seen that what Ouspensky says is what has here been said in the second paragraph above. There is thus no ultimate contradiction between the two Versions upon this point but there is certainly quite a difference between them in regard to what is considered as providing the first conscious shock. If in place of Ouspensky's own words we should write that this "consists primarily in self-remembering, and incidentally in observing the impressions received," we would have not only the superficial implication of his Version but likewise the understanding of it expressed directly to this inquirer by his own followers. As to the Oragean Version the case is explicit and has already been stated: that Self-Remembering by itself will accomplish nothing and that the cause of the actual transformation of the given physical substances is exactly the activity of Self-Observation, and neither one of its preliminaries nor anything else. Whether the error above discussed was ever Ouspensky's own or consists only in a misinterpretation on the part of his pupils, or in fact whether it exists at all, I cannot of course decide in any final sense. It is simply my conclusion from my own experiences that it does exist.

My opinion in this respect is reinforced by Ouspensky's own words, viz., "and in observing the impressions received." No impression can be observed in the sense of a genuinely organic Self-Observation by any pupil of the degree of those I met at Mendham or have previously met in the Gurdjieff work anywhere else; and the very phraseology quoted, evidences to me a lack of comprehension of the activity actually discussed. "Observing an impression" is observing a sensation (or else it is the attempt to observe some even foggier emotional or mental occurrence) and, as we have earlier seen, this is not really an observation at all but is equivalent, instead, to becoming more vividly aware of the occurrence of the sensation or impression. The only thing that can be observed in a correct sense is some current organic phenomenon; such an observation is made by means of sensations or impressions, which only mediate the self-observatory activity. To substitute the observation of impressions for that of organic phenomena first of all confuses the issue and secondly is at best a subjective manifestation closely resembling introspection if, indeed, it is not the same thing exactly. Until the object of observation is made specific and physically objective without possibility of doubt or verbal cavil, the activity itself remains as non-objective as its own object.

Observing an impression is the Introspective Fallacy with a vengeance. It is facile, though, and thus it is a lazy fallacy, too.

We have already remarked upon how easy it is to skip the hard, energetic, objective task and to slip into the pleasant daydream that introspection may be able to solve the difficulties, after all. Unfortunately (perhaps) that is not the case. Introspections, of course, can sometimes be difficult and unpleasant also; but neither does that alter the case, if you come right down to it.

The object of observation not only can, but must, be a physical, organic phenomenon of one's own body so clearly and universally recognized as to be open with equal ease either to instrumental checking or to that of other instructed and careful observers. Only so can there be any proper suggestion, let alone guarantee, of impartially objective success in the outcome. The distinction here made between introspective opinion and impartially objective knowledge is in plain fact so subtle and so difficult for *anyone's* apprehension in the usual terms that to me the failure to place the greatest emphasis upon this really extraordinary concept indicates the highest probability that both the crucial importance and the true meaning of the formulation have been lost upon the formulator.

In this kind of activity—that of the Fourth Way—introspection is not the technique advocated for the candidate or pupil; and introspection, whether or not accompanied by an admixture of Self-Remembering, remains introspection. Either that position is understood or it is not understood. In the Ouspenskian Version it does not appear to me to be understood.

This point is unusually important because it refers to something very important in any version of the Gurdjieff ideas, viz., the whole basis and beginning of the practical work that alone can lead to objective results in the case of the subnormal and undeveloped human being. The introspective misdirection of this first and basic step not only invalidates the very nature of the Hidden Secret, preventing its correct realization by the student, but likewise must of necessity then throw the predominant emphasis back upon the work of the Open Secret, which, merely by itself, is equivalent to little more than an advanced sort of Pelmanism or the self-interrogations of ordinary psychology. A great many persons—from those who study how to make friends and influence people to the victims of psychoanalysis—theorize about their own types, behaviors, past histories and so on, without ever in any way altering their status as subnormal or undeveloped human beings even when their conclusions of this kind happen to be unexpectedly correct. The successful prosecution of the work of the Open Secret will produce no fundamental change in semiconscious man.

These remarks, however, should not be construed as a criticism of the total Ouspenskian Version. That Version contains many very excellent formulations and with regard to a number of important topics it discusses competently matters either omitted altogether from the Oragean Version or which have received not nearly so adequate a treatment in the latter. Parachemistry, as it is related to human beings, is much more fully treated in the Ouspenskian Version, for instance, and the very illuminating formulation that it is the lower centres which are malfunctional in the undeveloped human, not the higher centres, is another example of a valuable contribution.

And there are other formulations that ought to recommend the Ouspenskian Version highly to any serious man seriously in search of this kind of information; but all these are therefore not apposite to this discussion. If all I had to say, consisted merely in my opinion that the Ouspenskian Version was perfectly and completely correct, the opinion itself would be both gratuitous and impertinent. It is because I have received the sober impression of the mentioned differences between the Oragean and the Ouspenskian Versions and just because I honestly consider those differences to be seriously important, that I have felt it proper to mention them at all. And obviously, if I am to mention them, I must do so as fully and clearly as I can.

Although I have therefore criticized the Ouspenskian Version (because I feel that in it a mistake of the most crucial ultimate significance is finding its initiation), it is likewise incumbent upon me to acknowledge the very courteous, helpful and hospitable treatment I myself have been accorded both at Mendham and elsewhere by the followers of M. Ouspensky. I do so acknowledge it with appreciation and gratitude. And if I am correct in supposing that his followers are augmenting the suggestion of an error which I think I have found in his formulations, it is also my testimony that they emulate him well in his essential and authentic courtesy.

For M. Ouspensky was a genuine gentleman in the exact sense. He was also, I think, an incorrigible mystic, no matter how much or how successfully he may or may not have striven against that tendency after his meeting with and his instruction by M. Gurdjieff. I do not know what caused the break between him and M. Gurdjieff; it may possibly have been this very slant of outlook which M. Ouspensky never lost. To me the latter seems to have been not what is sometimes called a scientific mystic but, instead, a religious mystic. The emphasis which he continued to lay upon such early Christian works as the Philokalia and the frequent references among his followers to East Indian works of a similarly religious rather than philosophical aspect seem to lend some substantiation to the opinion. For these reasons the Ouspenskian Version possesses a sort of overlay of religious enthusiasm and of mystical atmosphere very different both from the formulations of Gurdjieff and from the Version of Orage.

Now the combination of this semi-religious and semi-mystical attitude most definitely does not accord at all fully with the intellectual implications or with the practical work of the Fourth Way as set out in the doctrines of Gurdjieff. It is undeniable that religion itself is one, but another of the Ways, and mysticism may be an aspect of religion. But very surely the Way of Religion is not the Fourth Way; and the admixture of its enthusiasms (by some persons called fanaticisms) with the quite different attitude practiced by Gurdjieff and advocated clearly by Orage, not only estranges the natural candidate of the Fourth Way but equally misrepresents the essential and fundamental characteristics of its disciplines. In the case of the Ouspenskian Version this misinterpretation definitely exists in the plainly perceptible atmosphere of its formulations and to me it appears to have caused a geometrically increasing deviation from the original strictness and purity of the Gurdjieffian statement of the Hidden Secret, which doubtless was well enough known to M. Ouspensky at the time of his original association with M. Gurdjieff.

In any case those are my personal impressions in regard to the Ouspenskian Version and I have set them down here as honestly as I am able.

INDEX

art: 75, 105, 174, 181, 192–196, 198, 252, 255
    objective 174, 192–196, 198, 255
astrology: 21, 97–98, 254
automatism: 59–61, 63, 68, 87, 101
beings: 12, 22, 28, 38, 40–42, 44, 51–52, 59, 63, 70, 77, 82–83, 96, 100–101, 104, 109, 111, 133, 149, 175, 179–180, 186, 189, 192, 204, 208, 215–216, 221–225, 227, 231, 239–240, 250, 254, 256–257, 263–265, 273
biology: 21, 36–37, 42
Black Sheep, myth of: 64–67, 76, 87–88, 251
bodies: 56, 66, 113, 120, 162–167, 174, 207, 217, 220, 222–223, 225–226, 228–229, 234, 236, 241, 244, 249, 253
    four-dimensional 229, 245–247
Buddha: 67, 251
Buddhism: 39, 67
Calvin: 53
Carnegie, Andrew: 53
centres: 45, 47–48, 50–51, 53–55, 77–78, 80–83, 86, 106, 123–124, 151, 157–158, 160–165, 167, 173–174, 220–222, 252, 254, 256, 258–260, 262, 273
    functions of 80–82
    oppositions between 54
    sub-centres 161–162, 169, 177, 180, 187, 205, 220–222, 241, 252
chief feature: 99–101, 120, 125, 140, 220, 240, 251, 259, 261
Christ: 39, 67, 187, 193, 251
Christianity: 1, 18, 39, 68, 89, 98, 160, 163, 175, 185–186, 188, 193–194, 240, 258, 274
Comfort Bed, the: 186–187
common sense: 2, 17, 25, 51, 133, 135, 203
compassion: 182
Compton: 53
conscience: 174, 182–183, 262
consciousness: 7, 35–36, 40–43, 56, 58–59, 62–64, 67–68, 73, 75, 77, 80, 97, 103, 105–114, 118, 120–125, 129, 138, 147–152, 161, 171, 174, 178–180, 184, 189–190, 209, 218–222, 228, 231, 238, 244, 248, 251, 256–257, 260–261, 264–265

and values 109, 260
    cosmic 73, 103–104, 108–110, 178–179, 260, 265
    passivity of 59, 107, 152, 248
    self- 104–112, 119, 123, 125, 146, 148–149, 178, 183, 227, 260, 264
    waking 62–63, 76, 103–109, 123, 138, 149, 152, 160, 180, 183, 244, 260, 264
cosmic ray: 18, 69–71, 79, 201–204, 211–213, 217–219, 222
cosmoi: 206–207, 265
credulity: 7, 11, 30, 190, 202, 263
death: 8, 40, 48, 66–67, 72, 123, 162, 184, 187–188, 193, 239, 242–244, 246–247, 253, 269
definitions:
    actual 27
    art 192
    askokin 227, 250
    atom 209
    being 254
    belief 255
    carbon 211
    centre 45
    chief feature 99
    compassion 182
    constatation 81
    cosmic consciousness 260
    cosmic ray 69
    emotion 84
    essence 96
    eternity 238
    experiment 135
    faith 255
    food 215
    gross behavior 117
    heropass 229
    hope 255
    hydrogen 211
    "I" 208
    imagination, "creative" 75
    imagination, real 74–75, 239
    impossible 28
    incarnation 240, 258
    intuition 80
    knowledge 256
    "know thyself" 115

www.ingramcontent.com/pod-product-compliance
Lightning Source LLC
Chambersburg PA
CBHW020404100426
42812CB00001B/189